Approaches to Teaching Milton's *Paradise Lost*

Edited by

Galbraith M. Crump

The Modern Language Association of America
New York   1986

Acknowledgments: Reproduction of the illustrations accompanying Virginia Tufte's essay "Visualizing *Paradise Lost*: Classroom Use of Illustrations by Medina, Blake, and Doré" was defrayed by the University of Southern California's Raubenheimer Award. John Baptist Medina illustration reproduced courtesy of the William Andrews Clark Memorial Library, University of California, Los Angeles; Gustave Doré illustrations and William Blake, *The Temptation and Fall of Eve* (1807), by permission of the Huntington Library, San Marino, California; William Blake, *The Temptation and Fall of Eve* (1808), courtesy of the Museum of Fine Arts, Boston, Massachusetts.

Library of Congress Cataloging in Publication Data

Main entry under title:

Approaches to teaching Milton's Paradise lost.

  (Approaches to teaching masterpieces of world
literature ; 10)
  Bibliography: p.
  Includes index.
  1. Milton, John, 1608–1674. Paradise lost—Addresses,
essays, lectures. 2. Milton, John, 1608–1674—Study
and teaching—Addresses, essays, lectures. I. Crump,
Galbraith M. (Galbraith Miller), 1929–
II. Modern Language Association of America. III. Title.
IV. Series.
PR3562.A83   1986   821′.4   85-21390

ISBN 0-87352-493-4
ISBN 0-87352-494-2 (pbk.)

Cover illustration of the paperback edition: William Blake, *The Judgment of Adam and Eve*, illustration of book 10, *Paradise Lost*, 1807. By permission of the Huntington Library, San Marino, California.

Third printing 1992

Published by The Modern Language Association of America
10 Astor Place, New York, New York 10003-6981

Modern Language Association of America

Approaches to Teaching
World Literature

Joseph Gibaldi, Series Editor

1. Joseph Gibaldi, ed. *Approaches to Teaching Chaucer's* Canterbury Tales. 1980.
2. Carole Slade, ed. *Approaches to Teaching Dante's* Divine Comedy. 1982.
3. Richard Bjornson, ed. *Approaches to Teaching Cervantes'* Don Quixote. 1984.
4. Jess B. Bessinger, Jr., and Robert F. Yeager, eds. *Approaches to Teaching* Beowulf. 1984.
5. Richard J. Dunn, ed. *Approaches to Teaching Dickens'* David Copperfield. 1984.
6. Steven G. Kellman, ed. *Approaches to Teaching Camus's* The Plague. 1985.
7. Yvonne Shafer, ed. *Approaches to Teaching Ibsen's* A Doll House. 1985.
8. Martin Bickman, ed. *Approaches to Teaching Melville's* Moby-Dick. 1985.
9. Miriam Youngerman Miller and Jane Chance, eds. *Approaches to Teaching* Sir Gawain and the Green Knight. 1986.
10. Galbraith M. Crump, ed. *Approaches to Teaching Milton's* Paradise Lost. 1986.
11. Spencer Hall, with Jonathan Ramsey, eds. *Approaches to Teaching Wordsworth's Poetry*. 1986.
12. Robert H. Ray, ed. *Approaches to Teaching Shakespeare's* King Lear. 1986.
13. Kostas Myrsiades, ed. *Approaches to Teaching Homer's* Iliad *and* Odyssey. 1987.
14. Douglas J. McMillan, ed. *Approaches to Teaching Goethe's* Faust. 1987.
15. Renée Waldinger, ed. *Approaches to Teaching Voltaire's* Candide. 1987.
16. Bernard Koloski, ed. *Approaches to Teaching Chopin's* The Awakening. 1988.
17. Kenneth M. Roemer, ed. *Approaches to Teaching Momaday's* The Way to Rainy Mountain. 1988.
18. Edward J. Rielly, ed. *Approaches to Teaching Swift's* Gulliver's Travels. 1988.
19. Jewel Spears Brooker, ed. *Approaches to Teaching Eliot's Poetry and Plays*. 1988.
20. Melvyn New, ed. *Approaches to Teaching Sterne's* Tristram Shandy. 1989.
21. Robert F. Gleckner and Mark L. Greenberg, eds. *Approaches to Teaching Blake's* Songs of Innocence and of Experience. 1989.
22. Susan J. Rosowski, ed. *Approaches to Teaching Cather's* My Ántonia. 1989.
23. Carey Kaplan and Ellen Cronan Rose, eds. *Approaches to Teaching Lessing's* The Golden Notebook. 1989.
24. Susan Resneck Parr and Pancho Savery, eds. *Approaches to Teaching Ellison's* Invisible Man. 1989.
25. Barry N. Olshen and Yael S. Feldman, eds. *Approaches to Teaching the Hebrew Bible as Literature in Translation*. 1989.
26. Robin Riley Fast and Christine Mack Gordon, eds. *Approaches to Teaching Dickinson's Poetry*. 1989.
27. Spencer Hall, ed. *Approaches to Teaching Shelley's Poetry*. 1990.

28. Sidney Gottlieb, ed. *Approaches to Teaching the Metaphysical Poets.* 1990.
29. Richard K. Emmerson, ed. *Approaches to Teaching Medieval English Drama.* 1990.
30. Kathleen Blake, ed. *Approaches to Teaching Eliot's* Middlemarch. 1990.
31. María Elena de Valdés and Mario J. Valdés, eds. *Approaches to Teaching García Márquez's* One Hundred Years of Solitude. 1990.
32. Donald D. Kummings, ed. *Approaches to Teaching Whitman's* Leaves of Grass. 1990.
33. Stephen C. Behrendt, ed. *Approaches to Teaching Shelley's* Frankenstein. 1990.
34. June Schlueter and Enoch Brater, eds. *Approaches to Teaching Beckett's* Waiting for Godot. 1991.
35. Walter H. Evert and Jack W. Rhodes, eds. *Approaches to Teaching Keats's Poetry.* 1991.
36. Frederick W. Shilstone, ed. *Approaches to Teaching Byron's Poetry.* 1991.
37. Bernth Lindfors, ed. *Approaches to Teaching Achebe's* Things Fall Apart. 1991.
38. Richard E. Matlak, ed. *Approaches to Teaching Coleridge's Poetry and Prose.* 1991.
39. Shirley Geok-lin Lim, ed. *Approaches to Teaching Kingston's* The Woman Warrior. 1991.
40. Maureen Fries and Jeanie Watson, eds. *Approaches to Teaching the Arthurian Tradition.* 1992.
41. Maurice Hunt, ed. *Approaches to Teaching Shakespeare's* The Tempest *and Other Late Romances.* 1992.
42. Diane Long Hoeveler and Beth Lau, eds. *Approaches to Teaching Brontë's* Jane Eyre. 1993.
43. Jeffrey B. Berlin, ed. *Approaches to Teaching Mann's* Death in Venice *and Other Short Fiction.* 1992.

CONTENTS

PREFACE TO THE SERIES

In *The Art of Teaching* Gilbert Highet wrote, "Bad teaching wastes a great deal of effort, and spoils many lives which might have been full of energy and happiness." All too many teachers have failed in their work, Highet argued, simply "because they have not thought about it." We hope that the Approaches to Teaching Masterpieces of World Literature series, sponsored by the Modern Language Association's Committee on Teaching and Related Professional Activities, will not only improve the craft—as well as the art—of teaching but also encourage serious and continuing discussion of the aims and methods of teaching literature.

The principal objective of the series is to collect within each volume different points of view on teaching a specific literary work, a literary tradition, or a writer widely taught at the undergraduate level. The preparation of each volume begins with a wide-ranging survey of instructors, thus enabling us to include in the volume the philosophies and approaches, thoughts and methods of scores of experienced teachers. The result is a sourcebook of material, information, and ideas on teaching the subject of the volume to undergraduates.

The series is intended to serve nonspecialists as well as specialists, inexperienced as well as experienced teachers, graduate students who wish to learn effective ways of teaching as well as senior professors who wish to compare their own approaches with the approaches of colleagues in other schools. Of course, no volume in the series can ever substitute for erudition, intelligence, creativity, and sensitivity in teaching. We hope merely that each book will point readers in useful directions; at most each will offer only a first step in the long journey to successful teaching. We may perhaps adopt as keynote for the series Alfred North Whitehead's observation in *The Aims of Education* that a liberal education "proceeds by imparting a knowledge of the masterpieces of thought, of imaginative literature, and of art."

Joseph Gibaldi
Series Editor

PREFACE TO THE VOLUME

Following the guidelines set forth for the series, this volume addresses the challenges of teaching Milton's *Paradise Lost* at the undergraduate level. Several of those who provide advice do regularly teach Milton at the graduate level, however, and from that perspective offer insights that may prove useful in the more general context of undergraduate teaching. Likewise, the insights of the nonspecialist often prove illuminating to the specialist, for whom elementary questions have given way before the demands of a particularized, committed audience. If this volume allows us better to learn from one another, it will have fulfilled a valuable function. If it allows us better to serve the uninitiated reader, it will have accomplished the goal set for it by the series of which it is part. If it helps to maintain the presence of Milton's great achievement in all our consciousnesses, it will reinforce the general humanistic vision against the inroads of practicality that demand so much of our energy and attention.

The volume begins with an introduction considering the broad challenge of teaching *Paradise Lost* in our time. The main body of the work is divided into two parts, entitled "Materials" and "Approaches." The first deals with editions of *Paradise Lost*, required and recommended student readings, aids to teaching (recordings, films, and the like) and "The Instructor's Library," which lists reference works and background and critical studies. The discussion in the first part of the volume is based largely on information supplied the editor from teachers in the United States, Canada, and other parts of the world where *Paradise Lost* has a place in the curriculum.

The second part of the volume contains essays by seventeen teachers, who describe various approaches to teaching *Paradise Lost*. Comprehensiveness is not intended. Arousing interest most certainly is, together with creating challenges and looking at old problems in new ways.

An appendix of participants in the survey, a list of works cited, and an index complete the volume. The list of works cited does not include works referred to incidentally in the essays, such as Plato's *Laws* or Montesquieu's *Persian Letters*. Specialized books and articles related to specific teaching approaches, however, receive mention even though they may have no direct bearing on Milton or *Paradise Lost*. Though the listing of participants is seemingly but a nod of recognition on the part of the editor and the series, the volume would not have been possible without the generous support of those colleagues willing to share their insights and expertise with others. They gave graciously of their time and effort from busy schedules, and I thank them.

GMC

INTRODUCTION

Justifying Milton to the Modern Student

The sheer weight of Milton's presence makes it imperative that the teacher grapple with the problems attending his effective introduction to the modern undergraduate student of literature. There is little argument regarding the importance of Milton and his epic, as they summarize the great literary traditions filtering down to the Renaissance in England and as they provide the monument with which much later literature must cope, whether it sees that monument as something to emulate or execrate. Milton's influence on later poets and his debt to earlier ones define him as central to the study of English literature. Yet the scope and complexity of his epic challenge student and teacher alike. Our intellectual resources are meager in relation to the demands of the text. The very concerns that make *Paradise Lost* essential to an understanding of the English literature tradition also stand in the way of its general acceptance and comprehension as part of the modern literature syllabus. In scope it is difficult to fit into any survey format, even including that of the period course. Its demands on our intellectual background require the kind of preparation few of our students, nowadays, can bring to it. Yet *Paradise Lost* is Milton's supreme accomplishment. Despite its very real difficulties in form, background, and influence, teachers who pass over it for a selection of the shorter works both misrepresent Milton's achievement and ignore the major reason for his profound influence on the later development of English letters.

1

When we consider the significance of *Paradise Lost* on poetry from Pope to Eliot and beyond, we find ample arguments to justify teaching Milton's masterwork. But we hardly solve our presentational problems. In the eyes of Eliot and the New Critics, generally, Milton and his epic work threatened their literary enterprises, though they would not have put the matter in those terms. Eliot wrestled for more than twenty-five years with the problem of Milton's adverse influence on the growth of English literature. Modern readers may sympathize with Eliot and the critics more than with Milton in this regard. Milton threatens the literary and critical enterprises of today's readers as well. On the other side of the question, the positive, vitalizing worth of *Paradise Lost* to later poetry is evident. Works as significant and different as Pope's *Rape of the Lock* and Wordsworth's *Prelude* owe a considerable debt to *Paradise Lost*. Belinda is no less a latter-day Eve, suffering a prideful fall on the velvet plain at Hampton Court, than is Wordsworth a modern Adam, affirming "the earth is all before me," as he turns his back on the desolation of the city to re-create himself in nature.

It is equally certain that in *Paradise Lost* Milton sums up many of the vital concerns of literature and society that the Renaissance derived from classical and biblical traditions. Homer, Vergil, Dante, Tasso, Spenser—all stand behind Milton's masterpiece, as do Hebraic and Christian writers and commentators. Though these influences undeniably add their riches to the grandeur and value of *Paradise Lost*, they contribute as well to the difficulties that confront the modern reader. Contemporary transactional theories of reading receive a check in the immense cultural complexity out of which the epic evolves. The breadth of the work's achievement, debt, and influence makes *Paradise Lost* central to our understanding of English literature. It also makes it one of the most difficult texts to accommodate to an undergraduate literature course, whatever the format.

When we consider the poem's distance from modern sensibilities, we soon encounter problems arising from the historical and theological assumptions on which the poem rests. Many of the ideas Milton accepted as truths are alien to the modern reader. The same can be said of much sixteenth- and seventeenth-century literature, it is true, but few works of those periods lay such heavy claims on verifiable absolutes in thought, word, and deed. And few display a similar sweep in the canvas they cover. The heroic ideal, no less than the theological and historical, have been radically redefined since Milton's day, though the first, with its particular Miltonic emphasis on the everyday strengths of compassion and human resolve, provides

one way readers can negotiate the poem's somber, splendid landscapes of Hell beneath or Heaven above. But the blazes for that trail
only begin to appear to us relatively late in our journey. Much of the
way remains shrouded in darkness, imaginatively much less visible to
us than to our forebears.

In large measure the doctrinal, like the great synthesis of classical
and mythic materials, threatens to overwhelm our sensibilities. Does
one argue that Milton's theological concerns, like the weight of classical allusions, are givens ultimately subsumed in the sheer artistry of
the poem? Or does one doggedly pursue doctrine for its own sake,
administering it in even doses however little students may digest?
There are no easy solutions to such problems. The problems themselves shift with each new generation of students, equipped as they
are with whatever newfangledness is all the rage. A scant decade ago
broad ecumenical concern or pronounced religious unconcern made
Milton's theology a particularly troublesome challenge. Today a re-
surgence of fundamentalist principles in our society and throughout
the world has made the need again to confront hard, uncompromising religious ideas imperative to our well-being. And though another
decade may not see laughing Ceres reassume the land, it will surely
present new, equally difficult challenges to the teacher who would
mediate between Milton and the student reader. There is no easy
solution to the problem of shifting sensibilities. Perhaps the best we
can do is model ourselves on Raphael, the sociable angel, and seek
equivalent forms of discourse so that our fit audience, however few,
may see and understand. Though the tools and talents of our students
change, our responsibility remains the same, to discover the means of
communication without sacrificing the matter of human achievement
entrusted to our care.

It is evident, nevertheless, that just as the theological concerns
present in *Paradise Lost* challenge students' understanding and our
pedagogical skills, so the classical background of the *Iliad*, the *Odyssey*, the *Aeneid*, and a host of other, less well known works with which
Milton was fully conversant has receded farther and farther on our
students' imaginative horizons. Yet the endeavor to teach Milton—the
scholarly and humanistic enterprise itself—remains of utmost importance, even though it involves "translation" of the kind described by
George Steiner:

> Any thorough reading of a text out of the past of one's own lan-
> guage and literature is a manifold act of interpretation. In the
> great majority of cases, this act is hardly performed or even con-

sciously recognized. . . . When we read or hear any language-
statement from the past, be it Leviticus or last year's best-seller,
we translate. Reader, actor, editor are translators of language out
of time. . . . It is no overstatement to say that we possess civilization because we have learnt to translate out of time.   (17, 28,
30–31)

Clearly, the problems of language that a contemporary student faces
in reading Milton are not of the same order as those involved in actual
translation from a foreign language or even from a more distant form of
our own language. But the struggling student cannot be consoled as
easily with the notion that Milton's language, like Chaucer's Middle
English, is on the order of a foreign tongue. Milton seems perverse
rather than foreign. Students' needs and his seem of a different order
and nature. And these same students can find support for their point of
view—if they trouble to look for it—among numerous critics who,
with Dr. Johnson, consider Milton's language a "Babylonish dialect,"
constructed on the "pedantic principle of using English words with a
foreign idiom" ("Milton" 191). The real loss of language competence
that characterizes most Americans, student and teacher alike, exacer-
bates an already significant problem. Nor can we count on our students' being grammarians or rhetoricians. The difficulties that emerge
from these linguistic aspects of *Paradise Lost* are not, naturally, unrelated to matters of literary genre. The formal qualities of Milton's epic
arise out of an understanding of past epics, chiefly the *Aeneid*, and
they also manifest a particular attitude toward the worth and significance of the literary artifact, an attitude itself increasingly foreign to
the average reader of prose or viewer of television. The idiosyncratic
syntax and diction that Milton employs in his epic further complicate
understanding and appreciation of the formal characteristics of the
epic. How then is the teacher to deal with the impediments to sense
on the verbal surface of *Paradise Lost*?

In confronting these and related difficulties over the years, scholars
have sown forests of criticism where fields would have served. Bewil-
dering to the specialist, the mass of scholarship has become virtually
impenetrable for the nonspecialist who seeks help in presenting
Milton's epic to undergraduates. As often as not the scholar-critic,
instead of acting as a guide through the Miltonic landscape, is content
to clear a space in which to work a private patch.

Considering the multitude of difficulties hindering effective teaching of *Paradise Lost*, one might be inclined to seek out other works
that allow more efficient and effective teaching. Assigning *Paradise*

Lost to undergraduates might appear to be one of those "many mistakes which have made learning generally so unpleasing and so unsuccessful" that Milton himself complains of in his treatise *Of Education* (Wolfe, *Complete Prose* 2: 370). One might doubt the universality of *Paradise Lost*, especially in the light of the local, historical circumstances surrounding its conception and composition. But to doubt would be to commit a grievous error, causing irreparable losses to the profession of teaching the humanities. In *The Aims of Education*, Alfred North Whitehead claims "there is only one subject-matter for education, and that is Life in all its manifestations" (7). However difficult and removed from us *Paradise Lost* may appear to be, it provides a dramatic rendering of human activity as perceived in Western thought from Homer through the Renaissance and early Enlightenment. In the process it translates the mythic data of Hebraic and Hellenic thought into a concrete drama of shared concerns, lost opportunities, discord and debate that define the human condition and undergird all human aspiration.

Though it may be suspect to appropriate Milton's ideas in his own defense, it is reasonable to recall Milton's belief that "the end of learning is to repair the ruins of our first parents" (*Of Education*). Though we may question the concept of first parents, the need for reparation haunts our every action. In *Paradise Lost* Milton addresses that need, dramatizing human concern in the context of timeless behavior. Beyond recounting in imaginative and vivid detail the creation story as found in Genesis, he considers in human rather than merely doctrinal terms such matters as the troubled imperatives that characterize relations between men and women, the special demands of stewardship over nature and the self, the problems of freedom, choice, and responsibility. Moreover, *Paradise Lost* provides a comparative analysis of those Hellenic and Hebraic norms of accountability to which our culture, if we are to believe Matthew Arnold, owes a profound debt.

The creation story in Genesis, it has been argued, contributes to the subordinate position of women in Western society. In developing his poem, Milton lays himself open to charges of misogyny that derive as much from assumptions about Milton's private life as they do from facts of seventeenth-century social structures and the dramatic narrative of his poem. Yet Joan Webber has argued eloquently that Milton's epic is the first

> in which the active heroic role is shared equally between the sexes. . . . *Paradise Lost* is the first epic whose scene is, in

effect, the home, the woman's traditional sphere, rather than the world of warfare and quest outside. . . . While in most epics marriage or some analogous union is the symbol of fulfillment for which the hero strives, in *Paradise Lost* marriage is the main subject and theme of the poem. Although the setting in Eden seems far removed from ordinary life, much that happens there is commonplace. The poem traces the lives of a man and a woman from their first courtship through their first great disillusionment to their acceptance of life in the world that their descendants and Milton's readers know.   ("Politics of Poetry" 12)

Webber's view of these matters need not stifle discussion, as Joan Hartman's essay in this volume demonstrates. In areas such as this Milton seeks to make his poem an accounting of both divine and human motives. His method is that of dialogue and debate. And as we see from the poem itself, when dialogue ends, disaster looms. The consideration of the role of woman in human destiny is one of the concerns that ensures *Paradise Lost* a profound, continuing significance in Western thought.

Something of the same order of importance attaches to the poem's treatment of human relations with the natural world. Lynn White implicates Genesis and thus, indirectly, *Paradise Lost* as the distant source of the West's exploitative attitude toward the resources of nature: "By destroying pagan animism, Christianity made it possible to exploit nature in a mood of indifference to the feelings of natural objects" (1205).

In part 2 of this volume, Anne Prescott takes issue with the broad implications of such an indictment. But however we wish to modify the charge, the extended and dramatic treatment of human interaction with the natural world endows *Paradise Lost* with a long-range pertinence that is often overlooked. The implications of such interaction show themselves throughout the poem from the joy implicit in Milton's elaborate and inspired description of the creation itself to Eve's somber lament for the loss of her link with the garden world following the fall:

> O unexpected stroke, worse than of Death!
> Must I thus leave thee Paradise? thus leave
> Thee Native Soil, these happy Walks and Shades,
> Fit haunt of Gods? where I had hope to spend,
> Quiet though sad, the respite of that day
> That must be mortal to us both. O flow'rs,

That never will in other Climate grow,
My early visitation, and my last
At Ev'n, which I bred up with tender hand
From the first op'ning bud, and gave ye Names,
Who now shall rear ye to the Sun, or rank
Your Tribes, and water from th'ambrosial Fount?   (11.268–79)

These two subjects—relations between the sexes and the stewardship over nature and self—are basic to a full understanding and appreciation of the poem. Their significance for the contemporary reader reinforces the continuing value of *Paradise Lost* as an important document in the history of ideas. I do not suggest we see Milton's epic in the limited terms of its relevance to our times. Such a view is surely shortsighted. I wish rather to suggest the poem's fundamental resiliency as art and its ability through its richness to speak to any age in which human values are felt to be more than merely problematic.

Milton's concern for human freedom, dignity, and responsibility informs the structure and meaning of *Paradise Lost*. His own willingness to be held accountable is ubiquitous. Milton's valuing of the renewable resources of the human heart makes him weigh his age and condition in the scales of those timeless imperatives that animate all human activity. In the realm of science, for example, he investigates the problems attendant on the need to assimilate knowledge and faith, establishing by vivid analogy the rival claims of science and religion in the image of his near contemporary Galileo Galilei, whose struggle to proclaim the truth of science in the face of the reluctance of the Roman church made him a martyr to the religious power structure that could find no place for pure scientific investigation in the realms of its truth. Clearly, the role of scientific inquiry and the complex web of allegiances to which it must respond is a recurrent concern in the history of human thought. We may not be entirely satisfied with Milton's apparent judgment, voiced by Raphael in his monologue on celestial mechanics, but the poet's willingness to examine the conflicting claims of science and religion as he elaborates his narrative of loss and redemption characterizes the world of his poetry. Just as he inquires into the pervasive human problem of pain and loss by means of the courageous analysis of his own fallen state in Restoration London, so he analyzes the integrity of heart that prompts all significant reform in the face of physical or intellectual tyranny.

As noted earlier, it is difficult to separate out such matters from the general considerations of literary criticism. A sense of the importance of *Paradise Lost* inevitably leads to a critical reading of the poem itself. Recalling Whitehead's comment on life as the only subject matter for education, I would stress that coming to terms with a work of art as complex as *Paradise Lost,* a work arising from another and distant culture, amounts to much the same thing as coming to terms with any culture or set of cultural ideas different from ours. Encountering past or foreign values tests our own divergent set. Too often we think of life as our life, here and now, when all life teaches us that to comprehend no more than this is to fail utterly to grasp the essence of the human mind and human relations. A common mistake of student and teacher alike is to consider contemporary literature most relevant to her or his world. Nothing is further from the truth. Such a notion ignores the metaphysics of true belief; it embraces a fallacy of duration and subsists in ill-lasting monuments, as Sir Thomas Browne cautions. While the contemporaneous is often easiest to understand because of its closeness to us and our concerns, it is, for the same reason, often easiest to misread. Experience shows us that we do not profit from being reinforced in our own ideas and our own singleness of purpose. We need to reach for a broader grasp of the human condition in times and places other than our own, to translate, to carry over from one place to another the ideas of those different from ourselves in culture, background, and intellectual assumptions. I do not mean to imply we should appropriate those ideas merely; that is a colonialist impulse. Rather, we must seek to understand those ideas and use them to test the merit of our own ways and means. That action may prove to be the most compelling reason, finally, to find ways to assist the teacher in coping with the problems of presenting *Paradise Lost* to the undergraduate reader. Its bulk, complexity, and great demands make *Paradise Lost* an endangered poem. Yet how strange and barren the intellectual landscape would be without it. How much would be lost to the enterprise of teaching literature. Clearly, the effort to keep works of such magnitude before the student arises not from a vague desire to perpetuate the ungainly, the difficult, the erudite—too often the motives of a professional antiquarianism—but from a recognition of the essence and value of all humanistic endeavor.

Part One

MATERIALS

Galbraith M. Crump

Editions

However we react to reader-response theories of criticism, we do well to acknowledge the importance of the look of a text as it affects the reader. Though there is, of course, no substitute for an accurate, authoritative text, reading remains a strongly visual experience. As one who as an undergraduate struggled, not always successfully, with poets commonly presented in densely packed format, often on folio-sized pages in double column, I can still recall the depressing aspect. Difficult poets became daunting. Spenser, Shakespeare, and Milton, especially, suffered at the hands of parsimonious publishers. If as good humanists we would teach and delight, we would be well-advised to seek out texts that are at once authoritative and pleasing to peruse. Fortunately, today the instructor of Milton can choose from a wide range of texts that present the poet's work in a visually attractive format. As a result, and appropriately, decisions about textbook selection rest on such criteria as usefulness of critical apparatus and annotation, treatment of typographical characteristics of the early printed text, and practical matters like cost to students, hard or soft cover, and durability of binding. (With the great assortment of strong modern glues available, there is no reason why paperback books should fall apart even after continued use, but inevitably the products of some presses cast leaves with an autumnal abandon.)

What follows attempts to provide an objective guide to the various editions of Milton's poetry currently adopted by teachers, as reported by instructors in the survey that preceded preparation of the present volume. Throughout, I give attention to completeness and integrity of the text; the quality, quantity, and accessibility of editorial commentary and notes; and the general format of the book. Wherever possible, I include comments from individual instructors, when those comments illuminate some aspect of the usefulness of the text for teaching. Since instructors ought to select the edition most suited to the needs of their students, I have not made specific recommendations. My goal has been simply to help instructors make informed and appropriate selections.

The material is arranged in three categories—editions of the works of Milton, editions of *Paradise Lost* alone, and anthologies that include the poem. Full bibliographical information for works mentioned below is in the list of works cited that precedes the index.

Works of Milton

The edition of Milton's works most frequently cited in the survey is Merritt Y. Hughes's *John Milton: Complete Poems and Major Prose.* The cost of the volume argues against its use, according to some instructors. Yet some feel that the sturdy, hard-cover format, the clean printing, the generous margins, the numerous useful illustrations, and the comprehensive but not oppressive commentary are worth the cost. The main divisions of the book, the poetry and the prose, are organized chronologically, an arrangement that, Hughes argues, provides the "best substitute for the impossible royal road to an understanding of the development of the poet, the pamphleteer, and the amateur theologian" (vii). Hughes modernizes Milton's spelling and punctuation while retaining the most characteristic seventeenth-century typographical peculiarities. On the decision to modernize spelling and punctuation there is room for considerable argument, as Hughes admits in his prefatory remarks. If one puts aside for the moment Milton's own idiosyncrasies, the chief argument against modernizing punctuation arises out of our knowledge that rhetorical rather than grammatical principles governed seventeenth-century pointing generally and Milton's more particularly. Modernization obscures some of the phrasing and dramatic emphasis of the original, as Milton conceived those matters. Yet it is not always clear that the received pointing is Milton's own, and it is even less certain that the average modern reader will fully understand and be able to apply rhetorical considerations when confronting the poem or prose piece under consideration. Whatever may be a teacher's prejudices or preferences, however, he or she should consult Mindele Triep's authoritative study, *Milton's Punctuation and Changing English Usage, 1582–1676.*

Hughes provides critical headnotes for all the major poems and some of the minor works, though none for the prose. There are bibliographical headnotes for all the selections in the collection, however, plus a chronology of the main events of Milton's life and an appendix, which contains early biographies of Milton by John Aubrey, Edward Phillips, and an anonymous author (perhaps Cyriac Skinner). Latin texts are printed with English prose translations set alongside. In addition, Hughes offers extensive, authoritative footnotes throughout the volume. Though the commentary and footnotes have, over the years, become somewhat dated, they have essentially retained their value because most address concerns that stand apart from critical debate and relate to matters of abiding interest. Commenting on the edition in *Modern Language Review,* F. T. Prince feels, nevertheless, that an "amiable weakness of this edition is its determination to attach an equal value to every comment by every commentator . . . and the impression is left that every attempt at exegesis may be futile, however ingenious" (300). Still, there may be method to it. One might argue that, for most students approaching a text as challenging as *Paradise Lost,* such an Olympian overview licenses at least as much as it limits investigation. Summing up the merits of the Hughes edition, one respondent writes: "The excellent introductions, sensible footnotes, and the inclusion of significant prose works make this an outstanding teaching text for Milton."

Two other editions frequently cited by teachers surveyed are *The Complete Poetry of John Milton,* edited by John T. Shawcross, and *The Poems of John Milton,* edited by John Carey and Alastair Fowler. The former provides the student with all the poetry in an inexpensive paperback that is attractive but of less than adequate durability. It prints the Latin, Greek, and Italian poems with a literal translation by the editor. The edition contains a chronology of Milton's life, a reasonably comprehensive bibliography, and textual notes. Throughout, the volume is intelligently but sparsely annotated, providing relatively little help for the undergraduate reader. The text reproduces seventeenth-century sources, manuscript and printed, with precision.

If, as several teachers feel, the chief drawback of the Shawcross edition is the sparseness of its commentary, the opposite condition prevails in the edition prepared by Carey and Fowler. One instructor comments that, while the notes are useful, "I don't enjoy reading *Paradise Lost* or *Paradise Regained* in [this edition] because so little of the *poem* appears on a page; many of the pages are mostly notes, and this hampers one's reading pleasure." Writing of the edition for the *Times Literary Supplement* in 1969, the reviewer remarks that in the United States, where Hughes's edition has long commanded the field, "an editor of a recent anthology of Milton criticism thought Hughes too intimidating for English tastes ("Tercentenary"). Mr. Carey and Mr. Fowler have done nothing to allay such alarm and despondency. Professor Hughes required 308 pages for text and notes to *Paradise Lost*; Mr. Fowler takes up 606" (406). It should be added at once, however, that the notes for *Paradise Lost* are as illuminating as they are extensive, though at times too much reflecting the editor's scholarly penchants, particularly for numerology. Another problem with the edition is that its editors have not infrequently made decisions about the text, as if all the evidence were in. Thus, following the lead of William Riley Parker, they print *Samson Agonistes* as a work of Milton's middle years. The arguments concerning the date of composition of this poem are complex and surely unresolved by evidence thus far available to us. The editors' decision here is indicative of a rather general disposition on their part to deal cavalierly with matters of continuing critical debate. In using this edition, instructors and students need to exercise some caution. The text reproduced retains the original, rhetorical punctuation but abandons orthographic peculiarities.

Four other editions deserve careful consideration, according to teachers surveyed. Two are edited by Douglas Bush, and one each by Northrop Frye and B. A. Wright. Douglas Bush's edition, *The Complete Poetical Works of John Milton,* offers all the poetry, with prose translations of the Latin, Greek, and Italian poems, but prints no prose other than two brief autobiographical passages from Milton's prose tracts, supplementing the editor's fairly comprehensive introduction to the author's life and works. There are headnotes to the major selections, a glossary, and light but adequate annotation. One respondent writes of the relative merits of this edition that "it's the one that makes *Paradise Lost* look most like a poem and least like an exercise in scholarship." The text is modernized in spelling and punctuation, designed "for readers, not scholars." Bush also edits *The Portable Milton,* which contains complete texts of the major poems and many of the shorter lyrics. It prints *Of Education* and *Areopagitica,* in full, and autobiographical passages from other prose works. There is a lengthy introduction, chronology, and glossary of words and proper names. The text is modernized, and there are translations of the foreign language poems.

Instructors favoring Frye's Paradise Lost *and Selected Poetry and Prose* find its introduction and notes fully adequate to their needs. The prose selections are considered valuable in providing students with a more comprehensive sense of Milton's achievement as a writer than can be obtained from editions limited to the poetry. With respect to Wright's edition, *John Milton: Poems,* some feel that a major difficulty is the rather eclectic reformation of the text according to the original editor's perception of Milton's intentions. Editorially the principle is hard to justify, relying as it does on opinion at least as much as on firm evidence. Helen Darbishire's two-volume *Poetical Works of John Milton* elaborately argues the case and sets the modern standards for a reformed text. That hers and Wright's differ significantly will cause many readers to doubt the value of attempts at reformation in the first place.

In a slightly different category because of its contents is Christopher Ricks's edition, which contains *Paradise Lost* and *Paradise Regained.*

The texts are "partially modernized" in spelling but retain the original punctuation. The edition is introduced by a lively discussion of critical concerns past and present, a brief chronology, and a selected bibliography. The annotation is light and terse—at times too much so—to lessen the intimidation many students feel in Milton's presence.

From a bibliographical point of view, three other editions require mention, even though they are inappropriate as classroom texts. The standard edition is *The Works of John Milton*, under the general editorship of Frank A. Patterson. This eighteen-volume giant, the Columbia Milton, presents the text of Milton's work with full apparatus but without commentary. A separately printed two-volume index (Patterson and Fogel) provides a valuable subject guide. Despite the lavish enterprise, the edition is uneven and not always reliable. It has been, in part, superseded by the fully annotated, eight-volume *Complete Prose Works of John Milton*, under the general editorship of Don M. Wolfe. *John Milton's Complete Poetical Works, Reproduced in Photographic Facsimile* is edited in four volumes by Harris F. Fletcher. It includes facsimiles of manuscripts as well as of printed texts and could prove an extremely valuable teaching aid in studying Milton's methods and the growth of many of his poems, especially the shorter lyrics.

Texts of Paradise Lost

Instructors who teach only *Paradise Lost* and wish to use a text that isolates the epic have a broad range of choice. Merritt Hughes's edition of *Paradise Lost* is available in both hard and soft cover. Derived from the larger edition already discussed, the text has the advantages and disadvantages associated with the parent text. The same general observations apply to Alastair Fowler's edition of *Paradise Lost*.

Two other editions that deserve special consideration are the Modern Library College Edition, edited by William G. Madsen, and the Norton Critical Edition, edited by Scott Elledge. Madsen provides an excellent general introduction to the epic and a rather sparsely but intelligently annotated text. He modernizes spelling and capitalization but largely maintains the original rhetorical punctuation. The annotation in Elledge's edition, fuller than in Madsen's, is particularly useful in its treatment of the derivation of words and the background to many of Milton's more recondite allusions. Editorial considerations in relation to the text are the same as in Madsen. The edition contains a useful introduction to the poem, a selection of materials related to backgrounds and sources for the poem in Milton's own writing and in the Bible. The editor also provides extended notes on a number of topics and concepts especially pertinent to an understanding of the intellectual background of the epic, such as the structure of the cosmos, the scale of nature, and the fortunate fall. The edition concludes with a selection of criticism from the eighteenth century forward and an extended bibliography. In all, Elledge's is an attractive edition to use in the classroom, as a number of respondents point out, but, like all such critical editions, it has the drawback of packaging the poem, of making it thereby less a work for students to grapple with than one to accept on authority.

Anthologies

Although there is no substitute for reading and studying *Paradise Lost* in its entirety or in the context of Milton's other works, the particular demands of the survey or period course may make the anthology of literature a more satisfactory alternative textbook. In the survey and major authors course, two anthologies have risen above all the competitors, in the opinion of most teachers, as providing fullest coverage and most authoritative texts in a pleasurable format. These are *The Norton Anthology of English Literature*, under the general editorship of M. H. Abrams, and *The Oxford Anthology of English Literature*, under the general editorship of Frank Kermode and John Hollander; the names are similar, and the goals are certainly the same: to command a vast and lucrative market. In 1973, the reviewer for the *Times Literary Supplement* asked, rather naively, what "induced the Oxford University Press and academics" of high reputation "to undertake such an enterprise as this?" ("Corpus" 1337). One answer is clear. Whatever the motives, however, the results arising from these undertakings are more encouraging than one might have expected. And the continuing commercial struggle has produced handsome dividends for the average reader and student of literature, the minor stockholders, as it were, of industry's giants. Both publishers have been attentive, though Norton has been more assiduously so, to the reactions, suggestions, and demands of consumers. As a consequence, the Norton volumes have undergone revisions that have moved in the direction, generally, of more comprehensiveness and greater textual integrity. Compared with the anthologies of an earlier generation, the Norton and Oxford may be said greatly to have advanced the cause of teaching literature in the survey course.

The Norton has gone through four revisions, the latest being the fifth edition. The seventeenth-century section is edited by Robert M. Adams, who provides a modest selection from Milton's shorter poems "L'Allegro," "Il Penseroso," "Lycidas," and six sonnets; an extended excerpt from *Areopagitica*; and the complete *Samson Agonistes*. An intelligent abridgment of *Paradise Lost* offers books 1-3 and 9 complete; the remaining books appear in summary or abridged form, as follows: 4.1-407; 5.278-505; 6, summary; 7.1-39; 8, summary; 10.706-965; 11, summary; and 12.465-649. Providing general context, there is a lengthy introduction to the seventeenth century; a brief biographical introduction to Milton; headnotes to "Lycidas," *Paradise Lost*, and *Samson Agonistes*; extensive footnotes; and brief notes on bibliographical matters and poetic forms at the close of the volume. In addition, one significant virtue of this or any reasonably comprehensive anthology is the literary and critical context provided by the inclusion of work by an author's contemporaries and early critics. In the Norton, for example, besides the poetry of Milton's friend Andrew Marvell, with its complex literary and political concerns mirroring those of Milton, there are selections from such important critical response to *Paradise Lost* as Addison's *Spectator* essays and Dr. Johnson's analysis in his "Life of Milton." There are no illustrations in the Norton, apart from two at the back of volume 1, presenting images of the Elizabethan stage and the Ptolemaic universe. The endpapers of the volume present useful maps of England and London. A valuable recent addition to the anthology is a section entitled "Poems in Process," which reproduces a number of poems with manuscript revisions that allow a reader to study the creative rethinking underlying the final poetic result with which we are familiar. Representing Milton here, the editors have chosen a section from "Lycidas," contained in the Trinity College Manuscript.

The general editors of the Oxford anthology, Frank Kermode and John Hollander, are also responsible for the Renaissance section, including Milton. The overall format of this anthology is more pleasurable than that of the Norton, with fuller margins and less cramped layout, a handsome typeface, and better quality, more opaque paper. Like the Norton, the Oxford provides an extensive introductory note for the period and headnotes on the poets and major poems. The annotation is thorough and intelligent. There are bibliographical notes at the end of the volume and a glossary of literary forms and terms. One of the glories of this anthology is its rich gathering of illustrative materials—maps, portraits, emblems, and the like, as well as some representative musical settings. Despite these many merits, the Oxford has troubled many teachers because of its somewhat eccentric choice of texts. Oxford prints the same shorter poems as found in the Norton, plus the complete text of *Comus,* along with Henry Lawes's setting of "Sweet Eccho." Though this inclusion can certainly be justified, in and of itself, the decision becomes more problematic when one examines the abridgment of *Paradise Lost* that results. Books 4 and 9 are printed complete. The remaining books are either abridged or presented in synopsis. The editors also print *Samson Agonistes* complete, a brief segment from *Paradise Regained*— the denial of classical learning and philosophy—and conclude with a slender segment from the *Areopagitica.* On balance, the Norton selection is more satisfying for the reader concerned with *Paradise Lost* and the epic tradition.

Among other anthologies available for the survey course, two that are cited with some degree of regularity by teachers are *The Literature of England* and the two-volume *British Literature.* The former, edited by George K. Anderson and William E. Buckler, is a handsome book with generous white space and a pleasurable typeface. It contains an annotated chronology, brief headnotes, and footnotes. Selections from Milton's shorter poems are "On the Morning of Christ's Nativity," "L'Allegro," "Il Penseroso," "Lycidas," and six sonnets. *Samson Agonistes* is presented in full, and there is a brief excerpt "defending books" from the *Areopagitica.* Books 1, 2, 4, and 9 of *Paradise Lost* are printed in full, while the remaining books are represented by their arguments, merely. The editors also print the final ninety-two lines of the poem.

The two-volume *British Literature* is edited by Hazelton Spencer, in conjunction with Beverly J. Layman and David Ferry. The three editors are also responsible for the Milton material, consisting of selections from the *Areopagitica* and *Of Education,* seven sonnets, and the full texts of "L'Allegro," "Il Penseroso," and "Lycidas." Books 1, 2, and 9 of *Paradise Lost* are given in full, with extracts from books 4, 8, and 12 and the arguments from the remaining books.

Finally, an anthology that is widely used in surveys of world literature is the two-volume *Norton Anthology of World Masterpieces,* under the general editorship of Maynard Mack. The selections from *Paradise Lost,* edited by P. M. Pasinetti, are books 9 and 10. Though the text itself is slight, the general context of the volume allows for a number of illuminating juxtapositions and a sense of the broad epic tradition from which Milton set out in his poem.

Required and Recommended Student Readings

Among teachers surveyed, most stress close reading of the text of *Paradise Lost* and assign little or no reading from secondary sources. Those that do, however, usually argue that some knowledge of Milton's major sources and analogues is valuable and ought seriously to be encouraged. Chief among these texts are, of course, the Bible, the major classical epics, and various early myths. Many instructors place the King James Bible of 1611 or the Authorized Version of 1612 on reserve. These are presumably the translations Milton would have turned to most often, and a familiarity with the early chapters of Genesis, and parts of Job, and the Psalms, Isaiah, John, Romans, and Revelation is essential for students growing up in a profoundly secular age.

Students should also be encouraged to familiarize themselves with the *Iliad,* the *Odyssey,* and the *Aeneid,* understanding as a minimum the broad outlines of the narrative and some of the key passages that Milton had in mind in fashioning his epic. Numerous excellent translations of these texts are available; three particularly attractive verse renderings are those by Robert Fitzgerald. His superb translation of Vergil, in progress for many years, has only recently been published. Lacking firsthand acquaintance with the great epics of classical literature, students may be able to gain some sense of the grand epic tradition in which Milton wrote by consulting C. M. Bowra's *From Virgil to Milton.*

For many instructors, a translation of Ovid's *Metamorphoses* is also invaluable for students because it allows them to compare Milton's treatment of certain key myths, such as that of Narcissus, with the tone and treatment in the pagan work. Such a comparative study is often useful as the basis for student written work. Rolfe Humphries and Mary Innes produced attractive translations of Ovid's classic in recent years.

Among general reference materials of which students should be apprised is the *Oxford English Dictionary.* Historically organized, this dictionary is an excellent tool for both students and instructors seeking the special weight and meaning of individual words as Milton would have understood them or, indeed, redefined them in the course of his writing. To assist in tracking down the details of Milton's allusions, many instructors encourage their students to become familiar with the four-volume *Interpreter's Dictionary of the Bible,* edited by George Arthur Buttrick, and *A Dictionary of Biblical Allusions in*

English Literature, compiled by W. B. Fulghum, Jr. N. G. L. Hammond and H. H. Scullard edit *The Oxford Classical Dictionary,* while Mark P. O. Morford and Robert L. Lenardon are the compilers of an inexpensive guide, *Classical Mythology.*

Some of the many works presenting a clear statement of the historical background of the century are noted below in "Background Studies." Many instructors recommend Christopher Hill's *Milton and the English Revolution* as valuable in illuminating the political and religious climate in which Milton lived and wrote. For a general overview of intellectual conceptions that define the Renaissance mind, numerous respondents cite E. M. W. Tillyard's *Elizabethan World Picture.* C. S. Lewis's *Preface to* Paradise Lost is an eminently readable introduction to the concepts of the epic and to Milton's treatment of several moral and theological concerns. C. A. Patrides and Raymond B. Waddington edit the recent *Age of Milton,* an excellent guide to the intellectual backgrounds of the period, with eleven essays by scholars of authority.

The most accessible life is Douglas Bush's *John Milton: A Sketch of His Life and Works.* A. N. Wilson's *Life of John Milton* is also valuable as an introduction, as is James Thorpe's *John Milton: The Inner Life.* Graduate students should know William Riley Parker's excellent two-volume study, *Milton: A Biography.* It does not replace David Masson's monumental seven-volume *Life of John Milton,* but it is certainly more serviceable for student reading. John S. Diekhoff assembles autobiographical passages in *Milton on Himself,* and Helen Darbishire edits *The Early Lives of Milton.*

Four general works that offer useful supplements to the study of Milton are Marjorie Nicolson, *John Milton: A Reader's Guide*; James H. Hanford and James G. Taaffe, *A Milton Handbook*; Cecily V. Wedgwood, *Milton and His World*; and Don M. Wolfe, *Milton and His England.* The last two books offer a wealth of fine illustrative material. A similar work is Lois Potter's *A Preface to Milton,* containing many illustrations. It is especially good on the concrete details of Milton's world. John Broadbent is general editor of the Cambridge Milton for Schools and Colleges series, designed for the individual student but invaluable for instructors as well. Two volumes are especially relevant to our concerns. One is *John Milton: Introductions,* edited by Broadbent himself, with sections on various topics, such as Milton's life and times, the making of a seventeenth-century poet, science, the poet's Bible, iconography, music, and literary history. The companion volume, also edited by Broadbent, is Paradise Lost: *Introduction.* Topics include myth and ritual; the epic genre; the writing, publication, and editing of *Paradise Lost*; the worldview reflected in the epic; Milton's theology; structural and poetic patterns; and syntax and diction. Both books contain many valuable suggestions for stimulating, if at times controversial, topics for student investigation. Thus they offer student and instructor alike a rich quarry of materials for further refining. According to one respondent, intellectually the books are "great fun." G. K. Hunter writes an attractive introduction to *Paradise Lost* for the Unwin Critical Library series.

In the past, instructors have not infrequently had their students purchase a collection of modern critical essays to supplement reading. Unfortunately, most of these are no longer in print. As reference works for students to consult, however, they remain valuable. Arthur Barker's *Milton: Modern Essays in Criticism*, nineteen of whose thirty-three essays focus on *Paradise Lost*, presents an extensive and well-balanced array of critical approaches. C. A. Patrides's *Milton's Epic Poetry* contains sixteen essays, all but three on *Paradise Lost*, and an excellent annotated bibliography. Louis L. Martz edits a dozen essays in *Milton:* Paradise Lost: *A Collection of Critical Essays*. Martz's introduction amounts to a thirteenth essay. James Thorpe edits *Milton Criticism: Selections from Four Centuries*, and John T. Shawcross is the compiler of *Milton: The Critical Heritage*. Other collections worth consideration, though not all are as serviceable as those already cited, are Ronald D. Emma and John T. Shawcross, *Language and Style in Milton*; C. A. Patrides, *Approaches to* Paradise Lost; Allan Rudrum, *Milton: Modern Judgments*; and Thomas Kranidas, *New Essays on* Paradise Lost.

The above suggestions do not exhaust the possibilities of books useful to undergraduates and graduate students. Given the background, sophistication, and dedication of particular students, instructors will wish to peruse the additional books cited in "The Instructor's Library."

Aids to Teaching

Audiovisual aids available to supplement the study of Milton range from recordings and film strips to the art and music of Milton's age and that which immediately followed. Though many instructors feel that reliance on such materials, at any stage, detracts from the serious intellectual challenge of reading and responding to Milton, it is reasonable to remind ourselves that Milton and his early readers were themselves daily and profoundly influenced by music and art. They could hardly be expected to separate out the general aesthetic claims of their world in their own imaginative encounter with the specific demands of literature.

Great illustrators from Milton's contemporaries down to our own time—Medina, Blake, Doré—have sought to envision graphically the power and sweep of Milton's imagination. In *The Film Sense*, no less a practitioner of the film than Sergei Eisenstein considers *Paradise Lost* in terms of the cinema. While no filmmaker has actually undertaken the screening of Milton's epic, John Collier discusses the subject in *Milton's* Paradise Lost: *Screenplay for the Cinema of the Mind.* Justifying what he calls an "act of pillage," Collier cites as his primary objective "the making of a screenplay out of the most dramatic, spectacular and significant parts of Milton's epic, much as certain Romans built their lesser dwellings of materials quarried from the palaces and monuments of a greater past" (vii). Like the brilliant graphic representations of *Paradise Lost* by John Martin, the eighteenth-century English illustrator, the responses of Eisenstein and Collier remind us of the dramatic quality of Milton's epic, its engrossing visual and emotional content, and its very modern rather than old-fashioned visualization of a cosmos charged with vast dynamic energies. Regarding Martin, William Feaver's *Art of John Martin,* with 166 illustrations, is the definitive work.

The theatrical readings on the principal recordings of *Paradise Lost* do justice to the dramatic quality of the poem. Many instructors make their own tapes, however, to meet the special needs of their classrooms. The chief function of recorded selections, like in-class reading, is to help students overcome the apparent visual complexity of Milton's verse. One seeks to present not the "organ music" but the plain logical, rhetorical sense of the verse paragraph, which is visually intimidating to a modern eye raised on scant, uncomplicated journalistic paragraphs. Of recordings available, those most frequently cited by survey respondents are Anthony Quayle's reading of selections from the opening four books of the epic and readings by Tony Church and Michael Redgrave, among others, under the direction of George Rylands.

Filmstrips and television broadcasts are available but not in any quantity. The most interesting and useful is Don Taylor's fictionalized drama of aspects of Milton's life, *Paradise Restored,* a ninety-minute film in color that has been shown on public television in this country. Some instructors have found parts of Jacob Bronowski's *Ascent of*

Man useful in offering insights into the general intellectual background of the seventeenth century. The episodes most germane to *Paradise Lost* are "The Starry Messenger," and "The Majestic Clockwork," numbers six and seven of the series. Similarly, some of the central episodes of Kenneth Clark's series *Civilisation* provide valuable materials on the aesthetic concerns of the age. Episodes five, six, and seven, entitled "The Hero as Artist," "Protest and Communication," and "Grandeur and Obedience," illuminate *Paradise Lost*. (At this writing, Hugh Richmond is preparing a documentary television program on John Milton for the National Endowment for the Humanities for release late in 1985 or early 1986.)

The art and music of seventeenth-century Europe is invaluable in making emphatic the aesthetic context of Milton's poetry. The most useful introduction to the music is Winifred Maynard's essay, "Milton and Music," in Broadbent's *John Milton: Introductions*. In the same volume Joseph Trapp and Roy Daniells write on iconography and Milton's relation to Renaissance art, while John Dixon Hunt considers Milton's illustrators. The major studies in the visual arts as they affect Milton's work are Roland Frye's monumental *Milton's Imagery and the Visual Arts*, a work of exhaustive research and impeccable scholarship, and, more recently, Murray Roston's *Milton and the Baroque*, which Frye in his review appraises as "the most impressive and valuable correlation between the literary and visual Baroque with which I am familiar" (411). Returning to the musical context of Milton's work, I urge instructors to consider the value of playing selections from the music of the period as suggestive of the grand rhythms of *Paradise Lost*. Perhaps most characteristic and impressive is the work of Handel. A useful reference is R. M. Myers's study, *Handel, Dryden, and Milton*. A pioneering work is *Milton's Knowledge of Music* by Sigmund G. Spaeth. Two important works, one specifically related to Milton and the other more general, are E. Brennecke, *John Milton the Elder and His Music*, and John Hollander, *The Untuning of the Skies: Ideas of Music in English Poetry, 1500–1700*.

The Instructor's Library

This section lists essential reference materials that an instructor should consult in preparation for teaching *Paradise Lost*. The list is not exhaustive, nor is it meant to take the place of the instructor's own investigation of materials. It may best be considered as an annotated list of significant research tools frequently cited by teachers responding to the survey on *Paradise Lost*. I have felt free to supplement those suggestions, particularly with notable works of recent scholarship that have not yet generally assumed a place alongside the indispensable standard works in the field. Because of space limitations I cite relatively few journal articles. The reader is urged to explore the various journals that typically contain Milton scholarship, as well as the standard bibliographies and reviews of current scholarship.

Reference Works

The wealth of critical material relating to Milton that has accumulated in the past two centuries has been fully documented, to 1968, in three standard reference books: David H. Stevens, *Reference Guide to Milton from 1800 to the Present Day*; Harris F. Fletcher, *Contributions to a Milton Bibliography: 1800–1930* (addenda to Stevens); and Calvin Huckabay, *John Milton: An Annotated Bibliography, 1929–1968*. Douglas Bush provides extremely valuable and wide-ranging bibliographies for Milton and the seventeenth century generally in *English Literature in the Earlier Seventeenth Century*, part of the Oxford History of English Literature; he also compiles and writes the section on Milton in A. E. Dyson's *English Poetry: Selected Bibliographical Guides*. There is an excellent annotated reading list in C. A. Patrides's *Milton's Epic Poetry*. James Holly Hanford edits the Goldentree Bibliography on Milton, which is perhaps the handiest guide to use but is not as thoroughgoing as some of the others. Annual bibliographies that cover Milton include the English Association's *Year's Work in English Studies*, a selective annotated guide that lags about three years behind the current date. The Modern Humanities Research Association's *Annual Bibliography of English Language and Literature*, the *MLA International Bibliography*, and *Studies in Philology* are all extremely valuable listings. Among the many journals that ought to be consulted for articles on Milton are *Milton Studies* and the *Milton Quarterly*.

In addition to the standard biographies cited earlier, a number of other, more specialized studies provide insights into the poet's life and works. J. Milton French edits *The Life Records of John Milton*, and Jackson C. Boswell investigates the books that Milton owned, knew, and read in *Milton's Library*. Donald L. Clark's *John Milton at St. Paul's School* analyzes the course of study and pedagogical practices under which the young Milton would have been educated. William Riley Parker presents documents in *Milton's Contemporary Reputation,* and Leo Miller inquires into the authenticity of images of the poet in *Milton's Portraits.* Allan Gilbert compiled a *Geographical Dictionary of Milton.*

Linguistic aids include the previously mentioned *Oxford English Dictionary.* Edward S. Le Comte compiles *A Milton Dictionary* and *A Dictionary of Puns in Milton's English Poetry,* a pioneering work but less than comprehensive. There are concordances by John Bradshaw and by William Ingram and Kathleen Swaim. Gladys W. Hudson compiles a computerized concordance to *Paradise Lost.* Two other general reference tools providing a wealth of materials relating to the poet and his work are *A Milton Encyclopedia,* edited by William B. Hunter, Jr., with John T. Shawcross and John M. Steadman, in eight volumes. Merritt Y. Hughes and John Steadman are general editors of the *Variorum Commentary on the Poems of John Milton* (in progress), with the volume on *Paradise Lost* not available at this writing.

Background Studies and Critical Works

Numerous works illuminate the history—social, political, and religious—of Milton's age and provide excellent background materials for the study of Milton's epic. The two volumes of the Oxford History of England that cover the period of Milton's life are Godfrey Davis's *The Early Stuarts, 1603–1660* and George Clark's *The Later Stuarts, 1660–1714.* Both works contain extensive bibliographies. In the New Cambridge Modern History, volume 4, *The Decline of Spain and the Thirty Years War, 1609–59,* is edited by J. P. Cooper, while F. L. Carsten edits volume 5, *The Ascendancy of France, 1648–88.* Godfrey Davis compiles the *Bibliography of British History: The Stuart Period, 1603–1714;* J. S. Morrill's *Seventeenth-Century Britain, 1603–1714* surveys and updates bibliographical materials. John Roach edits *A Bibliography of Modern History* to supplement the New Cambridge Modern History. Volume 2 of G. M. Trevelyan's four-volume *Illustrated English Social History* is valuable as a repository of illustrative materials for the Miltonic period. J. A. W. Gunn's *Politics and the Public Interest in the Seventeenth Century* and Barry Coward's *The Stuart Age: A History of England, 1603–1714* are useful general works to consult. G. M. Trevelyan's *England under the Stuarts* provides a useful survey with a whiggish, that is, Miltonic, bias. With a strong Marxist flavor, Christopher Hill writes illuminatingly on the period. Beside *Milton and the English Revolution,* noted earlier, stand his *Puritanism and Revolution, Society and Puritanism in Pre-*

Revolutionary England, Intellectual Origins of the English Revolution, and *The World Turned Upside Down: Radical Ideas during the English Revolution*. Hill's deep interest in and knowledge of the poetry of the century make these historical studies unusually informative and illuminating for the student of Milton despite their particular political slant. Cecily V. Wedgwood also writes extensively on this century, focusing on the turbulent Civil War period: *The King's Peace: 1637–1641, The King's War: 1641–47*, and *A Coffin for King Charles: The Trial and Execution of Charles I*. Two more general studies by the same author are *Seventeenth-Century English Literature* and *Poetry and Politics under the Stuarts*; both works broadly survey their subjects without pretending to great depth.

Under the heading of the history of ideas a great deal of valuable scholarship has accumulated in the past half-century. Two of the first modern scholars to work in this area were Hardin Craig and A. O. Lovejoy. Craig's *The Enchanted Glass: The Renaissance Mind in English Literature* and its sequel, *New Lamps for Old*, catalog and consider the furniture of the Elizabethan mind, with special emphasis in the latter on the relation of Elizabethan to modern sensibilities. Lovejoy's influential work is *The Great Chain of Being*; more specialized studies are "Milton and the Paradox of the Fortunate Fall" and "Milton's Dialogue on Astronomy." Another scholar who contributed impressively to this area throughout his career is Don Cameron Allen. His study *The Legend of Noah: Renaissance Rationalism in Art, Science and Letters* shows how the claims of reason and science served gradually to liberate artists and writers from a strict dependence on the biblical narrative. Of particular interest for us is Allen's analysis of the reasons for Milton's elaborate and traditional account of the flood in *Paradise Lost*. Allen's subsequent works include *The Harmonious Vision*, six essays on the general subject of the unifying theme in Milton's oeuvre; *Doubt's Boundless Sea: Skepticism and Faith in the Renaissance*; and *Mysteriously Meant: The Rediscovery of Pagan Symbolism and Allegorical Interpretation in the Renaissance*. Herschel Baker investigates the rise and decay of Christian humanism in the Renaissance in two important studies, *The Dignity of Man* and *The Wars of Truth*. Baker pays special attention to Milton's use of reason and the Anglican-Puritan controversy as reflected in the poet's work. Douglas Bush's *The Renaissance and English Humanism* contains a chapter on Milton. J. B. Bamborough offers an extensive study of Renaissance psychology, *The Little World of Man*, which considers the human being's place in nature and theories concerning body and soul. Another study providing important background information for

Milton is Victor Harris's *All Coherence Gone,* which examines the idea of decay in nature as manifest in Renaissance thought. Leo Spitzer's *Classical and Christian Ideas of World Harmony,* William Madsen's "The Idea of Nature in Milton's Poetry," and Harry Levin's *Myth of the Golden Age in the Renaissance* are of broadly related interest. Margaret Wiley's *The Subtle Knot: Creative Skepticism in Seventeenth-Century England,* Ernst Cassirer's *Platonic Renaissance in England,* Hiram Haydn's *The Counter-Renaissance,* Robert Hoopes's *Right Reason in the English Renaissance,* and Rosalie L. Colie's *Paradoxia Epidemica: The Renaissance Tradition of Paradox* examine various aspects of the intellectual traditions to which Milton was heir. Samuel Kliger's *The Goths in England* studies seventeenth- and eighteenth-century patterns of thought, while Laurence A. Sasek investigates the Puritan viewpoint in *The Literary Temper of the English Puritans.*

The history of science, especially as it impinges on the literature of the seventeenth century, is the subject of R. F. Jones's *Ancients and Moderns: A Study of the Rise of the Scientific Movement in Seventeenth-Century England.* The standard work on astronomy in the period is *Astronomical Thought in Renaissance England* by F. R. Johnson. Marjorie Hope Nicolson greatly enhances our understanding with three excellent studies: *The Microscope and the English Imagination,* a work that was preceded by journal essays listed in works cited at the end of this volume; *The Breaking of the Circle: Studies in the Effect of the "New Science" upon Seventeenth-Century Poetry;* and *Mountain Gloom and Mountain Glory: The Development of the Aesthetics of the Infinite.* Other works that offer valuable insights into the development of scientific thought are A. C. Crombie's *Augustine to Galileo: The History of Science, A.D. 400–1650,* T. S. Kuhn's *The Copernican Revolution: Planetary Astronomy in the Development of Western Thought,* S. K. Heninger's *Touches of Sweet Harmony: Pythagorean Cosmology and Renaissance Poetics* and *The Cosmological Glass: Renaissance Diagrams of the Universe,* and Walter Curry's *Milton's Ontology, Cosmology, and Physics.* Lynn Thorndike's *History of Magic and Experimental Science* provides, among other things, a valuable insight on the troubled yet productive relation of the arcane and the practical. E. A. Burtt analyzes the rise of the new science in *The Metaphysical Foundations of Modern Physical Science,* an important early work in this field. Basil Willey considers the role of ideas in poetry and religion in *The Seventeenth Century Background;* he discusses Milton's epic in the chapter "The Heroic Poem in a Scientific Age." In *Milton and Science* Kester Svendsen studies medieval and Renaissance encyclopedias as they provide a general background for Milton's ideas and illuminate the metaphoric rather than scientific use he made of these ideas in fashioning his epic.

Among works seeking to relate Milton and *Paradise Lost* to their classical and Continental contexts are Bowra's *From Virgil to Milton*, cited earlier, and Gilbert Highet's broad survey, *The Classical Tradition: Greek and Roman Influences on Western Literature*, which glances at Milton's work. Francis C. Blessington's Paradise Lost *and the Classical Epic* investigates "the dynamics of the relationship" between Milton's epic and the major classical models. An extremely valuable and comprehensive work, it defines the ways Milton reworked the classical vision and, as a result, "extended and fulfilled" it in terms of his own poetry. Joan Webber's *Milton and the Epic Tradition*, which received the Milton Society's James Holly Hanford Award, surveys the epic tradition in Homer, Vergil, Dante, Ariosto, Camoëns, Tasso, and Spenser, as these writers influenced Milton and were, in turn, "redefined" in Milton's epic. (Webber's essay "Jumping the Gap: The Epic Poetry of Milton—and After" represents work on which she was engaged at the time of her death.) Irene Samuel's two studies, *Plato and Milton* and *Dante and Milton: The* Commedia *and* Paradise Lost, provide a useful survey of Milton's debt to these writers in his thought and poetry.

F. T. Prince's *The Italian Element in Milton's Verse* is a standard work but is only partially concerned with *Paradise Lost*. Ernst Curtius's *European Literature and the Latin Middle Ages* reaches forward into our period in its pursuit and study of recurrent images and motifs, while Jean Seznec's *The Survival of the Pagan Gods: The Mythological Tradition and Its Place in Renaissance Humanism and Art* surveys a tradition that bears significantly on Milton's art and thought. Three other works of interest are Davis P. Harding's *The Club of Hercules: Studies in the Classical Background of* Paradise Lost; Thomas Greene's *The Descent from Heaven: A Study of Epic Continuity*, which deals with the convention of heavenly epiphanies in the epic tradition and contains a chapter on Milton; and Leo Spitzer's standard account, *Classical and Christian Ideas of World Harmony*.

There is a vast amount of valuable work concerned with the religious context of *Paradise Lost*. A sampling of the field is all that is possible to offer here. The titles are set out alphabetically by author: John Armstrong, *The Paradise Myth*; Arthur Barker, *Milton and the Puritan Dilemma, 1641–1660*, considers the development of Milton's thought as evidenced by the prose pamphlets and discusses the dilemma of how to establish a reformation that would allow freedom of conscience, and vice versa; J. L. Blau, *The Christian Interpretation of the Cabala in the Renaissance*; Mary Irma Corcoran, *Milton's Paradise with Reference to the Hexameral Background*, shows that Milton's concept of nature and humankind was fundamentally religious rather than merely humanistic; Austin Dobbins, *Milton and the Book of Revelation: The Heavenly Cycle*; J. M. Evans, Paradise Lost *and the Genesis Tradition*; Harold Fisch, *Jerusalem and Albion: The Hebraic Factor in Seventeenth-Century Literature*; Harris F. Fletcher, *Milton's Rabbinical Reading*; William B. Hunter, C. A. Patrides, and J. H. Adamson, *Bright Essence: Studies in Theology*; and Lee A. Jacobus, *Sudden Apprehension: Aspects of Knowledge in* Paradise Lost. Despite the subtitle, this work is a comprehensive investigation of all dimensions of knowledge, a broad and important area for the study of *Paradise Lost*.

Additional titles are Maurice Kelley, *This Great Argument: A Study of Milton's* De doctrina *as a Gloss on* Paradise Lost; Watson Kirkconnell, *The Celestial Cycle: The Theme of* Paradise Lost *in World Literature with Translations of the Major Analogues*; Burton Kurth, *Milton and Christian Heroism: Biblical Epic Themes and Forms in Seventeenth-Century England*; C. A. Patrides, *The Phoenix and the Ladder: The Rise and Decline of the Christian View of History*, *Milton and the Christian Tradition*, and *The Grand Design of God*, which like Patrides's earlier titles places Milton's thought within the context of the providential view of history, examining that view as manifest in the works of the early church fathers down to Milton's own day; Leland Ryken, *The Apocalyptic Vision in* Paradise Lost; Howard Schultz, *Milton and Forbidden Knowledge*; James Sims, *The Bible in Milton's Epics*; D. P. Walker, *The Decline of Hell: Seventeenth-Century Discussions of Eternal Torment*; Robert West, *Milton and the Angels*, a comprehensive study of angelology and Milton's use of its ideas and doctrines in his epic. Arnold Williams, *The Common Expositor: An Account of the Commentaries on Genesis: 1527–1633*, examines various commentaries on Genesis compiled during the sixteenth and seventeenth centuries and their influence on Milton's time.

In addition to several titles mentioned earlier on the subject, a number of excellent surveys on aspects of the arts will prove useful to the instructor preparing to teach *Paradise Lost* with an eye to its broad aesthetic context. (Readers ought to consult the essays in this volume by Virginia Tufte and Anne Prescott for more detailed information about texts related to art and gardening.) Some standard works are Beverly Sprague Allen, *Tides of English Taste (1619–1800): A Back-*

ground for the Study of Literature, the two volumes containing a wealth of illustrative material; Stephen Behrendt, *The Moment of Explosion: Blake and the Illustration of Milton;* Calvin S. Brown, *Music and Literature: A Comparison of the Arts*; Terry Comito, *The Idea of the Garden in the Renaissance*; Roy Daniells, *Milton, Mannerism, and Baroque*; Gretchen Finney, *Musical Backgrounds for English Literature: 1580–1650*; Ernest Gilman, *The Curious Perspective: Literary and Pictorial Wit in the Seventeenth Century*; André Grabar, *Christian Iconography: A Study of Its Origins*; Miles Hadfield and J. C. H. Hadfield, *Gardens of Delight*; Jean H. Hagstrum, *The Sister Arts: The Tradition of Literary Pictorialism and English Poetry from Dryden to Gray* and *Sex and Sensibility: Ideal and Erotic Love from Milton to Mozart*; James Hall, *Dictionary of Subjects and Symbols in Art*; Robert Hughes, *Heaven and Hell in Western Art*; Erwin Panofsky, *Studies in Iconology*; Marcia Pointon, *Milton and English Art*; Mario Praz, "Milton and Poussin"; Roy Strong, *The Renaissance Garden in England.*

Scholarship related to Milton and his epic has accumulated in such vast quantities over past decades that any listing appropriate to this volume must be highly selective. Instructors are advised to consider the standard bibliographies cited earlier for a more comprehensive listing. Most of the works that follow are those frequently named by respondents as valuable for the teacher. I have added to the list a few recent titles of special interest. Robert Adams appraises Milton criticism in *Ikon: John Milton and the Modern Critics.* Theodore Banks's *Milton's Imagery* is an early but still useful study, as is Robert Bridges's *Milton's Prosody.* A later study is William B. Hunter, "The Sources of Milton's Prosody." Ernest Sprott's *Milton's Art of Prosody* is a very useful work, supplanting Bridges in thoroughness and systematic analysis. Other early critical studies that have remained valuable are Douglas Bush, Paradise Lost *in Our Time*; David Daiches, *Milton*; John Diekhoff, *Milton's* Paradise Lost: *A Commentary on the Argument*; H. J. C. Grierson, *Cross Currents in English Literature of the Seventeenth Century*, which investigates the tensions between humanism and Puritanism in Spenser and Milton; Grierson's *Milton and Wordsworth: Poets and Prophets. A Study of Their Reactions to Political Events* provides a valuable analysis of the great Romantic poet through the medium of Milton and his influence. Raymond Havens also studies Milton's impact on later poets in his pioneering work, *The Influence of Milton of English Poetry.* Edward S. Le Comte investigates verbal and psychological patterns in Milton's poetry and thought in *Yet Once More*; a more recent work is his *Milton and Sex.*

Grant McColley writes about sources and literary patterns in Paradise Lost: *An Account of Its Growth and Major Origins*. Ants Oras canvasses a range of opinions in *Milton's Editors and Commentators from Patrick Hume to Henry John Todd (1695–1801)*. In Paradise Lost *and the Seventeenth-Century Reader* Balachandra Rajan describes the advantages of approaching Milton's epic as far as possible in the spirit of the contemporary reader; his more recent *The Lofty Rhyme: A Study of Milton's Major Poetry* includes brief but cogent chapters on *Paradise Lost* as seen in the larger context of Milton's oeuvre. Denis Saurat's *Milton: Man and Thinker* remains useful, though much of it is now dated in matter and method. E. M. W. Tillyard wrote extensively on Milton over a long and brilliant career. His study *Milton* was followed by *The Miltonic Setting: Past and Present* and *Studies in Milton*. All three works, like his *Elizabethan World Picture*, have been frequently reprinted. A. J. A. Waldock defends the continuing validity of Milton's epic for our time in Paradise Lost *and Its Critics*. George Whiting's *Milton's Literary Milieu* and *Milton and This Pendant World* consider aspects of the contemporary setting of Milton's work.

Among studies published in the last twenty-five years, the following selection represents a variety of approaches developed by critics building on the groundwork of previous scholarship: Boyd M. Berry examines the relation between Puritan writing and Milton's epic in *Process of Speech: Puritan Religious Writing and* Paradise Lost. Dennis Burden's *The Logical Epic: A Study of the Argument of* Paradise Lost is a convincing discussion of the intellectual qualities inherent in Milton's epic as they reinforce the logical and coherent argument mounted in support of the providential order of the universe; Jackson Cope suggests an approach that can make the epic more accessible to the modern reader in *The Metaphoric Structure of* Paradise Lost; Robert Crosman's *Reading* Paradise Lost is in the critical tradition of Stanley Fish and Joseph Summers, arguing that to read the epic is to engage in collaboration with the poet; Galbraith Crump, *The Mystical Design of* Paradise Lost, examines the ways in which Milton's epic relates to the fourfold method of allegorical interpretation deriving from biblical exegesis; Joseph Duncan investigates the various traditions that lie beyond *Milton's Earthly Paradise: A Historical Study of Eden*; William Empson's *Milton's God* is, at times, outrageous but never for a moment dull; Anne Ferry defines various authorial strategies in *Milton's Epic Voice: The Narrator in* Paradise Lost.

In *Surprised by Sin: The Reader in* Paradise Lost, Stanley Fish initiates a fruitful pedagogical method of analysis that investigates the

ways Milton involves the reader in making moral choices and accepting responsibility for those choices no matter how wise or foolish.
Michael Fixler studies Milton's apocalyptic thought and expectations
in *Milton and the Kingdoms of God,* a survey of the development of
Milton's thought and its final resolution in *Paradise Regained.*
Northrop Frye's *Anatomy of Criticism* lays the groundwork for any
number of studies of *Paradise Lost* concerned to trace its mythic backgrounds and patterns. His *Return to Eden: Five Essays on Milton's
Epics* is mainly devoted to *Paradise Lost,* though one essay discusses
Paradise Regained. Helen Gardner's *Reading of* Paradise Lost is a
stimulating account of the "permanent greatness" of Milton's epic.
Christopher Grose considers influences in *Milton's Epic Process:* Paradise Lost *and Its Miltonic Background.* A number of James Holly
Hanford's finest essays on Milton are reprinted in *John Milton: Poet
and Humanist.* Another important collection of essays by a distinguished Miltonist is Merritt Hughes's *Ten Perspectives on Milton.*

Other valuable studies of Milton and *Paradise Lost* include the
following: *The Living Milton,* edited by Frank Kermode, with essays
on aspects of *Paradise Lost* by David Daiches, Donald Davie, and
Kermode; John R. Knott, Jr., *Milton's Pastoral Vision: An Approach to*
Paradise Lost; Thomas Kranidas, *The Fierce Equation: A Study of
Milton's Decorum,* a comprehensive and rewarding study of the subject in Milton's poetry; Jon S. Lawry, *The Study of Heaven: Matter
and Stance in Milton's Poetry*; Barbara Lewalski, *Protestant Poetics
and the Seventeenth-Century Religious Lyric,* an important work
studying the alternative tradition to the Catholic poetics of meditation
treated by Louis Martz's *Poetry of Meditation*; Michael Lieb, *The
Dialectics of Creation: Pattern of Birth and Regeneration in* Paradise
Lost and, more recently, *Poetics of the Holy: A Reading of* Paradise
Lost. Isabel MacCaffrey's Paradise Lost *as "Myth"* is a full and illuminating study of mythic patterns and impulses in Milton's masterpiece.
William Madsen's *From Shadowy Types to Truth: Studies in Milton's
Symbolism* examines the effect of biblical typology on Milton's epic
imagination. Louis Martz's study *The Paradise Within* discusses the
influence of meditational exercises on the poetry of Vaughan, Tra-
herne, and Milton. His important work *Poet of Exile: A Study of
Milton's Poetry,* about half of which is on *Paradise Lost,* deals with
themes that permeate Milton's epic in the chapters "The Power of
Choice," "The Trials of Faith," and "The Diffusion of Good." Diane
McColley considers the poet's concept of the first woman in *Milton's
Eve.* The last of Earl Miner's trilogy of books on the various modes of
seventeenth-century poetry, *The Restoration Mode from Milton to*

Dryden, considers public and narrative modes of poetry in the second half of the century; especially valuable is the way the discussion sets *Paradise Lost* in its poetic and intellectual milieu. Christopher Ricks's *Milton's Grand Style* brilliantly treats the poet's style, language, and syntax, at once attacking the various critics, especially those of this century, who find Milton's language ineffectual and analyzing that language in detailed ways that prove very useful in the classroom.

Other works of considerable interest are Herman Rapaport, *Milton and the Postmodern;* Hugh M. Richmond, *The Christian Revolutionary: John Milton;* William Riggs, *The Christian Poet in* Paradise Lost; John M. Steadman, *Milton and the Renaissance Hero, Milton's Epic Characters: Image and Idol,* and *Epic and Tragic Structure in* Paradise Lost; Arnold Stein, *Answerable Style: Essays on* Paradise Lost and *The Art of Presence: The Poet in* Paradise Lost. A book frequently cited by teachers is Joseph H. Summers's *The Muse's Method: An Introduction to* Paradise Lost; it has been characterized, reasonably, as one of the best modern studies. Walter Watkins provides a useful introduction in *An Anatomy of Milton's Verse* and includes a chapter on *Paradise Lost.* In *The Thesis of* Paradise Lost George Wilkes considers how the weight of the poem's argument is balanced equally in the twelve books of the poem. Joseph Wittreich has written extensively on Milton's influence on the Romantics. His *Romantics on Milton: Formal Essays and Critical Asides* was followed by *Milton and the Line of Vision* and *Angel of Apocalypse: Blake's Idea of Milton.* B. A. Wright's *Milton's* Paradise Lost: *A Reassessment of the Poem* is a broad and generally useful introduction to the epic.

Part Two

APPROACHES

INTRODUCTION

In the following pages seventeen teachers and scholars offer advice on teaching *Paradise Lost*. All but one regularly confront the epic in the classroom. Some have done so for decades, while others have been teaching only for a few years. All agree on the importance as well as the difficulty of presenting *Paradise Lost* to the modern undergraduate. All agree too that there is no simple or single solution to the challenge of teaching a work as complex as Milton's masterpiece. What they offer are not answers but possibilities. Teaching is in large measure an art of improvisation, yet improvisation can only be successful when it is wrought from a deep commitment to the work in hand, along with a thorough understanding of its nature.

The essays in this volume represent a variety of approaches, some orthodox and some unabashedly unorthodox. What they have in common is the desire to illuminate *Paradise Lost* and make it more accessible to the modern reader, whose tools for reading the epic are rather less comprehensive than Milton hoped for in his fit audience. The discussions envision the teaching of *Paradise Lost* in various formats, in different settings, and at several levels of instruction. Unifying each approach, if only tacitly, is the need to ask the question put by Michael Levy and his colleagues in the northern reaches of Wisconsin: "Will it work here?" All consider that whatever techniques are used, they must fit the strengths and weaknesses of the particular students who happen to settle into the seats flanking the podium.

The first group of essays provides a general overview of the epic and its presentation to students. Elizabeth McCutcheon offers a number of "mapmaking" devices by which students can be encouraged to immerse themselves in the world of the poem. Anna K. Nardo, Michael M. Levy, and John Wooten offer approaches tailored to their own specific teaching situations. Underlying the three essays is the exhortation that teachers should recognize the special strengths students bring to a reading of *Paradise Lost* and build on them rather than decry deficiencies. Concluding the section, Joseph E. Duncan summarizes a "three-pronged" method of teaching *Paradise Lost* that moves through the mythic or archetypal, the historical, and the personal. His primary goal is "to lead students to realize that the modes of thinking and posing questions in *Paradise Lost* belong not only to past cultures but to their own and to themselves as individuals."

The next section offers several specific approaches to *Paradise Lost*. Ellen S. Mankoff explains how she prepares her students for the epic by having them read some of Milton's sonnets, in which the large problems of language and style in the epic can be confronted in a more limited and precise context. Leslie E. Moore challenges the teacher's normal role as guide and mediator, offering instead a pedagogical model that "incorporates the student's experience of feeling lost within, overpowered by, and even hostile to the poem." This model, she argues, is one the text prepares us for and one that encourages the student to think in terms of narrative conventions, linguistic processes, and imaginative exploration. Eugene D. Hill offers illuminating ways of dealing with the "mazes of sound" that characterize Milton's prosody. Robert W. Halli, Jr., and George Klawitter consider the special problems of time limitations when teaching *Paradise Lost* in a survey course for nonmajors. While admitting the injustices the survey forces instructors to commit, they suggest ways to mitigate the offence. Virginia Tufte discusses using the illustrators of Milton to enable the student both to visualize *Paradise Lost* more directly and to recognize the limitations of visualization in comparison with the complexity of Milton's own imagination. Two essays present what some may think are radical approaches to the traditional materials of Milton's epic. Joan E. Hartman explains how she confronts the vexing but vital question of Milton's treatment of Eve in particular and the sexes in general in the epic and prose works. And Herman Rapaport offers an admittedly unusual approach stressing "for heuristic purposes that *Paradise Lost* is a novel with the facade of an epic."

The third section offers some suggestions on how to teach the background and contextuality of *Paradise Lost*. Hugh M. Richmond considers the general contexts of the poem—the history of its ideas—so as to enable students better to grasp its meanings and implications. Sanford Golding provides ways in which a teacher can effectively use the literature and criticism immediately surrounding the publication and early response to Milton's poem. Anne Lake Prescott shows how the theme of stewardship in *Paradise Lost* is at once relevant to present ecological concerns and integrally tied to Renaissance notions about the proper relation of art and nature. Finally, William Malin Porter, a sometime teacher of *Paradise Lost* and a full-time classicist, addresses the difficulties of Milton's many profound allusions to classical literature.

Though the selection of essays is intended to be representative of the challenges, problems, and possibilities that face teachers, it cannot hope to touch on all the concerns raised by such a complex work. In the end, the essays will have been useful if they serve to raise questions rather than provide answers. In reading the responses of teachers to the original fact-finding survey with which this anthology began, I was struck by the number of times teachers commented on the value of confronting the questionnaire. Whatever its merits or demerits, the questionnaire forced them to consider in a new light what they did in the classroom and how much they invested in the enterprise. Time and again, respondents remarked on the value *Paradise Lost* had for them. The words of one may be allowed to stand for the thoughts of many: "I hadn't fully realized how much teaching the work meant to me." Too often we think of our commitment to *Paradise Lost* as one rooted in professionalism. For most of us, when we think carefully about it, our professional interests are the least the poem means to us. As teachers our real desire is to help our students share something of the poem's imaginative richness. If the following essays contribute in some degree to the realization of that goal, they will have fulfilled their function. Beyond that, our best efforts must be to let the poem emerge.

GMC

GENERAL OVERVIEWS

Getting to Know *Paradise Lost*

Elizabeth McCutcheon

Everyone who teaches *Paradise Lost* must have faced the question raised by a notice in the May 1983 issue of *PMLA* advertising a prose rendition of the work. Is *Paradise Lost* "a closed book to this generation" because of its language and its style? At about the same time that I saw this advertisement, I attended a symposium on cross-cultural experiences in the arts at the East-West Center in Honolulu. As I heard interpreters, performers, and teachers struggle with the problem of how best to present the art forms of one culture to another, I realized anew that, as teachers of a seventeenth-century poem, we too are engaged in a cross-cultural experience. I also realized how fortunate we are to have Milton's language and with it the opportunity for a direct encounter with the magnitude and power of epic that this language provides. It seems to me, in other words, that Milton's language is inseparable from the poem, that it can open doors, instead of closing them, and that our role as teachers is not to simplify *Paradise Lost* by offering a diluted or predigested form of it but rather to develop a variety of ways that will let our students experience a truly inexhaustible text. Admittedly, *Paradise Lost* asks a great deal of its readers. But, like all great works, it gives much more than it asks. Addressing fundamental issues about the nature of good and evil and the human condition, it exercises its audience and encourages growth through the tests and experiences it embodies. To read Milton's epic is to be challenged, chastened, transformed, and renewed. As one of my students wrote, "I would not like to have gone through life without experiencing *Paradise Lost*."

There is always, of course, an immediate and all too practical problem: time. In comparison with other Renaissance epics, *Paradise Lost* is short. But its language is so rich, its form and substance so all-encompassing, that students need a great deal of time to integrate their reading of it, weighing one part in relation to another and discovering how much greater the whole is than the sum of the parts. Over the years, I have increased the number of class meetings devoted to *Paradise Lost* in the one-semester upper-division undergraduate course on Milton that primarily concerns me here. In effect, *Paradise Lost* has become both the center and the culmination of things Miltonic, and I give it relatively as well as absolutely more time than I give any of Milton's other works, important though each of them is. Since the length of the semester has not changed, I have had to treat some of his other writing in less detail. This was a hard decision to make, but I would argue that *Paradise Lost* is its own justification and that the opportunity to experience an epic in its original language is a unique one for many students.

Time is stretched in another way, since I ask students to read *Paradise Lost* at least twice in the course of the semester, in addition to the rereading they do while they work on their *Paradise Lost* paper (written on a topic of their choice and handed in only after we have finished our discussion of the poem in class, so that the paper also encourages them to integrate their experience with the poem). One reading is book by book and parallels the syllabus and class discussion: ideally, this includes an overview. But this is actually a second reading, for students read *Paradise Lost* on their own during the first part of the semester, while in class we are reading and discussing Milton's earlier poetry and his prose. If they wish, they may keep journals or other records of their initial impressions, responses, questions, discoveries, and so on, so that they will have personal accounts of their reading before class discussion begins. They also have a focal point for this preliminary reading. Borrowing from John Huntley, whose useful exercises I am paraphrasing here, I assign two projects, due when we actually start to discuss the epic: a time chart and a map or maps of Milton's geography. The time chart means unraveling Milton's narrative structure. Students must unscramble the events and arrange them in chronological order, noticing the different stages on which action takes place—heaven, hell, the world, and the cosmos surrounding it—and those events that actually occur as well as those that are dramatized within the narrative time span or included by allusion, report, forecast, prophecy, or retrospection. This exercise allows students to sense the nuclear center of the poem's action, seemingly spread over thirty-three days, and the action's infinite circumference, with its mysteries (at once epic and divine) of beginnings and endings, or of primal oneness and that moment when God is "All in All." After students have completed these time lines, incidentally, I direct them to the introduction by Carey and Fowler as a kind of cross-check and a complement to the introduction in their own text. The map or maps are supposed to be simple diagrammatic representations of Milton's imagined landscapes and geography; in fact, some students go further and create dramatic illustrations in color. Later in the semester, we look at a quite different kind of mapping, in Byard, which includes a diagram of the flights of Satan, the Son of God, and the angels (but not the metaphoric flights of the narrator) as they move between heaven, earth, and hell in each of the twelve books.

A few of my students find the mapping exercise frustrating. They like the challenge of puzzling out Milton's clues about the physical structure of hell or heaven or Eden, but they protest what they feel are the limitations of a static visual medium. From their point of view, the time chart has proved the more satisfying of the two projects. In fact, mapmaking allows them to discover for themselves the dynamic energy of Milton's descriptions. I would agree, however, that the time chart is the more important project and the one I would choose if students felt overworked doing both: alternatively, they themselves could choose one of the two exercises. In any case these projects motivate students and facilitate discovery through model making in a medium other than Milton's. They also require active participation and markedly reduce student anxiety. For many students, Milton is a particularly formidable poet, at least by reputation, and their initial encounters with some of Milton's earliest poems do not necessarily counteract their preconceptions. But so long as students are intimidated by Milton, it is hard for them to become engaged in the text or to develop an understanding of the poem, much less enjoy it. The projects are nonthreatening and specific; success is virtually built into them. Meanwhile, students are becoming familiar with Milton's language and with the workings of his mind and imagination and can build on this first reading of the epic, along with the context provided by their other reading in Milton, when they return to *Paradise Lost* in midsemester. A preliminary reading also solves an otherwise perennial problem: how and when to read the footnotes that accompany the text (either of the editions I use, Hughes's *Milton* [1957] or [1962], is copiously glossed). Because students have more time to absorb the text and because they know they will be returning to it later in the semester, the problem simply seems to solve itself.

I have talked about models the students make. Milton too had models—the various genres or literary kinds that he absorbed and transformed in the course of composing his poetry. I find it helpful to stress both the way that a particular form frames experience, giving us what Rosalie Colie (*Resources*) has called potential images of life, and the ways that Milton changed and enlarged every form he worked with. More specifically, I use Milton's sonnets as an introduction to some aspects of *Paradise Lost*. Because the sonnet is such a brief form, students can easily see it whole and can understand how what the seventeenth-century poet would have called decorum affects language and style. We also discover how Milton broke down the "walls" of traditional sonnet form to achieve the orbicular effects that Wordsworth later admired so much. And we think about Milton's variations on the heroic sonnet and his concern with the nature of a truly heroic act or stance. These are by no means the only things we talk about—I do much with the parallelism and antitheses that take place in sonnet dialectic, for example—but the sonnets do seem to provide, in microcosm, views of Milton's ways with form.

We ask comparable questions about epic experiences and epic form when we come to *Paradise Lost*. What is an epic, and why did Milton prefer it to the drama or tragedy that he earlier intended to write? The answers given at this point are still preliminary, of course, especially since, in Milton's hands, the epic itself becomes encyclopedic and includes so many other genres and, hence, so much of life. But, stimulated by their time charts, students already have some sense of the poem as a whole and a lively interest in its structure and sequence of events. What is especially important at this point is their recognition that every aspect of epic is interrelated. Fundamentally we are here concerned with epic expansiveness and magnitude, structure, multiple foci and shifting perspectives, the nature of heroic action and how it is tested or shown, parodies and inversions of the truly heroic, Milton's varied and various styles, narrative voice, character, and the energy of his language—all as manifestations of his epic imagination. Obviously discussion can take many different directions; in 1979, for example, soon after the operatic version of *Paradise Lost* by Krzysztof Penderecki and Christopher Fry had been performed and reviewed, we found ourselves giving even more thought than usual to Milton's handling of time and space in book 1. Noting the relatively little (albeit extremely important) external action that is Satan's in the earlier part of the book and the intensely dramatic and long-sustained psychological activity, we wondered how Miltonic time and space could be handled in a stage production.

Because of Milton's cosmic scope and because we are so often thinking about many different things at once as we watch Milton's epic unfold, I begin to hand out a series of outlines, one for each book of *Paradise Lost,* which students can juxtapose with their time lines, so that they have two different but complementary chartings of the poem. These outlines are concrete extensions of Thomas Greene's discussion of epic norms and structure. I have blocked out the panels of action by line references, identifying each occurrence of the two sorts of scene that characterize so much epic action—the executive and the deliberative—and noting some of the many similarities and differences among them.

Originally I prepared one of these outlines while I was thinking about a question raised by a student who wanted to know how the blind poet could have held so much material in his head. As I blocked out the various scenes, I realized that a brief outline of the panels of action—I keep the length of the outline for each book to between one and two typewritten pages—was a particularly good way for students to see parts in relation to other parts and to the whole of *Paradise Lost.* Because the movement between executive and deliberative is inherent to epic, an outline of it avoids imposing an arbitrary pattern on students' experience of the poem or obscuring generic inclusiveness. Yet the outline allows them to sense subtle modulations in sequential movement and various ways that Milton handled narrative action. It facilitates the identification and discussion of Milton's strong images, like the temple, used metaphorically at the beginning of book 1 and literally at the end, with the building of Pandemonium. And it underscores the dramatic, psychological, and spiritual dimensions of Miltonic epic—hence Milton's preference for dialogue. It also encourages the balancings and rebalancings between passage and passage and book and book that are so necessary for a fuller understanding of the experiences the blind bard narrates. Obvious examples include Eve on her creation and Adam on his; exemplars of obedience and disobedience; the fall of Satan and of Adam and Eve; Adam and Eve's pastoral love story and tragic fall; and Satan's refusal to repent and the whole course of repentance that book 10 traces in Adam and Eve. Less obvious, perhaps, are juxtapositions and shifts of the sort we find at the beginning of book 3, where the poet portrays two different ways of experiencing the divine; first we hear the narrator's hymn and only then do we have a deliberative scene. So "Hail holy Light" checks any too quick rejection of Milton's God as a school divine and precipitates a major question: in what sense does one "see" or know God? To ponder a question like this is to think, too, about the nature of both language and reality and the different ways that characters in the poem see and understand. In short, these outlines turn the students back to the text; by illuminating the reverberations, oscillations, and movements (large and small), they also help to keep us on track, so to speak, as the focus of the discussion shifts, reflecting the interests and interaction of text, students, and teacher at a particular time.

There are, of course, a great many other ways that students can be encouraged to experience Milton's text. I want to mention just a few that I have found particularly helpful. Some of my students have trouble reading Milton because they simply cannot hear his language and its rhythms. Yet we know that, in the Renaissance, reading was not altogether silent; moreover, Milton writes for and appeals to the inner ear, and his iambic pentameter lines, his plays on sound and sense (as in *sole, soul, sol* at the beginning of book 4), the rhythms of speech that characterize each of the speakers, et cetera, are essential to the poem. I try to stress the aural aspects of *Paradise Lost* by reading aloud myself, by encouraging students to do so, and by playing tapes of the poem. I am selective in what I play in class, but I always include some of Satan's speeches, since I lack his resonance: in fact, my students one year gave me the "sweetest Satan of the year" award. I play passages by other speakers, too—enough to whet the students' appetites. At that point I direct them to the Listening Center to hear more of Argo's *Paradise Lost* tapes, which include book 1, complete, and selections from every other book except 8 and 11. Although there are other recordings, I like the Argo—part of their English Poets series—because it is a dramatic reading, with a different voice for each speaker. My students' chief "complaint" is that there is not enough; they would like to have *all* of *Paradise Lost* on tape.

Hearing Milton allows for an immediate awareness of his auditory imagination; we also talk about how his language involves the other senses. Wayne Shumaker has discussed this topic so comprehensively that examples on my part are unnecessary. I shall mention just one. Toward the end of book 1, the narrator exalts, or purports to exalt, the beauty of the lamps in Pandemonium:

from the arched roof
Pendant by subtle Magic many a row

>Of Starry Lamps and blazing Cressets fed
>With *Naphtha* and *Asphaltus* yielded light
>As from a sky.   (726–30)

In Honolulu, trucks with bubbling tar pots are a common sight and smell; once students sense the way that this passage moves in two directions at once (and catch Milton's sly sense of humor), they are ready for more serious "surprises" and unsettlings. Similarly, the rich eroticism and the muscularity of his words disabuse them of any lingering idea of Milton as a dour Puritan, so that Milton's language, far from being a barrier to understanding, is what one of my students called a "turn-on."

Finally, I like to use iconographic material both to focus on crucial images and motifs and to open the discussion of traditions and contexts (including the theological) that might otherwise seem arcane. Inevitably the subject turns to a consideration of the changes Milton makes—changes that are fundamental to an understanding of the poem. Much of this material is now accessible in Roland Frye (*Milton's Imagery*), and the *Milton Quarterly* is a good source of illustrations selected with an eye to the classroom. When I began teaching *Paradise Lost*, however, there was far less interest in Milton and the visual, and I made my own collection of slides, postcards, illustrations photoduplicated from Renaissance books, cartoons, even advertisements: anything that had some connection with biblical and classical story in *Paradise Lost*. (My model was the iconographic files at the Warburg Institute, in London.) Because my teaching now is process oriented, I typically circulate a few particularly relevant illustrations each time we meet. I use the elaborate frontispiece to Genesis from the Geneva Bible (1583) to launch a discussion of Reformation attitudes toward the relation of human beings with God. Adam and Eve are on either side of the tree of knowledge (with the snake entwined around it), the tetragrammaton overhead, the plenitude of the created world about them, while banners and mottoes spell out the rhythm of creation, fall, and restoration, with the hope of eternity through faith in Christ's death. Aesthetically, this image is vastly different from Milton's depiction, and we also question what Milton does with the "Desire to knowe" theme; in fact, I later hand out a sheet on the serpent-knowledge question as well as asking students to read the early chapters of Genesis. Nevertheless, the illustration gives students who are sometimes quite unfamiliar with Christian doctrine, much less its history, a visual and conceptual grounding. Similarly, the beautiful Medici tapestries in Florence and Milton's creation scenes are reciprocally illuminating, while medieval and Renaissance scenes of the fall and expulsion prompt discussion of Milton's radical rethinking of the nature of Satan and the relation between Adam and Eve and between them and God as they are led out of paradise, hand in hand with the angel.

In these and other ways I try to encourage students to immerse themselves in the poem and to experience it for themselves. Individual students inevitably respond differently to any one approach or method, as they do to *Paradise Lost*. When I asked students a few years ago what seemed to them most vital and valuable about their reading in Milton, I was struck by the range of answers. One talked about Milton's reaffirmation of the individual's dignity as a creature who could make choices instead of being a victim of fate: this student found the sense of responsibility exhilarating. Another liked Milton's reworking of myth, another his dedication and the commitment he made to his art, another the power of his vision. Still another wrote passionately about Milton's sense of pain and loss and how he not only struggled with suffering but could integrate it into a fuller view of life. But no matter how different their responses were otherwise, they also singled out Milton's language, what one student called the overwhelming beauty and challenge of the poetry itself.

Their Faith Is Strong, but Their Prose Is Weak: Teaching *Paradise Lost* at Louisiana State University

Anna K. Nardo

I don't have to make *Paradise Lost* relevant to my students. Two vignettes may suggest why.

First, standing on a bench at noon outside the student union, a conservatively suited evangelist wields a Bible and exhorts a crowd of over a hundred students. Some heckle, but others listen intently and accept the leaflets distributed to the crowd. This scene is repeated frequently throughout the school year with evangelists old and young, black and white.

Second, four hundred faculty members and students, many having marched from campus in the sweltering Louisiana heat, assemble outside the bishop's residence. A former Jesuit English professor reads a measured letter protesting the removal of a young priest and his liberal order from the Catholic student center. From a distance, the gathering might resemble a sixties peace demonstration. But there are no slogans on placards or chants of protest rhetoric. Instead, the crowd prays for the bishop's better understanding of Vatican II, sings "Yahweh, I know you are near," and receives instructions on petitioning papal legates.

Obviously, sin, redemption, and the complexities of church governance are live issues at LSU; my students still recognize Milton's world. Although they seldom elect a Milton course, the base for teaching *Paradise Lost* is here.

Students generally encounter the epic in a sophomore survey course, one option that fulfills a literature requirement. English majors must take a course in either Milton or Chaucer, so some approach *Paradise Lost* as vocational training for teachers. Thus students' resistance to difficult requirements and Louisiana's rank as the fiftieth state in adult literacy pose challenges to the advantages of teaching *Paradise Lost* at LSU. After providing a profile of our students, I will present a strategy for using their genuine strengths while strengthening their weaknesses—a strategy that may be transferable to other state universities with rural students and to urban universities with Catholic populations.

Students at LSU generally fall into one of four categories: (1) Cajuns from rural south Louisiana—French Catholic inheritors of a living folk culture; (2) Italian and French whites from New Orleans, many of whom attended Catholic schools; (3) rural and urban whites from north Louisiana belonging to Baptist and more fundamentalist congregations; and (4) blacks—urban and rural, Catholic and Protestant—with a rich and poetically oral, but not highly literate, culture. Fundamentalist students tend to know the Bible, both testaments, but lack a systematic theology. Catholic students tend to have a mythic sensibility and some recognition of New Testament passages but little ability to articulate doctrine or locate biblical allusions. Probably because of vestiges of southern respect for the classical education, Louisiana high schools often teach classical mythology, and Milton classes may include one student who knows a little Latin. Few students, however, have a sense of history.

This background produces strengths that prepare LSU students to read *Paradise Lost*: an interest in and knowledge of Christianity and the Bible; a respect for and, at least, minimal acquaintance with classical studies; and, especially among blacks and some Cajuns, a sensitivity to oral eloquence that attunes them to the magniloquence of *Paradise Lost* read aloud. The weaknesses of some students are serious but not insurmountable: little background in history, a devaluation of literature in comparison to more narrowly practical subjects, and an inability to write well.

To introduce the course, I entice students to enjoy *Paradise Lost*, while I fill in the gaps in their background. In a series of lectures in the semester course on Milton and in one lecture in the survey course, I review the history of the period, with colorful details of, for example, the clipping of William Prynne's ears; narrate the events of Milton's life, emphasizing his heroic preparation for writing a masterwork; and illustrate with slides the cosmology of his universe. This frank attempt to entertain with storytelling and visual aids usually pays off in students' curiosity. Everyone loves a story, and the background of *Paradise Lost* makes a good one.

In the semester course, students do not read Milton's long epic until they have surveyed his early poetry and selections from the prose. The first unit prepares them for *Paradise Lost* by attending to Milton's syntax and diction, by requiring a brief essay (1,250 words) on some aspect of Milton's use of allusion in either "Lycidas" or the sonnets, and by introducing in the minor works key themes of the epic, for example, the journey out of darkness into light. Because of time pressure in the survey course, I use lectures on "Lycidas" and selected sonnets to introduce Milton's ornate style, allusive density, and thematic complexity.

Once we are ready, I reiterate that *Paradise Lost* is the culmination of all our preparation. Although my reverence for a poem bemuses some students, enthusiasm is catching and those who have not already dropped the course are by now curious. Before they read book 1, I give them five basic rules for Milton's moral universe:

1. God, by definition good, created the universe *ex deo*, not *ex nihilo*.
2. As a result, the universe may be conceived as an infinitely expanding circle of goodness.
3. No created being can get outside the circle without achieving nothingness or nonbeing.
4. Goodness includes free will.
5. Evil arises from free will and eventually destroys itself or turns into goodness.

A diagram on the blackboard provides students with an easily remembered spatial model of this moral universe.

Although they are encouraged to raise questions and objections to these rules, I refuse to respond at this point, noting specifically who asked what and promising that Milton will eventually answer each question. So when students read the opening conversation between Beelzebub and Satan, they are prepared to detect Satanic lies. Then in the following weeks, as the epic addresses their initial queries (such as "Can Satan be saved?" or "Why would a good God place the tempting fruit in the garden?"), I lead whichever student raised the question to find the answer Milton provides.

Presenting the basis of Milton's ontology and ethics as a model with rules serves two functions. First, it moves fundamentalists beyond quotations of isolated scriptural passages and Catholics beyond a vague mythic sensibility toward systematic theology. Because of Milton's systematization of a personal and sometimes heretical theology in *The Christian Doctrine*, Protestants can sympathize with his attention to scripture. Because of his deep reading in the church fathers and his emphasis on free will, Catholics can learn to regard his anti-Catholicism as more historically and politically than theologically significant.

Second, introducing Milton's ontology and ethics as a model with rules helps forestall theological wrangling by distancing his beliefs from the students' and the instructor's. Fundamentalists need not assert their doctrines self-defensively, because Milton's creed is not being preached, only studied. Also their biblical knowledge makes these students valued participants in class discussion, and they are generally satisfied with this role. Furthermore, my students seem comfortable with the concept of a rule-governed universe because the literature they read for pleasure is science fiction and fantasy, which establishes premises to set alternative worlds in motion. Some students leave my course complimenting Milton on his superiority to J. R. R. Tolkien or Frank Herbert. In this business, we take what rewards we can get.

After the introduction, I avoid lectures and lead class discussions instead. Students knowledgeable about the Bible, classical mythology, or Latin etymologies and students who recognize the issues raised in preparatory phases of the course become the class experts in these fields. If I am lucky, a kind of class cohesiveness develops as members respect each others' strengths. Generally, however, LSU students do not perform well when discussion depends wholly on their own resources; a structured series of questions is more successful in leading them to discover key interpretive points. To stimulate and focus discussion, I present a question with each reading assignment. As they read, students take notes toward an answer, for they know they may be asked to write a thirty-minute response during the next class. Never knowing when they must write, they come to class prepared for a lively, focused discussion.

Because the survey course can devote so little time to *Paradise Lost*, this technique of emphasizing key questions is helpful, making it possible—if not ideal—to teach a substantial part of the epic, not just the usual books 1 and 2, in a brief time slot. For each day's reading assignment, survey students receive five to eight questions, on any of which they may be asked to write. Since they must prepare notes toward answers, these questions define the content of class discussion for three to four days.

By drawing attention to major interpretive issues, this technique also confronts my students' literacy problems. When reading for the answer to a well-defined question, students feel less overwhelmed by Milton's complexity. Certainly graduate students should read for independent discovery, but many LSU undergraduates need a structure before they can profit from free reading or discussion. This technique also gives students frequent writing practice. Some who are insecure about their writing prepare not merely notes but drafts of short essays for every assignment. On days when they must write, the students with first drafts use the thirty minutes for a guided workshop on revision.

Such short essays already focused by the assigned question help students concentrate on organization, detailed support for their answers, and mechanical correctness. Later when they must present a term paper, this training should prevent unfocused, disorganized, vague, or illiterate work. Composing several short essays alerts students to my standards for writing and alerts me to which students need individual conferences before they begin the term paper. As rigorous as some students find the daily preparation for writing and the frequent essays, they tend to like *Paradise Lost* more because they are writing about it. Patients who pay seventy-five to one hundred dollars an hour for psychoanalysis believe in the method; likewise, students who invest so much mental energy in Milton's poem take it as their own.

After such structured writing, students must determine their focus for a final paper on a single narrow topic in *Paradise Lost*. Because they sometimes lack sophistication in evaluating what they read and may feel that such critics as C. S. Lewis, John Steadman, Stanley Fish, and Mary Ann Radzinowicz have left nothing to say, I request that undergraduates use no critical sources. Instead, I ask them to consider a problem or idea that has not been explored sufficiently in class, to reread for a solution or clarification, and to focus on a limited aspect of their findings that can be developed adequately in a maximum of twenty-five hundred words. For example, one fundamentalist student recently argued from biblical echoes in the poem that the primary cause of Adam's fall was idolatry; another student, a Vietnam veteran and "biker," analyzed images of frustrated sexuality associated with Satan. This final project tests whether students can use their own resources, not my structuring and interpretations, to find an entry into Milton's complex poem and whether they can communicate their vision in a focused, organized, specific, and literate analysis.

Because my methods are neither innovative nor shocking, they can be transferred to schools without the peculiarities of south Louisiana culture. Rural Protestants in large southern or midwestern state universities and urban ethnic Catholics in city colleges probably bear a family resemblance to LSU students. These student populations may know more history and less classical mythology than mine or have a different racial mixture, but this approach depends less on such details than on a fundamental belief: instead of despairing over students' supposed incompetence and disinterest, I respect the strengths that can make *Paradise Lost* live for them. We need not oversimplify the great epic in English for our students; we can use what they know to teach them what they don't.

Paradise Lost in Northern Wisconsin

Michael M. Levy

For the last four years I have been part of a committee at the University of Wisconsin, Stout, formed to assess and recommend new approaches to the teaching of basic composition and literature. We have discussed sentence combining and process writing, reader-response theory and structuralism, all with an eye toward finding practical applications, approaches that work. Each theorist we have read and talked about has had such an approach, of course, which he or she puts through its paces, complete with theoretical underpinnings, numerous excerpts from student writing, and a plenitude of scholarly cross-referencing. Our committee has learned quite a bit from this research, and several of the new methods have been tried with varying degrees of success; but one thing has remained consistent over virtually the whole course of our study. Almost always, forty-five minutes into the discussion of some newly published article or highly touted book, we have found ourselves sitting back, looking from one colleague to the next, and sighing. Eventually one of us has uttered the invariable words, "But will this work at Stout?"

Too often, it seems to me, the fashionable approaches to teaching literature and composition come from the major universities. This is only to be expected, perhaps, since it is to such places that the most talented or publication-oriented people tend to gravitate, but it has the unfortunate result of skewing our sense of what is or is not teachable, our sense of how well an approach to a piece of literature, *Paradise Lost* for example, will work. True, the best schools are now admitting students of suspect literacy. High-powered scholars at research-oriented universities are being forced to deal with fundamental grammatical and cultural ignorance to an extent that would have astonished them just fifteen years ago; but what of the smaller and less prestigious colleges and universities? What approaches will work in a college classroom where virtual illiteracy is the rule, where the two or three students who can actually write grammatically or who actually read for pleasure, even if only best-sellers, are immediately hustled into honors classes?

The University of Wisconsin, Stout, is such a school, as, in fact, are most colleges in this country. We tend to forget, perhaps, that for every prestigious, research-oriented university there are a dozen places like Stout, schools that may lack graduate seminars in *Paradise Lost* but that nonetheless teach literature. It is the instructors at these schools who are most in need of practical approaches to Milton's poetry. Virtually any teaching method will work with the most advanced and best students, but what will work with the rest?

I have no theories to offer, no well-chosen and carefully arranged examples of student work, no scholarly documentation. With more than 120 students a semester, most of them in writing courses, most of them marginally literate at best, I have not the leisure to prepare such an elaborate presentation. What I do have, I think, is a number of useful, specific observations on what will and will not work in the attempt to teach *Paradise Lost* to students of the type Stout attracts, students with some intelligence but virtually no cultural or literary sophistication and little interest in gaining such sophistication.

Escape to Wisconsin. Several years ago this phrase gained great popularity as a bumper-sticker slogan and, despite recession, acid rain, and the threat of nuclear-waste storage sites, it still sums up the attitude of many of the state's citizens. Northern Wisconsin in particular is seen as a kind of Eden, complete with its own mythology of silent conifer forests, hunting, fishing, snowmobiling, and innocence. The University of Wisconsin, Stout—which specializes in home economics, education, and industrial technology—draws its students from across the country, but the bulk of its admissions are from Wisconsin and Minnesota, young men and women who to a surprisingly great extent share this Edenic view of their locale. Heaven is a resort on Lake Chetek or a canoe trip on the Boundary Waters. Fulfillment is getting your first buck. Most students, if asked, will admit to the Lutheran faith, but it is a kind of foggy, homogenized Lutheranism that differs hardly at all from the equally vague Methodism or Catholicism of their peers elsewhere. I mention this not to denigrate the quality of my students' faith—it is often very strong—but to bring out the fact that few of those to whom I have taught *Paradise Lost* have had any insight into the specifics of their religions, into what makes them Lutherans as opposed to Methodists or, for that matter, Catholics. Nor do many of them have any real knowledge of either the Old or the New Testament. They come to *Paradise Lost* lacking virtually all the extensive historical, literary, mythological, and theological information necessary to a thorough or even partial understanding of the poem. It is important to remember, however, that even though my students lack this knowledge, they are not blank slates. Their worldview may be a simplified amalgam of Wisconsin Edenic, homogenized Protestantism, and, of course, mass media culture, but it is a worldview, a strongly held one at that, and it can either impede or aid their understanding of Milton's epic.

Stout has neither an English major nor a course in Milton, but *Para-*

dise Lost, or selections from it, are taught in both our freshman honors course and our Early English Literature Survey. The syllabus for the latter is fairly standard: *Beowulf* and selections from the *Canterbury Tales,* both in translation; a book of *The Faerie Queene; Dr. Faustus;* a Shakespeare play or two; a miscellany of lyrics by Marlowe, Donne, Herbert, and others; and, at the end of the semester, just when everyone is beginning to think about Christmas vacation, a big chunk of *Paradise Lost.* I use the exerpts in *The Norton Anthology of English Literature,* partly because, as such anthologies go, the Norton is excellent, partly because I have little choice. Stout, like many smaller schools, has a textbook library from which we are required to make our assignments. I can also ask each student to buy up to ten dollars' worth of extra reading material, usually a writing handbook or a Shakespeare play not in the anthology.

My syllabus is invariably chronological, and my lectures heavily emphasize historical and cultural context, both what was happening at the time the work was written and why. To my mind the standard New Critical position, with its emphasis on the work itself, its tendency to exclude or minimize both historical background and authorial intent, is simply not very useful on an undergraduate, nonmajor level. Equally problematic are approaches that use the currently fashionable reader-response theories, with their tendency to deny even the work, their belief that the work exists primarily as it is re-created in the reader's mind. While both of these critical methods have obvious value for the theorist and the advanced student, they do not satisfy the needs of the basic first-time reader of literature. Many college instructors, trained as we were at schools where New Criticism was the established orthodoxy, forget that we can ignore historical context in our own interpretation of a literary work only because we already know that context; unnoticed, it is the foundation on which our critical perceptions are built. Freshmen reading *Macbeth* for the first time, however, cannot truly comprehend the horror of Duncan's murder if they do not understand the concept of the divine right of kings. Their tendency, putting the act into their own contexts, will be to see the crime in terms of the most recent overthrow of a modern dictator. Such a naive student response can be used to gain a handle on *Macbeth,* but it is not sufficient in itself. Cultural context, the realization that Macbeth's crime is not merely political assassination but also sacrilege, is necessary.

Similarly, a heavy emphasis on the primacy of the reader's response can also cause problems. Reader-response theory can give instructors useful insights into how their students will react to a poem and why they will react that way. It also works well when dealing with what we may call the educated reader, the person whose analysis of a work may differ from one's own, but only within well-defined limits. But few of the students I have taught in the Early English Literature Survey, or even in Honors Freshman English, qualify as educated readers. How, after all, is one to answer a student who thinks she has conclusive proof, based partly on her ignorance of theology and partly on her failure to look up two words in the *Oxford English Dictionary*, that George Herbert is a pagan? Or, for that matter, with the student who interprets "The Grand Inquisitor" as anti-Christian because he thinks its author, being a Russian, must be a Communist? When faced with such totally ludicrous student analyses, one cannot help realizing that, to prove useful as a teaching tool, reader-response approaches, like other recent critical approaches, actually do require a cultural context, shared historical knowledge, background information that my students just do not have.

What exactly do they need to know about *Paradise Lost*? How can we approach the poem successfully?

First, students must be made aware of the concept of the Renaissance. They must understand both that period's new emphasis on humanism and the related conflict between pagan and Christian knowledge. This conflict permeates *Paradise Lost* and, unless one has a basic grasp of its roots, it is impossible, I think, to comprehend either Satan's attitude toward God or, for that matter, Milton's attitude toward his poem. (I have found, by the way, that the current conflict between fundamentalist Christianity and secular humanism provides a convenient entry into the topic.) Further, students must be aware of the general historical situation: the Puritan revolt against what was perceived as a corrupt church and court; the commonwealth, a dream that eventually went bad; Milton's own position as an embittered older man, formerly at the center of power, now living on sufferance. These materials must be covered briefly, of course, and brevity often leads to oversimplification, but I do not think that matters. Obviously the modern student is going to approach *Paradise Lost* or any Renaissance work with a twentieth-century sensibility, but if the poem is to have anything like its intended effect, the student must have something contemporary with that poem to hold on to. Even oversimplifications, if generally accurate, are better than nothing.

Why this insistence on bringing Milton himself into a basic discussion of *Paradise Lost*? Why this flouting of the intentional fallacy? As important as teaching students facts about the poem, as important as making sure that they understand the poem, is making them interested in it, helping them to take pleasure from it. This purpose may seem obvious, but it is frequently forgotten. When a teacher does his or her best to present a work of literature to a class and is greeted with blank incomprehension, it is discouraging; but how much more discouraging it is to meet bored comprehension and expressions that say "so what?" Too often these two states seem to be our only choices. What we need are methods that will allow students not only to understand *Paradise Lost* but to appreciate it, and biography, judiciously used, can lead to such an appreciation. Admittedly *Paradise Lost* is not the most obviously biographical of poems, but Milton is there throughout, his hopes, his frustrations, his scars infusing the entire work.

My experience has been that for most of my students the very idea of writing a poem is incomprehensible. It is not just that they are not interested in poetry or that they would not want to compose a poem themselves. Often they honestly do not understand why anyone would want to write a poem, they are curious to know the reason, and they can be hooked by an examination of this question. Why would anyone write a poem? Why would anyone devote the years necessary to composing an epic poem like *Paradise Lost*? Why would Milton write such a poem? Biography thus provides an entry to the work.

Inexperienced readers tend to personalize everything, tend to see everything in terms of themselves. When interpreting a character's motivations or actions my students often ask themselves how they would have responded in the given situation. This way of responding is the source, I think, of that frequently heard student critique of great works of literature: "I didn't like it. It wasn't realistic." The character who does not act exactly as the student would have acted, as anyone from northern Wisconsin (which is to say the world) would have acted, is dubbed unrealistic. If this student tendency is kept in mind, another effective approach can be developed. It can be useful to forget temporarily Milton's great poetry (which very few undergraduates in my experience have really been able to appreciate), his magnificent epic structure (ditto), and his complex theological arguments and to concentrate straightforwardly on his characters, primarily Satan, Adam, and Eve. (I have had little success with either God or Christ.) Milton, after all, had a genius for characterization through a combination of self-betraying monologue and ironic authorial comment, and my students have been able to pick up on this. Some of the best experiences I have had in the classroom, rare moments of excitement, have involved student attempts to grapple with Satan as a character. Why did he rebel? Why did he lie to the other fallen angels? To what extent is he lying to himself? On two occasions I have had students develop something very like Blake's argument for Satan as hero of the poem and debate it with enthusiasm.

What else works? Dare I mention the *Star Wars* approach? To the extent that my students read at all, they often read science fiction and fantasy. There are always several people in my classes, usually the brighter ones, who are familiar with J. R. R. Tolkien or Arthur C. Clarke, and they have all seen films like *Star Wars* and *Return of the Jedi*. Fans of science fiction like to refer to what they call a "sense of wonder," the feelings raised by descriptions of strange and wonderful surroundings, bizarre situations, magical transformations—in short, what filmmakers call special effects. *Paradise Lost* is a poem of magnificent language and serious theological debate, but it too is a work of special effects. The poem could never be filmed without gutting its language and intellectual content, but if it were, what a spectacle it would be. Nothing in *The Lord of the Rings* can rival for sheer sense of wonder the initial scenes in hell, Satan's flight through chaos, or the battle in heaven. These are the scenes most easily accessible to many students, and I consider it no vulgarization of the poem to discuss them in terms of special effects, science fiction, and spectacle. Milton's primary purpose in writing *Paradise Lost* may have been to justify the ways of God to man, but, obsessed with fame as he was, he also had few objections to "wowing" his audience.

A final approach with which I have had some success is to treat the poem not as a work of art but as a religious document. As mentioned earlier, few of my students know very much about their religion, but most do consider themselves religious, and many in fact have a pious streak. Further, their literary naïveté makes it difficult for them to differentiate between Genesis itself, the various bowdlerized Bible stories they vaguely remember from childhood, and Milton's epic. Their reverence is thus directed not so much at the Bible, at Genesis, as it is at an amorphous, generalized concept of the creation story. The specifics, what is in fact biblical and what is in fact folk or Miltonic elaboration, do not seem to matter to them greatly. Therefore, students can often be induced to approach *Paradise Lost* with something of that extra attention that one reserves for the holy. It might be argued that, since Milton's poem is not the Bible, this conception is a falsification of the text. The fact is, however, that the students are going to confuse the two in any case. The key is gaining their attention, giving them reasons to care about the poem. If, a few years later, they cannot remember whether a specific event is biblical or Miltonic, my only response is to be glad that they remembered something.

Paradise Lost as historical document, disguised biography, character study, fantasy, religious work: it might be argued with some accuracy that several of these approaches are tangential, that I seem to be downplaying or even ignoring the importance of teaching such more central topics as the poem's language, structure, and ideas, but such is not my intention. I have no desire to advocate the teaching of an exclusively trendy, mass-cult Milton, nor do I wish to push the teaching of some watered-down Milton for the illiterate; rather, I am trying to work with the minds placed before me in a classroom located far away from the nearest ivory tower. Actually, I undoubtedly spend as much time on the standard topics relevant to *Paradise Lost* as anyone can afford to in a survey class. If I give them short shrift here, it is only because I do not feel that I have anything particularly novel to share, any approaches to these topics that work particularly well. Is there a really effective (or even moderately effective) way to get students like those I teach at Stout to appreciate the language of Milton's poem? Can the concept of the epic be made meaningful to students who have never heard of Homer or Vergil? Is it possible to bring the scenes between God and Christ to life for the average sophomore majoring in hotel and restaurant management? I do not know. My purpose here has simply been to suggest a few openers, approaches to *Paradise Lost* that I believe will work on even the most basic college level.

Teaching *Paradise Lost* at the United States Naval Academy

John Wooten

Students at the United States Naval Academy are likely to take seriously many of the things that most concerned Milton. I can depend, for example, on a fairly serious amount of religious belief. Almost half of the student body is Catholic. My students also tend to pursue ideals of discipline and obedience with more Miltonic zeal than do students at other colleges and universities. If there is anything my students understand, it is the tension between freedom and restraint. Religion, discipline, obedience, freedom: these are all significant Miltonic words. Theoretically, then, Milton is less foreign and less anachronistic than he might be at other schools. But despite such affinities, *Paradise Lost* is hard to teach well, even here. Nonmajors find the poem difficult, as do any number of the 200 English majors who might study the poem in one of several majors courses. My students are thus not very different from their peers in civilian dress who are reading the poem elsewhere. What follows is first my characterization of what makes the poem a challenge to all twentieth-century readers and then some specific suggestions for meeting the challenge in the classroom.

Paradise Lost is, especially today, an intractable poem. It does not bend easily to adapt itself to currently popular notions about morality, politics, religion, or love. It stubbornly asserts its large ideas and its grand style in the face of the generally parochial predispositions and prejudices of modern readers. Milton did not casually identify a "fit audience . . . though few" (7.31) as his best expectation of the poem's public reception. The phrase—something like the poetic equivalent of the gauntlet thrown down before medieval combat—conveys in miniature the intellectual and imaginative challenge the poem is and was meant to be. To do justice to the subject, teaching the epic has to communicate some of Milton's aggressive truths. Sensitive students, I find, are not fooled by efforts to make the poem an innocuous artifact in the genteel museum of English literary history. To pretend that Milton has no intention of communicating truths for which he is asking intellectual, moral, and imaginative assent is to distort one of the most consistent features of his entire literary career. The prejudice that splits apart the imaginative poetic experience and the didactic aims of the poet is a modern, not a Renaissance, one. (Students are not usually so hostile to didactic poetic strategies as their often more skeptical professors are.) Any teaching of the poem, however designed and executed overall, should confront its didactic, assertive qualities. Otherwise, we enact before our classes a cowardice in the face of Milton's unique challenge, a cowardice that is a disservice both to our students and to the poem. I would prefer that students intensely dislike the epic for very clear reasons based on what it is rather than "like" it for hazily perceived things that it essentially is not.

At the Naval Academy, I teach *Paradise Lost* in three courses: The Literature of Classical and Christian Ideas, The Renaissance Mind, and The Poetry of John Milton. In my Milton course, I focus on Milton as (1) a Renaissance poet, (2) a seventeenth-century man, and (3) the major native influence on English eighteenth-century and Romantic poetry. My largest aims are to educate students about the Renaissance context of Milton's life and works; about the tensions, conflicts, and advances in his own country during its intense religious and political struggles; and about his unique contribution to English and world literature. I organize as follows:

1. The sonnets: introduction to the poet, his times, and varieties of Renaissance style
2. "On the Morning of Christ's Nativity": Renaissance tropes and individual talent
3. *Comus*: virtue and the masque tradition
4. "Lycidas": the classical pastoral, mortality, and seventeenth-century religious conflict
5. *Paradise Lost*: achievement and stress in Milton's major poem
6. *Samson Agonistes* and Milton Agonistes
7. *Paradise Regained* and Milton's "Calm of Mind, All Passion Spent": toward the eighteenth century and beyond.

In teaching *Paradise Lost,* I try to help my students see the poem as a brilliantly imaginative narrative energized by aggressive religious, philosophical, moral, and aesthetic views. To demonstrate what I mean in my outline by "stress," I concentrate on five areas: (1) Milton's attitude toward women, (2) free will and obedience, (3) human stewardship of the world, (4) the nature of evil, and (5) the style of the poem. "Stress" in these areas involves Milton's emphases on certain ideas, the tensions created by the working out of those ideas in the poem, and the stress the reader may feel in reaction to the pressures the poem creates. Examined one at a time, such topics take one to the heart of Milton's challenge to the reader, and students come to

see (and, one hopes, respect) how little complacent reassurance or
cheap comfort the poem gives. Consider the topics individually:

1. *Paradise Lost* does not reinforce the current feminist wisdom
about the proper or ideal relations between men and women. Milton's
initial description of Adam and Eve in Eden gets to the heart of the
matter: they are, we are told,

> Not equal, as thir sex not equal seem'd;
> For contemplation hee and valor form'd,
> For softness shee and sweet attractive Grace,
> Hee for God only, shee for God in him.   (4.296-99)

To many readers today, perhaps nothing in the poem seems at first
glance as dated as this bald declaration. But has the sexual revolution
achieved all its aims? Should it? I find that the debate about the
traditional dogma Milton espouses is far from over. At the Naval Academy women were only recently allowed to attend, they are over-
whelmingly outnumbered, and, like Eve, they frequently feel like
second-class citizens. The issue of whether women should be given
combat roles brings student convictions and prejudices to the fore in
ways perhaps unavailable to civilian schools. The issue focuses the
mind and heart wonderfully. Current platitudes about the equality of
men and women and the differences between them are held up to
sometimes scorching light in the heat of discussion. One of the intellectually satisfying aspects of teaching Milton here is to confront students with the liberal-conservative tensions in Milton's art. Eve's relation to Adam and its larger didactic significance, Milton's portrayal of
unfallen and fallen sexuality, and his attitudes toward the related issues of order and individuality, of hierarchy and freedom—in a marriage and in society at large—are of great interest to students at a
school like the Naval Academy, where hierarchy, freedom, obedience,
and sexual stereotypes are daily issues. I like to use Milton to challenge some of my diehard conservative students—and my diehard
liberal ones too. Conservative-minded students can be shown, to good
effect, the revolutionary effect of Milton's radical political sympathies
on his life and art. Liberal students can be helped to understand
Milton's profound commitment to classical and Christian values, or, to
put it another way, his deep response to the achievements of the
Western European tradition. Milton was intensely alive to the past in
the present for the sake of the future.

2. *Paradise Lost* does not offer placating extenuating circumstances
to those who would moderate harsh issues of freedom and responsibil-

ity. Milton's fierce insistence on free will raises questions my students like to ponder about various modern determinisms—Marxist, Freudian, and Darwinian ones, for example. Students here tend to have an intense belief in the freedom of their wills, and they find Milton reinforcing on that score. But Milton is not simplistic about such a complicated matter, and close analysis of how in book 9 Adam and Eve actually fall is salutary in expanding student understanding of the larger issue and of Milton's specific moral and psychological insights. I ask students to consider the complementarity of the two falls: The central danger for Eve seems to be narcissism, a potentially disastrous introversion—an ego problem, if you will; Adam's danger is one of extroversion, a problem of the id: passion. (Yet once more, opposites attract, I point out.) God, Superego Extraordinaire, completes the scheme. Students find such a triadic pattern helpful because it allows them to build a series of comparisons and analogies on the foundation of modern psychological metaphors. They begin to understand better Milton's dramatization of the psychological, emotional, and, from the divine standpoint, immoral pressures that impinge on free will. After such analysis, they appreciate more deeply the tension between Milton's unwavering insistence on virtuous obedience to a divine standard, on the one hand, and, on the other, his wisdom about how certain complications of personality make such obedience difficult.

3. *Paradise Lost* offers no optimistic vision of humankind's supposedly rational stewardship of the world. Issues of war and peace are one good way to approach this subject. At an institution that is training students to organize and potentially execute violence on an unprecedented scale, such issues are especially relevant. I may begin by asking students to compare and reconcile two passages from the poem. One is the impassioned antimilitarist passage in book 11 when the archangel Michael sums up the martial spirit at its most sinful:

> For in those days Might only shall be admir'd,
> And Valor and Heroic Virtue call'd;
> To overcome in Battle, and subdue
> Nations, and bring home spoils with infinite
> Man-slaughter, shall be held the highest pitch
> Of human Glory, and for Glory done
> Of triumph, to be styl'd great Conquerors,
> Patrons of Mankind, Gods, and Sons of Gods,
> Destroyers rightlier call'd and Plagues of men.   (689–97)

The other is from Abdiel's speech in book 6:

> nor is it aught but just,
> That he who in debate of Truth hath won,
> Should win in Arms, in both disputes alike
> Victor; though brutish that contest and foul,
> When Reason hath to deal with force, yet so
> Most reason is that Reason overcome.   (121–26)

My students read themselves as they read Milton, of course. They generally find that Milton's ideas are not easily reducible, and neither are their own. If they eventually arrive at a better understanding of a "just war" theory, the better for the nation, for then their admirable patriotism has been enriched by some serious wrestling with the moral and immoral reasons for going to war.

4. *Paradise Lost* gives no quarter in its insistence that the word "evil" is not outdated jargon created by puritanical killjoys. The poem flies in the face of those too tolerant souls among us who open wide their arms to the world and exclaim in pale echo of Alexander Pope that "whatever is is right." Milton's poem contends that much that is is wrong—terribly wrong. Here some understanding of Milton's absolutist viewpoint is crucial. Today's moral relativism is so pervasive, even among many who are nominally religious, that it generally goes unchallenged. Our culture has achieved a level of tolerance that makes it increasingly hard for many students to feel visceral outrage at serious criminal or immoral acts, much less feel that something significant can be done to correct such wrongs. Milton's revolutionary spirit, his radicalism, is rooted in an unblinking vision of evil in its many forms. But it is also balanced by his hard-earned knowledge of human failure, disappointment, and weakness. This tension—between supreme moral vision and an intensely hurtful life experience—is another essential source of stress in the poem, and this stress is of compelling interest when revealed to students. The Urania invocation to book 7 is one of many passages that can be used as a locus for discussion of this subject. In that invocation, one finds language tense with such various feelings as spiritual transport ("above th'Olympian Hill I soar"), pain ("though fall'n on evil days"), anger ("drive far off the barbarous dissonance / Of Bacchus and his Revellers"), and prayerful anxiety ("So fail not thou, who thee implores"). Milton's tolling repetition of the word "evil" in lines 25 and 26 makes the tension I have just described quite manifest.

5. Finally, the poem's style—diction, imagery, syntax—demands stamina of a kind rare in the language. Samuel Johnson, no slouch when it came to alert and generally intelligent reading of poetry,

confessed in "Milton" that he was quite exhausted by the attempt to meet the aesthetic, emotional, moral, and intellectual requirements of the poem's language. Not surprisingly, students often fare much worse. Many at first find the style either smotheringly uniform, or bombastic, or simply impenetrable. One way to address the problem is to look closely at the kinds of stylistic variety in *Paradise Lost.* For example, the poem contains quiet poetic passages of ravishing (and quite accessible) lyric beauty such as the pastoral episodes in Eden that include Adam and Eve's exquisite love poetry. Forcefulness and massiveness are not the only sensations created by the poem's epic verse. Milton's poetic art is characterized by a "grateful vicissitude" (to use his phrase for heaven's joyfully various pleasures) that includes wonderful modulations in language and tone. The myth of the smothering uniformity of Milton's style can be exploded by comparing, to give only one example, how Adam addresses Eve before the fall and how he speaks to her after it. Before the fall, he says: "Sole partner and sole part of all these joys, / Dearer thyself than all" (4.411–12). After the fall, we read: "Out of my sight, thou Serpent" (10.867). Yet one should not go too far with this kind of thing, because finally the poem does make a unified impression—but in the way a baroque church does. Saint Peter's Basilica in Rome contains many separable and quite different architectural, sculptural, and artistic elements, but the major effect of the whole is one of splendid power and aggressive grandeur. Milton's poem is a massive Protestant poetic parallel to the Catholic assertion of power in the Vatican. And just as in the Vatican the normal and commonplace, when found, seem lifted onto a higher level of reality, the style of *Paradise Lost* analogously transforms the objects it touches. For example, an elephant appearing before Adam and Eve "to make them mirth" wreathes "his Lithe Proboscis" (4. 345–47). It is important to help students see the point of "Lithe Proboscis"—the wit of it, if nothing else. The deliberately clumsy, slightly unwieldy bigness of the phrase is the charming poetic equivalent of an elephant's brand of playfulness; it is not bombast. Milton, like Michelangelo and Bernini, does inflate (at least to the modern prosaic sensibility), but an epic style is rather pathetic, like an unfilled balloon, when not filled with the proper inspiration. To give another example: When God in book 7 commands the angels to "inhabit lax" (162) while he sends the Son on his mission to create the universe of human beings, students need to appreciate that the Latinism is of the essence in understanding Milton's special challenge to the reader—or, to put it more sympathetically, is of the essence in understanding the special pleasures Milton's poetic style offers readers who desire a change from ordinary language. One can get an easy laugh by translating "inhabit lax" into "hang loose, boys," but if students are not helped to see the serious implications of the gulf between their generally narrow, slang-filled use of language and Milton's grand style, then the teacher's flippant cleverness will only have done harm to all concerned. When Milton recharges words like "inhabit" and "lax" with the spirit of their Latin ancestry, he transforms etymological knowledge into poetry of a high order. A linguistic bridge is built between two great cultures, the Latin and the English, and, in the process, rich poetic connotations are created by means of the linguistic illusion. It is no ordinary task to create omnific words spoken by the "Omnific Word" (7.217). In this context, students can be asked, sometimes with excellent results, to "lower" the style of a passage in the poem. Discussion of the dramatic differences between Milton's original and the student's travesty can be entertaining as well as illuminating. A student's prejudices and limitations can be exposed—Milton's too perhaps—in a context that is generally fun and revelatory for all concerned. In any case, in a modern world that seems increasingly in danger of being swamped by the trivial, the transitory, and the decadent, Milton's "monument to dead ideas" (to quote Walter Raleigh) written in language "far removed from common use" (to quote Samuel Johnson) can be surprisingly successful with students—*if* the teacher will attempt the negative capability required to convey well the poetry's unique qualities.

In conclusion, I would ask colleagues to consider the possibility as they prepare to teach *Paradise Lost* that Milton's statements about the aims of education in his pamphlet on that subject are still relevant to what many if not most students hope to learn as they prepare for adult life and, in any event, express ideas that explain as well as any could Milton's hopes for his poem's place in the culture he wished to shape and has shaped:

> The end then of learning is to repair the ruins of our first parents by regaining to know God aright, and out of that knowledge to love him, to imitate him, to be like him, as we may the nearest by possessing our souls of true virtue, which being united to the heavenly grace of faith makes up the highest perfection.

> I call therefore a complete and generous education that which fits a man to perform justly, skilfully, and magnanimously all the offices, both private and public, of peace and war. (Hughes, *John Milton* 631, 632)

A Three-Pronged Method of Teaching
Paradise Lost

Joseph E. Duncan

My method of teaching *Paradise Lost* incorporates three different approaches to the poem: the mythic and archetypal, the historical, and the personal. All these approaches lead students back to themselves. I explain these in an introductory lecture and elaborate on them when the class is studying particular sections; in discussion I encourage students to raise questions or to make comments relating these approaches to particular problems or passages.

My major aim is to help students realize that the modes of thinking and posing questions in *Paradise Lost* belong not only to past cultures but to their own and to themselves as individuals. While contexts and issues change, readers of Milton's epic poem can still share imaginatively in some of the most profound and enduring of human experiences. The framework of allusion relates readers to the mythic and the historical; the readers relate the inner experience of Satan, Adam, and Eve to themselves and to the experiences of other literary characters. I hope that students will be more deeply touched by *Paradise Lost* than by anything they have previously read. Some are.

Finding parallels between this work and various mythologies and archetypal theories is not only endlessly fascinating (especially for students who have had a mythology course); it also demonstrates that *Paradise Lost* is universal, that it is about everyone. I cite the *Gilgamesh Epic* because of its ancient origins and interesting overlapping with the Bible: its paradisal mountaintop garden of Siduri, its flood story, the fall of the natural man Enkidu, Gilgamesh's discovery of death, and his loss of the plant of life to the serpent. In taking up book 4 of *Paradise Lost,* I mention that paradises are also described in the mythologies of India, Iran, China, Greece, Rome, and Scandinavia as well as in the modern mythologies of Faulkner and Tolkien. I read Ovid's account of the golden age. Classical mythology suggests the parallel between Satan's rebellion and the war of the titans against the Olympian gods. A different, more sympathetic conception of Satan comes from comparing him with Prometheus. Falls are described in the account of the stages of human history and in the stories of Pandora, Proserpina, and Phaeton. Rebirth or regeneration is reflected in the stories of Adonis, Narcissus, and characters in other fertility myths. Less familiar mythologies, such as those of the African Nuer and the South American headhunters, tell of a lost paradise that was once in close contact with heaven.

One can find numerous parallels between *Paradise Lost* and the conceptions of some of the better-known archetypal critics such as Mircea Eliade, Joseph Campbell, Carl Jung, Maud Bodkin, and Northrop Frye.

Milton's paradise enjoys what Eliade, in his anthropological approach to archetypes, calls "the prestige of the Center," enduring in the realm of the sacred, as distinct from the profane (*Myth* 12). It represents the sacred marriage on the sacred mountain; Eliade saw mountains as symbols of the concentrated presence of God. Milton's depiction would reflect human nostalgia for "a mythic past transformed into an archetype"—paradise (*Images* 16). Campbell has reminded us that goddesses of life have presided for millennia over gardens, sometimes as the bride of the serpent (70–72).

In the archetypal interpretations of Jung (primarily in *Archetypes*), devil figures like Satan are symbols of the shadow archetype within the unconscious. Jung also discusses the devil figure as the trickster. Two of Jung's views of paradise are relevant for Milton's paradise: as a symbol of the mother archetype, associated with life and fertility, and as a symbol of integration. Our yearning for the mother as symbolized by paradise is a search for rebirth and redemption. Despite the differences in the terms and values of Milton and Jung, Milton's Adam and Eve experience the kind of psychological integration and development that Jung calls individuation—a psychological version of the fortunate fall. They consciously accept forces within their unconscious, including their shadows and the parts of their psyche representative of the opposite sex (Jung's anima and animus). In teaching book 9, I distribute an excerpt from the essay "The Undiscovered Self," in which Jung claims that "the case is far graver" than the church's conception of original sin or "Adam's relatively innocent slip-up with Eve" (296–98). Current newspaper accounts often make the same point.

In an application of Jungian conceptions to literature, Bodkin discusses Milton's paradise as a part of the paradise-hades archetypal pattern, found also in Coleridge's "Kubla Khan." The pattern of death and rebirth, which she examines in Coleridge's *The Rime of the Ancient Mariner,* also appears in *Paradise Lost,* while Christ is the type of the sacrificial tragic hero. Some of the complexity and ambiguity in the relations between God and Satan are provocatively elucidated by seeing Bodkin's antithetical patterns: Satan is serpent, God is savior; or Satan is Promethean hero, God is alien despot.

For Frye, *Paradise Lost* would exemplify the archetype of the quest, as Adam loses paradise and the tree of life, wanders in the wilderness of the world, and is restored to Eden by the Messiah. *Paradise Lost* would also be an example of a human being's loss and regaining of identity, which for Frye provides the "framework of all literature" (*Educated* 55). The imagery of paradise reflects Frye's "analogy of innocence" (*Anatomy* 151–53), found in works like *The Tempest* and *Songs of Innocence*. After the fall, Death becomes Frye's recurrent "cannibal giant" (*Anatomy* 148).

Besides perceiving that *Paradise Lost* possesses the kind of reality reflected in myth and archetype, students also need to understand that it reflects a historical reality accepted by Milton and most of his contemporaries. I tell students that for a society accepting the Bible as the ultimate authority, it was easier to believe that the human race originated with Adam and Eve than it is for our own society to believe that the human race originated from a globule of protoplasm. As shown by genealogical charts (like those in early editions of the Authorized Version), it was natural to believe that Adam and Eve were just distant grandparents. Walter Raleigh insisted that it was as important to locate paradise for readers of Genesis as to locate the Holy Land for readers of the gospels. One can show students copies of elaborate maps indicating the position of paradise and of title pages depicting Adam and Eve in paradise (see Duncan, *Milton's Earthly Paradise,* and Williams).

The historical interpretation—whether understood through belief or a suspension of disbelief—gives a new reality and importance to Adam and Eve as historical figures. It also forces us to think about our cultural origins and about ourselves as descendants and as ancestors of future descendants. Students are surprised to realize how many cultural beginnings are described in *Paradise Lost*: natural law, language, knowledge, work, rest, marriage, the family, the church, the state, and of course sin and redemption. The historical interpretation of Adam and Eve in paradise, an introduction to sacred history, helps prepare students for the interpretation of history in books 11 and 12. More important, it leads us straight forward to a fallen world—our world.

Instead of 1066 and 1492, students need to think of the events in the great world drama of Christian history. On the first day of class and on successive occasions I draw a chart across all the blackboard available showing paradise, the fall, Christ, the millennium, final judgment, and the new heaven and new earth. I also present *Paradise Lost* as a drama in three acts: act 1—Before the Fall; act 2—The Fall and Its Consequences, and act 3—Redemption. Through the structure of the poem and the early allusions to the fall, the destruction of sin, and the redemption (as in 1.301–13, 381–501, and 3.250–65), we see these acts simultaneously.

The historical interpretation raises many questions—questions that Milton had to answer and that we should also try to answer. What is a life of innocence like? What choices does one make before, at the time of, and after a fall? How is it possible to fall from a life of innocence into sin? Does the fall of Adam and Eve shed light on how a baby can grow up to be a member of the Mafia? How much free will does one have? How can one experience regeneration? Class discussion can be more exciting if we feel that the choices of Adam and Eve—or of some progenitor—have given us the world we inherit. How will our choices affect the world we leave?

The third approach I use is the personal. Personal experience can help one to understand *Paradise Lost,* but *Paradise Lost* can also help one to understand the experience of oneself and others. Once students perceive this two-way process, they provide some of the best ideas for teaching and for their own writing. The personal approach includes the autobiographical, the relation of the reader to the experiences in *Paradise Lost,* and the literary, the relation of fictional characters to the experiences in Milton's epic.

Every mature person has a lost paradise within. Everyone confronts temptation and choice; everyone falls, or loses innocence. Many also experience some kind of regeneration, perhaps through becoming a born-again Christian, or falling in love, or having a baby, or finding a mission (Margaret Atwood's *Surfacing* provides a good modern example of rebirth). The relations between God and Satan, Adam and Eve, are the counterparts of innumerable relations today. Some students prefer to see Adam and Eve as the faculties in a person. Almost all readers can find themselves in *Paradise Lost* or find *Paradise Lost* in other literary works.

In discussion or in personal papers, students can compare themselves with Adam and Eve or even with the devils of book 2 who organize into activity groups after Satan departs. Those with creative interests may try writing a modern version of a scene from *Paradise Lost,* such as a speech by Satan, the fall, or the separation or reconciliation of Adam and Eve. They not only make the connection between Milton's characters and themselves, but they appreciate Milton more after encountering firsthand the problems of literary composition. They may also explain how a modern version is like or unlike Milton's.

Paradise Lost deepens our understanding of relations between parent and child, husband and wife. A student suggested thinking of God as a loving parent who delights in giving to his children but who knows they must grow, assume responsibility, and make their own decisions. In insisting that love must be a free choice, Milton's epic reflects the joy and sorrow of parenthood and of matrimony. It also shows the joy—and the end—of childhood and of the honeymoon.

Applying concepts of structural and transactional analysis to *Paradise Lost* relates it to enduring problems and raises questions about the action from a new perspective. What characters at what times have the ego functions of the adult, the parent, and the child? When are pairs of characters in the four life situations (I'm OK, You're OK; I'm not OK, You're OK; I'm OK, You're not OK; and I'm not OK, You're not OK)? (See Berne, esp. 75–78, and Thomas A Harris, 38–59, 65–77, and 257–71.) A "complementary transaction" occurs when Adam's parent responds to Eve's child after her dream in book 5. In what transactions is communication impeded? Do Satan, Adam, and Eve have imagined "life scripts" that they want to follow? Adam envisions himself as progenitor, but is having children important in the drama Eve imagines for herself?

I want students to realize that what is called universal in *Paradise Lost* is still with us in the twentieth century, even in popular reading. Two works familiar to many students and easily related to *Paradise Lost* are William Golding's *Lord of the Flies* and John Knowles's *A Separate Peace*. Both describe modern falls. If *Lord of the Flies* reflects modern psychology, politics, and warfare, are there comparable elements in *Paradise Lost*? Can anything in Milton's epic be related to Simon, who is convinced one must seek out evil? The central episode in *A Separate Peace* involves a tree and a fall. Gene feels guilt like that of Satan and Adam after he has caused his friend Finny to fall from a tree, but Finny is a Christ figure who both teaches and forgives.

In investigating the relation of *Paradise Lost* to some less familiar works, students can make genuine and original contributions to literary criticism. One paper developed a fascinating comparative study using Golding's *The Inheritors*. Whereas Milton deals with a mythical and theological interpretation of the fall, Golding deals with a fall in modern anthropological terms. A Neanderthal man, totally innocent because he can neither remember nor anticipate, is corrupted and then exterminated by Homo sapiens, whose superior knowledge leads to the experience of evil. Watching from a tree, Lok and Fa learn of drunkenness, lust, and cruelty. The Neanderthal man and woman were not sufficient to have stood, and at the end, without promise or grace, they seem abandoned by their evolutionary goddess.

I was skeptical when a Tolkien buff suggested an extended comparison between *Paradise Lost* and *The Lord of the Rings*. As the paper asserts, however, "Tolkien deals with the same basic materials as Milton—the theme of temptation, man's mortality, and the fate/free will problem—and creates a totally original universe parallel to that of *Paradise Lost*." The relations are numerous and complex. Satan has his counterpart in Saruman, once the White, who falls through a betrayal motivated by pride, retains vestiges of his former glory for a long time, and is finally reduced to crawling. Adam's counterpart is Frodo, the most important representative of the innocent hobbits and their paradisal Shire. With his actions foreknown by the One, does Frodo steal the ring of his own free will? But Christ has no counterpart, unless Frodo himself is a Christ figure.

American literature offers a variety of opportunities for this kind of study. In papers comparing *Paradise Lost* with "The Man That Corrupted Hadleyburg" and *Letters from the Earth*, one student observed that both Milton and Mark Twain "would probably cringe at the comparison," and the other said that such a comparison offered "unusual insights" and "a different perspective." In the irreverent *Letters* God's punishment of Adam and Eve is seen as totally unjust. Perhaps T. S. Eliot would also have cringed at the comparison of *Paradise Lost* and *The Waste Land*. Other students have compared *Paradise Lost* to Hawthorne's *The Scarlet Letter* and to Dreiser's *An American Tragedy*. Not surprisingly, works of Milton and Faulkner can be compared extensively. Both writers present the inception and consequences of an original sin that brings spiritual bondage. Both delve into the past. In Faulkner's work the wilderness is lost and the Civil War is like a descent into hell. Isaac McCaslin is unsuccessful in playing the role of Christ. Students have worked out revealing comparative studies using a piece of adolescent fiction called *The Butterfly Revolution*, by William Butler, and Carson McCullers's *The Heart Is a Lonely Hunter*. Recently, a student showed the similarities in *Paradise Lost* and James Baldwin's *Go Tell It on the Mountain*. From Baldwin's perspective the top of the mountain—redemption—can be reached only by means of a journey through hell to personal responsibility—a journey made successfully by his major character, John Grimes. Eve's desire to get away from Adam and to try out her independence may be compared to the feminist heroine's desire to escape her husband or lover, as in Marilyn French's *The Women's Room* and Francine du Plessix Gray's *Lovers and Tyrants*.

Continental literature also offers some interesting parallels with *Paradise Lost*. In Hermann Hesse's *Demian* the boy Emil Sinclair experiences childhood innocence and then a period of doubt and torment in which he swings between the worlds of light and darkness, but in Hesse's interpretation the boy is redeemed through discovering the synthesis of these two worlds within himself. One must lose innocence to gain this new inner harmony. The figure Demian, a new Christ, and Demian's mother, Frau Eva, a new Eve, along with the dark satanic Kromer, are the chief characters influencing Emil. Albert Camus's novel *The Fall* carries themes and problems of *Paradise Lost* into a modern world in which God is passé, everyone (including Christ) is guilty, and it is always too late. The fall of the central character, Jean-Baptiste Clamence, occurs when he ignores a suicide at a Parisian bridge. The student making the comparison concludes that "modern man," as represented by Clamence, is closer to the fallen Satan than to the fallen Adam; his city is a Dantesque hell and he is unable to endure the thought of innocence in others. When two good students undertook comparisons of *Paradise Lost* with Samuel Beckett's *Waiting for Godot* and André Malraux's *Man's Fate*, I was dubious; but the results showed again how basic the problems and characters in *Paradise Lost* really are. Another paper, entitled "The Rise as Fall," examined works interpreting the loss of innocence as a necessary step in human or individual development. Within this focus, Clamence in Camus's *The Fall* experiences a moral rise from a natural self-absorption to an existential awareness of failings and responsibilities. In Hesse's *Journey to the East*, H. H. finds that what he had thought was the disastrous end of his journey was really only the beginning.

A teacher's greatest hope is that students will continue to remember a class and to profit from it. I have evidence that some of my students do. Although the mythic and archetypal, historical, and personal are only three of the many possible approaches to Milton's epic, I am convinced that they lead students to think of and remember *Paradise Lost* as a living embodiment of the ways humans have experienced— and continue to experience—both the long quest of the human race and the quests of their own individual lives.

SPECIFIC APPROACHES

Approaching *Paradise Lost* through a Reading of Milton's Sonnets

Ellen S. Mankoff

Although I teach *Paradise Lost* in several different courses at Kenyon College, including upper-level courses in Renaissance literature, I find teaching Milton's epic to the freshmen in my introduction-to-literature class especially rewarding. Unlike the upper-level students, the freshmen have not specifically elected to study *Paradise Lost* and usually stand in awe of the text, never imagining that the seventeenth-century English epic might speak to them as familiarly as, say, a modern American novel. That it does—that the students become passionately involved in a text that, indeed, turns out to be about themselves—is what makes the course so exciting for me. Every time I teach the poem I share their sense of discovery, and I discover the work anew. Although *Paradise Lost* is probably the most challenging work we read all year, I teach it fairly early on, as a four-week high point in the first semester, after two weeks on Robert Fitzgerald's translation of the *Odyssey* and six weeks on lyric poems in *The Norton Anthology of Poetry*. If Milton's language is difficult for freshmen, so much the better—it is not a difficulty above their years, and I can assure them that after reading *Paradise Lost* with care they will be able to master the rest of the literature we read with relative ease.

I begin the year with Homer and with English and American lyric

74

poetry because I want my students to have at least some shared experience of literature before we read Milton. The idea of—indeed, the reality of—this shared experience is extremely important, for I teach what might be called a reader-response version of *Paradise Lost*. I believe that the reader is the focus of Milton's poem, that we experience our fallen condition in the difficulties of reading the poem, that Milton's aim is to reeducate us, or, as Milton writes in *Of Education*, "to repair the ruins of our first parents" (Hughes, *John Milton* 631). In reading and responding to the poem "incorrectly" and in being corrected by the poet, we come to a better understanding of the limitations of our understanding; we also sharpen our perceptions and clarify our vision. Anyone familiar with the work of Stanley Fish will recognize my huge debt to him: I rely on *Surprised by Sin: The Reader in* Paradise Lost and "Interpreting the Variorum" throughout this essay and use them as a base for my teaching. Though I first read Milton in one of Fish's seminars and can hardly imagine reading Milton any other way, I teach a reader-response method because it works—and it works with phenomenal success.

What does it mean, however, to teach a reader-response method? After all, one of the tenets of reader-response critical theory is that the interpretive assumptions we bring to a text structure and largely determine our experience of that text; therefore it would seem that to teach any literary work successfully by this method, we need to know rather precisely what our students' interpretive assumptions are. What expectations do they share when approaching Milton's (or any other) text? To what interpretive community do my freshmen belong? In teaching practice, at least as differentiated from critical theory, these questions are easy to answer, for as teachers we are clearly responsible for creating many of our students' expectations, for informing them with certain assumptions; our classrooms function as small interpretive communities that reflect the larger and ever-changing worlds of literary academia. (This, of course, is something students have always known: we have all been asked, "What do you *want* in this essay?" and even if some of us try to disabuse our students of the notion that there is one particular kind of essay or answer we "want," they soon learn—from the grapevine, from classroom discussion, from the comments on their written work—that Professor X favors detailed stylistic analysis, Professor Y is interested in feminist readings, and Professor Z wishes them to concern themselves with the large mythic structures underlying a work.)

I choose the *Odyssey* as the basis of our shared experience (although the *Iliad* or the *Aeneid* would serve equally well) so that I can be sure my students are familiar with epic conventions and concerns, with classical conceptions of heroism and of the relations of mortals and gods. Reading Homer also gives my students an opportunity to begin to familiarize themselves with classical mythology or at least to learn where in the library to go—whether to Ovid or to the *Oxford Classical Dictionary*—if they want to know more about Athena or Minos or Persephone. From the weeks spent on lyric poetry and the accompanying discussions of imagery, allusion, form, meter, sound, diction, syntax, tone, and convention, I know my students will be able to bring to Milton's long poem the interpretive techniques they have practiced in reading—word by word by word—many shorter poems. These eight weeks offer only a minimal background in the epic and in techniques of close reading, but even this background provides us a shared vocabulary with which to approach *Paradise Lost*. (Here I might add that I sympathize with Robert Crosman, who complains that Fish's model reader in *Surprised by Sin* is a "seventeenth-century Christian reader . . . of the Puritan persuasion" [12].) I can always count on some of my students to know the Old and New Testaments and on many to know the first chapters of Genesis. They have all learned how to use the *Oxford English Dictionary*, and the excellent introduction and notes (required reading) to Merritt Hughes's edition of *Paradise Lost* provide more background.

I argue that, as teachers of *Paradise Lost*, we cannot expect to find "fit audience"—or even a few fit readers—in our classrooms; instead, we must fit our readers for Milton's text. Fortunately Milton makes our task easy, for his poem offers so many models of education—of learning and of teaching. No matter what expectations we bring to Milton's poem, we find them (and ourselves) subverted, challenged, overthrown as the poet attempts to teach us to read the world and ourselves anew.

As an introduction to the revisionist methods of *Paradise Lost* and as transition from the lyric poetry we've been reading, I spend several class hours on Milton's sonnets 7, 19, 20, and 21. Sonnet 20 ("Lawrence of virtuous Father virtuous Son") introduces them to the peculiarly Miltonic texture of classical and biblical allusion—with the Horatian Favonius clothing the lily from Matthew in the second quatrain—and to the concept of the "thing indifferent." (See Fish, "Interpreting" 466–68, for the argument that follows.) We spend most of our time on the last two lines: "He who of these delights can judge and spare / To interpose them oft, is not unwise." The discussion usually shapes itself as a debate about the "intended" meaning of "spare" in line 13: does it mean "refrain from," and is Milton, like a

Stoic philosopher, warning us away from the delights of wine and music? Or does it mean "afford," and is an Epicurean Milton urging those same delights on us? Because the students expect a stern and unyielding Milton, they usually prefer "refrain from," but after a backward glance to the "Lily and the Rose, that neither sow'd nor spun," they side with "afford." They know from reading Shakespeare's sonnets that not all sonnets resolve themselves neatly; they can accept ambiguity and paradox, but they are pleased at being able to decide on a stable interpretation of the close of this sonnet. When I ask them to paraphrase these lines, however, a new problem emerges—or perhaps the former problem loses its force. For as soon as we judge as best we can which meaning of "spare" Milton intends—and all I am sure he intended was our difficulty—we are confronted with the double negative of "not unwise" and are made to realize that in important ways our debate was irrelevant. The delights of this world, Milton would tell us, are things indifferent in themselves: we are not unwise if we judge them correctly, but only in our proper use of God's gifts might we be judged wise.

The experience of involving ourselves in irrelevant debate over unimportant distinctions that finally collapse occurs again and again in *Paradise Lost*, sometimes in the time it takes to read one line, sometimes over the course of a book. The "fruit" of the first line is initially read figuratively, as the "result" of human disobedience, then becomes the literal fruit "of that forbidden tree" in line two, and then regains its meaning as the result of disobedience when those results are made explicit in lines three and four. By forcing us to concentrate on "fruit," to make an interpretive choice, Milton encourages us to forget our "first disobedience"—until those interpretive distinctions collapse, making us face our mistake. This sequence will recur throughout the poem: we will be tempted to blame someone or something other than ourselves—Satan, God, Adam, Eve, or even the fruit—for our fall. A larger example of the irrelevant debate occurs, of course, in books 1 and 2, when the fallen angels debate whether force or guile, open war or wiles would be the better strategy in their renewed attempt against heaven. As Satan, Belial, Mammon, and the rest present their arguments, it is nearly impossible not to get involved, not to side with one devil or another, until we find Satan commending *us*: "Well have ye judged, well ended long debate" (2. 390). In the rhetorical thrills of the debate we forget, or choose to forget, exactly what we've been debating, just as Eve in book 9 will forget God's one command as she too thrills to Satan's eloquence. As we look back more closely in class at the inconsistencies in and motivations of the arguments, and as we pay more attention to narrative comment, students are always surprised that they did become so involved. But they never fail to become so. Especially after our recent reading of another "study of revenge," the *Odyssey*, it is easy for the class to respond to Satan and involve itself in his dilemmas. The class time spent on books 1 and 2 offers a good occasion to discuss Miltonic allusion to other epics as parody, and parody curiously double-edged: that is, we come to understand both that Satan is not a type of the good leader who risks his own safety rather than endanger his crew, and we see the classical definition of heroism itself undercut simply because Satan is so easily comparable to Odysseus, preparing the way for the Christian redefinition of heroism later in the poem.

The last two lines of sonnet 21 ("Cyriack, whose Grandsire on the Royal Bench"), easier for the students than sonnet 20, also briefly engage them in syntactical debate: some students will assume for a moment at least that we are to refrain from "the cheerful hour" rather than from the "superfluous burden." At this point a disapproving rather than mild God is still the figure they expect to encounter in Milton's poetry; a heaven-ordained, God-sent pleasure is still an unexpected event. Later, when we read the descriptions of the beauties of Eden, and of Adam and Eve and their amorous play in book 4, students are still likely to mistrust, responding with the carnal knowledge of fallen humanity to the spotless innocence of paradise. We think ill of all this good, as Satan does, until the narrator's reprimand tells us that the guilt is in ourselves, not in the yet sinless Adam and Eve: "Then was not guilty shame: dishonest shame / Of Nature's works, honor dishonourable, / Sin bred . . ." (4.313–15). And we will continue to forget and be reminded, to mistake and be corrected, throughout the course of the poem. Our tendencies to misinterpret God's will or word, or to be seduced to such misinterpretations, to err, and then to judge ourselves even more harshly than would God (for example, Adam's and Eve's accusations of each other and self-recriminations after the fall) are also suggested in sonnet 21 with the mention of "our Laws, / Which others at their Bar so often wrench."

The interpretation or acceptance of God's will or word is an issue at the very hearts of sonnets 7 and 19, and just as Milton warns against wrenching, willful mis- or overinterpretation in sonnet 21, so he urges simple acceptance of God's will—whether or not we understand it— in sonnet 7 ("How soon hath Time, the subtle thief of youth"). This poem is full of characteristically Miltonic ambiguities. Lines 5 and 6, for instance, have been paraphrased by my class to opposite meanings. One paraphrase is: Perhaps my appearance is false, for although

I have arrived near to manhood in years, I am far from maturity. Another paraphrase is: Perhaps my appearance of not having achieved anything (because my buds and blossoms do not show) is deceptive, for I am arrived near to manhood even though it may not look that way. After all, "inward ripeness" may "much less appear" simply because it is inward. "Endu'th" in line 8 can mean both "is inherent in" or "clothes"—and therefore is a good Miltonic word to point up the difference the poet often finds between internal qualities and external attributes and the difficulty we often experience in distinguishing the two. Once the octave of the sonnet seems to lie open to two opposing interpretations, we move on to the sestet, hoping for resolution—which indeed we find, although the sestet is full of ambiguities of another sort. The class usually notices the seemingly disordered syntax of "less or more, or soon or slow," and "mean or high," in lines 9 and 11, and decides that if the order of the words in these phrases does not matter enough to keep them consistent, the values they represent must not be too important to the poet. And indeed, a concern for position, first or high, turns out to be characteristic of Satan in *Paradise Lost,* while God's angels, no matter what rank, sing in one voice and sit "in order serviceable," and God's son knows he will not "lessen or degrade" his own nature "by descending to assume / Man's" (3.303–4). Another troublesome feature of the sestet is the vagueness of the "it"s and "all"; the attempt to determine their antecedents turns out to be a difficult, even impossible task. (For the critical history of this problem, see Hughes and Steadman 2.2: 372–73.) Oddly enough, in spite of the seeming vagueness of the sestet, most students readily grasp its meaning—or at least the meaning of the last two lines: "All is, if I have grace to use it so, / As ever in my great task-Master's eye." The difficulties of the poem collapse when we read this statement of faith and responsibility, and the class again feels that Milton has caught them in yet another irrelevant debate, for God's "time" cannot be translated into human terms. I begin teaching this poem by placing it in the context of other great lyric poems about the passage of time (recently read in class): just as we will analyze Milton's implicit and explicit criticisms of epic conventions, here the class has the chance to see how Milton manipulates the conventions of this great lyric tradition. The differences between God's eternal moment and our sense of fleeting time, God's complete vision and our limited sight, are suggested in this sonnet, which prepares the way for Raphael's conversation with Adam in *Paradise Lost* and certainly Raphael's responses to Adam's astronomical "doubt" in the beginning of book 8.

Sonnet 19 ("When I consider how my light is spent"), linked in many ways to sonnet 7, is the last I teach before moving on to *Paradise Lost*. Familiar with the figures of Tiresias and the blind poets and singers of the *Odyssey*, my students have already discussed the themes of physical and spiritual vision, blindness and insight, outer darkness and inner light; this sonnet prepares the way for the great proem of book 3. Sonnet 19 quite literally addresses the problem of interpreting texts (or perhaps the problem of interpreting texts quite literally); the speaker of the poem has misinterpreted at least one of Christ's parables by reading it too literally, in spiritual darkness. Year after year my students give witness to the experience of reading lines 6–8 described by Stanley Fish: they first assume that the questioner of line 7 will be the Maker, returned and chiding, rather than the speaker of the poem. As Fish notes: "This assumption does not survive line 7—'Doth God exact day labor, light denied,'—which, instead of chiding the poet for his inactivity, seems to rebuke him for having expected that chiding" ("Interpreting" 473). When we discover in line 8 that the questioner is instead the poet, angry at God's demands and deprivations and simultaneously aware of his own foolishness at rebuking God, the reader becomes aware of his or her own faulty assumptions and misreadings. That is, the reader's experience in misinterpreting those central lines is perfectly described by the speaker of the poem, who has ironically already been cast into the "outer darkness" he fears. The speaker misinterprets and is then graced with a better understanding of God's will; readers misinterpret and are also given a chance to correct themselves. I look back at this poem when I teach the end as well as the beginning of book 3, when Uriel, "the sharpest-sighted spirit of all in Heaven," not only fails to detect Satan but actually points him the way to paradise. Most of my students are quick to blame Uriel—as we are all quick to blame others—and are then confronted with Milton's statement that hypocrisy is "Invisible, except to God alone" and that Uriel's mistake is a sign of his innocence, for "goodness thinks no ill / Where no ill seems" (3.684, 688–89). Again, the ill is within us, for jumping too quickly to a conclusion, for assigning blame where none belongs, for failing to recognize God's will. Patience in sonnet 19 also looks forward to "the better fortitude / Of Patience and Heroic Martyrdom" (9.32), as well as to another kind of heroism so important in *Paradise Lost*. On leaving Adam at the end of book 8, Raphael advises: "Stand fast; to stand or fall / Free in thine own Arbitrement it lies" (640–41).

Although these sonnets do prepare my students for the large and small interpretive cruxes of *Paradise Lost*, linked as the short poems are to the longer one in imagery, theme, syntactic structure, reliance on and revision of poetic convention, *Paradise Lost* still, of course, surprises and overwhelms the class. We fall again and again in the text of Milton's poem, finding ourselves now "in wandr'ing mazes lost" and then corrected to a straighter path and clearer vision. That my students insist on discussing "Providence, Foreknowledge, Will, and Fate, / Fixt Fate, Free Will, Foreknowledge absolute" (2.559–60) even in book 9 shows how easy it is to learn and to forget—and to learn again. Books 11 and 12, traditionally experienced as disappointing anticlimax, become for my students a review, as Adam's instruction by Michael remodels their own instruction by Milton. Adam's vision is now as clouded as our own has proved to be, but the last books bring new understanding and new hope. "Let mee / Interpret for him," volunteers Christ, speaking of fallen man to his Father (11. 33–34). As Adam learns to read human history, so have we been learning to interpret our world and our responsibilities; my students have been learning never to rest secure in their reading strategies and interpretive assumptions. When Adam correctly interprets the covenant, Michael responds, "Dext'rously thou aim'st" (11.884): although the poem teaches us our limitations, it also challenges us to overcome them, to choose carefully, to think actively, to aim dextrously. If we accept the challenge, Milton gives us the chance to leave the world of his poem as fit, perhaps even heroic readers. My class finishes *Paradise Lost* early in the year, but for the rest of the course Milton's poem remains an interpretive principle, a model, a guide, and—I hope—a paradise within.

Moments of Delay:
A Student's Guide to *Paradise Lost*

Leslie E. Moore

Student readers of *Paradise Lost* might well empathize with Satan's predicament in book 2 as he crosses the "wild Abyss" to search for a place of rest:

> *Chaos* and *ancient Night,* I come no Spy,
> With purpose to explore or to disturb
> The secrets of your Realm, but by constraint
> Wand'ring this darksome Desert, as my way
> Lies through your spacious Empire up to light,
> Alone, and without guide, half lost, I seek
> What readiest path leads where your gloomy bounds
> Confine with Heav'n. (2.970–77)

Wandering the "darksome Desert" of Milton's verse, students may find themselves "Alone, and without guide, half lost"; they read the poem under constraint rather than by choice. In their difficult journey through Milton's empire, they search for the "readiest path" out of the poem and ask directions from anyone crossing this path, be it Chaos or ancient Night.

When faced with this situation, teachers respond almost instinctively with an act of guidance. Like Raphael and Michael, Milton's angelic professors, we tell stories about the poem and paraphrase its difficult sections or offer a more direct and doctrinal supervision; in either case, our students react like Adam in book 11: "I follow thee, safe Guide, the path / Thou lead'st me" (371–72). Our instincts are in large measure correct, for we are following a pattern established by Milton, who either casts his characters as guides or shows their desire to lead others toward salvation or destruction. Yet we may think twice before continuing this pattern, especially if we plan to lead our students quickly and efficiently through the poem's fabric of "mazy error." Sin and Death, for example, may assault the abyss by building a "broad and beat'n way," but Milton reminds us that this smooth and easy path leads directly to hell. Warned against taking the shortest route, we are likewise cautioned against haste by Eve's experience in book 9. "If thou accept / My conduct, I can bring thee thither soon," promises Satan, and when Eve acquiesces, he makes "intricate seem straight" and guides her "swiftly" to the forbidden tree (629–32).

Though it is not my intention to cast Milton teachers as Sin or Satan (or as Chaos and Night, for that matter), the temptation to provide a ready and easy way through *Paradise Lost* could limit the scope of our teaching and lessen the pleasure of our first-time readers. But what if we refocused our pedagogy and introduced students to the very problem we experience as teachers and critics: how do we chart a path through *Paradise Lost*? The poem ends with Adam and Eve searching for a place of rest; we would begin our classes by asking students to take responsibility for their own journey through the poem, just as Satan chooses to travel through chaos, Uriel through the heavens, and Abdiel through Satan's scornful legions.[1] We would ask students the same questions we ask ourselves: what determines a choice in *Paradise Lost*, and what does it mean to choose a particular path or journey—or interpretation—over another?

Introducing students to Miltonic choice is no small task, for choosing is one of the poem's most enigmatic activities. Nevertheless, there are moments in *Paradise Lost* when the poem itself aids us in our teaching, moments when the text pauses between conflicting interpretations and asks us to consider what it means to choose. These "moments of delay" usually follow a confident presentation of a system, relation, or doctrine: suddenly, an odd figure or troubling simile will appear, as if from nowhere, and proceed to examine or call into question the concept just established.[2] In the larger narrative, these moments are the origin of a matrix of paths, some complementary, others antithetical, which offer a series of competing perspectives on the justification of God's ways to men.[3] Such moments conflict, almost sharply so, with a search for the "readiest path."

An alternative method for teaching *Paradise Lost* would introduce students to this ever-changing series of paths, to the "darksome Desert" of figurative choice that forms the space of the poem. Initially we would take the more traditional stance of guide (partly because our students expect it), but we would provide guidance that is actually a form of mediation. We would guide until our students learned to choose for themselves what decisions to make, what paths to follow. In an ideal situation, the dynamics of the classroom would be transformed from an encounter between student and teacher—as so often happens with the texts of the traditional canon—to an encounter between student and text, with the teacher becoming less important as students learned to define a figurative choice.

Having gained more confidence and independence, students would find their creation of a path through *Paradise Lost* more stimulating than the "readiest path" of our steady guidance. For this method at once incorporates their experience of feeling lost within, overpowered by, and even hostile to the poem, while demonstrating that such reactions are far from abnormal and that much of the text prepares for and even elicits such responses. They would admit that part of the point is to be lost and "without guide." And they would begin to imagine the magnitude of Satan's loss, the depth of Adam's fall, the despair of Eden's destruction in books 11 and 12.

I

No other section of *Paradise Lost* tempts us to guide like the account of Eden in book 4. Though paradise contains "In narrow room Nature's whole wealth, yea more, / A Heaven on Earth" (4.207–08), students tend to miss or ignore its beauty because they are bothered by Eden's limitations and boundaries. They see its high wall rather than wondrous abundance. When we see our students' disappointment, we try to convince them—often unsuccessfully—that paradise is just as exciting as hell, Pandemonium, or chaos and that the "loss of Eden" is indeed significant. Book 4 thus poses a genuine pedagogical problem: though Eden appears to be accessible, it is actually a most mysterious image, so much so that students rarely know how to approach it.

To solve this problem, we can use the moment of delay to help students discover what makes Eden "Eden." We can show them how Eden is defined, altered, or even threatened at such moments of choice, and we can suggest that paradise not only is something lost but also is an interpretive center linking Milton's fallen and unfallen realms, his satanic, angelic, and human characters. Students would learn that what intrigues them in books 1 and 2, the potential for rebellion and deviation, also exists in book 4; that the poem's fallen and unfallen imagery is more closely intertwined than the sharp break after book 2 implies; and that choosing something—be it a path or an interpretation—entails loss as well as gain, losses that may surpass the imagined gains.

Teachers might begin their discussion of Eden by asking students how a moment of delay works in a Miltonic text. The great set piece describing the garden's water system, for example, may appear to be an unlikely source for such moments, but it offers at least two examples of delay—places where the text hesitates between alternative paths and presents its readers with a choice. In so doing, the passage illustrates the dilemma of trying to construct an imaginative space both richly figurative and consistent with the definition of Eden as "unfallen." Lines 223–63 of book 4 are one long sentence—which is one reason students have trouble with it: they keep looking for a period to break the flow of Milton's verse, but it appears only belatedly, a reminder of the river's endless cycle:

> Southward through *Eden* went a River large,
> Nor chang'd his course, but through the shaggy hill
> Pass'd underneath ingulft, for God had thrown
> That Mountain as his Garden mould high rais'd
> Upon the rapid current, which through veins
> Of porous Earth with kindly thirst up-drawn,
> Rose a fresh Fountain, and with many a rill
> Water'd the Garden; thence united fell
> Down the steep glade, and met the nether Flood,
> Which from his darksome passage now appears,
> And now divided into four main Streams,
> Runs diverse, wand'ring many a famous Realm
> And Country whereof here needs no account,
> But rather to tell how, if Art could tell,
> How from that Sapphire Fount the crisped Brooks,
> Rolling on Orient Pearl and sands of Gold,
> With mazy error under pendant shades
> Ran Nectar, visiting each plant, and fed
> Flow'rs worthy of Paradise which not nice Art
> In Beds and curious Knots. . . .   (4.223–42)

Students can gain some control of this passage if they look for images that conflict with the initial description of the river, which rises from an underground fountain, flows through the garden in various rills, and falls "united" to rejoin the "nether Flood." The moment of delay begins when the "nether Flood" divides into four main streams and "Runs diverse, wand'ring many a famous Realm." Seasoned readers of Milton half expect an epic catalog to follow, as it would in book 11, a list of the numerous kingdoms such streams traverse. Instead, there is an oddly self-conscious decision not to pursue the image—"whereof here needs no account." The choice not to speak, not to fall into diverse realms, ensures that Eden will stay in its place, "in narrow room."

Yet such a choice provokes a crisis: for the description of the natural, self-renewing river disappears and is replaced by a brief meditation on the limits of art in creating unfallen gardens: "But rather to tell how, if Art could tell." The images that follow in lines 237–42 break with the earlier pattern; they lose their fluidity and "harden" into gemlike entities or crystallized metaphors. The fountain of line 229 is transformed into a "Sapphire Fount," the rills into "crisped Brooks" that roll on "Orient Pearl and sands of Gold." This is the static, unrealistic—and artful—Eden that students find so troubling. The choice not to pursue the four rivers into realms beyond Eden leads to a stratification of metaphor; not too surprisingly, the passage ends with flowers arranged in "curious Knots." Here a second pause appears, and only when Milton reopposes art with nature and reintroduces the original river metaphor ("but Nature boon / Pour'd forth profuse on Hill and Dale and Plain") can the passage continue and conclude by reuniting all the waters.

Though a poet may initially establish a cyclical water system, he may always wander or imagine deviation, and it is this potential that creates the aura of fragility and instability in paradise. For students who sigh at the end of book 2, who expect a bleak future of doctrine, history, astronomy, and horticulture, passages like this may cause them to reconsider the complexity of choosing, even in an unfallen world. The testing and breaking of boundaries are inherent characteristics of Miltonic language, and not only of Satan's attempt to repossess his "native seat." Thus my concern that we as teachers neither circumscribe the poem's boundaries in advance nor delineate its spaces too clearly, saying, "This is fallen, this is unfallen"; for we are then doing for our students what they can do for themselves—determining what it is that constitutes a fall.

II

If students are given only one class on Eden, the Eden of book 4, they may discover that paradise contains a series of potential choices; and yet they may never connect the description in book 4 to other representations of Eden in *Paradise Lost*. A second class on Eden might, therefore, discuss how paradise reappears in different guises and how each of these representations develops from a moment of delay. For each moment initiates a larger movement toward narrative, formed either by transgressing boundaries to explore new worlds or by respecting boundaries to work within an established space; each moment not only marks a choice or decision but provides a source from which narrative grows. To teach this concept, we would ask students first to describe how these moments expand into anti-Edens or approximations of paradise and then to think about the ways these different perspectives are related. In pedagogical terms, students would create an interpretation of *Paradise Lost* by tracing the development of a major image. As they learned to recognize Eden in different contexts and circumstances, they would begin to see how all these "Edens" work together to form a narrative of the garden's birth and destruction.

The notion of a paradise appears long before book 4—in fact, we first hear of Eden in a rumor. Thinking of the heaven he has lost and surveying the hell around him, Satan remarks to Beelzebub,

> Space may produce new Worlds; whereof so rife
> There went a fame in Heav'n that he ere long
> Intended to create, and therein plant
> A generation, whom his choice regard
> Should favor equal to the Sons of Heaven:
> Thither, if but to pry, shall be perhaps
> Our first eruption, thither or elsewhere.   (1.650–56)

Satan greets the news by planning a possible "eruption" from hell to infiltrate the newly created space. He wishes to leave his place to tamper with unknown realms—precisely the process we saw in book 4, where Milton considers leaving the bounded space of Eden to follow its rivers to foreign lands. The chance that Eden might exist is reason enough to leave hell; but this rumored paradise also serves as the model or source for the poem's first anti-Eden, Pandemonium, which rises like an "Exhalation, with the sound / Of Dulcet Symphonies and voices sweet" (1.711–12), with music rivaling the airs of paradise. Eden is thus introduced dialectically: at first a neutral space, it contains the potential for imaginative generation by God or for imitation and eruption by Satan.

The development of Eden as an imaginative space is continued in the invocation to book 3, where the narrator describes his wanderings through an interior garden: "Yet not the more / Cease I to wander where the Muses haunt / Clear Spring, or shady Grove, or Sunny Hill" (26–28). The words are echoed later, both in Raphael's account of the earth's creation in book 7 and in Eve's lament at her departure in book 10. But for the moment, the narrator-poet contemplates the space created by the rumor of "new Worlds" and goes on to imitate the dual pattern established in book 1: "So much the rather thou Celestial Light / Shine inward, and the mind through all her powers / Irradiate, there plant eyes" (3.51–53). Like God, the narrator intends to "create, and therein plant / A generation"; like Satan, he expects a kind of eruption, here a breaking of the boundaries that limit his mind, a dispersal of the mists that obscure his vision.

If one aspect of Milton's "great Argument" entails a battle over the use of space, then this battle will not only concern Satan's attempt to raise the "standard of ancient Night." It will also include the poet's decision to give space to certain kinds of imagery and to question the relation between certain kinds of figuration and the larger narrative or argument. Our students can learn how this process works by engaging in a similar activity: as they try to define a concept and defend it, they will discuss competing representations and perhaps choose one above all others or agree to disagree. Together, they will create interpretations of the poem—much like those potentially existing in the moments of delay. Moreover, they will be working on the question that haunts our reading of *Paradise Lost*: if we follow the rivers away from the central fountain, how far can we travel and still remain in Eden?

III

Yet these images of Eden are not developed in isolation, apart from a particular context: it is Satan, for example, who initiates the narrative of Eden and becomes the first to tamper with its history. A third class on Eden might well demonstrate how the garden is linked to Milton's entire cast of characters, who each try to create their own version of Eden. Much of the drama of the poem, its "great Argument" in fact, derives from these conflicting attempts to determine a path for the Edenic narrative. Students usually engage in this conflict by taking sides with Milton's characters, reading the poem from the perspective of a favorite angel or devil. They need to learn, however, that each character offers only a partial vision. Favoring or excluding any one view will limit their ability to build an interpretation, since all these visions—whether satanic, angelic, or human—contribute to our understanding of paradise. We would begin, therefore, by asking students to explore each character's vision of the garden and then to link these different re-creations to one another. And we would ask them, finally, to make the larger connection between choice and loss. Does Eden represent something that, when confronted by any revision, will always perish?

Sin and Death may seem an unlikely pair to include in a class on Eden; nevertheless, their bridge linking earth, heaven, and hell is a parodic and frightening extension of the "curious Knot" of art in book 4, a stratifying of natural images into mineral metaphors:

The aggregated Soil
Death with his Mace petrific, cold and dry,

As with a Trident smote and fix't as firm
As *Delos* floating once; the rest his look
Bound with *Gorgonian* rigor not to move,
And with *Asphaltic* slime.   (10.293–98)

In a work of "wondrous Art," Sin and Death crowd together elements
"Solid or slimy" and drive them "shoaling towards the mouth of
Hell." Faced with the abyss of chaos, they re-create its space into what
is for them an Eden, a bridge that will bring them to the decaying
garden. In the architecture of Sin and Death, students may see a
paradigm emerging, one that details how a "loss of Eden" occurs and
shows what a fallen Eden looks like.

What Sin and Death finish in book 10 is shown at its origin in book
4, when Milton first describes Eve in the garden. Her wish to differentiate the space—"Let us divide our labours" (9.214)—is anticipated
in the moment of delay following Milton's careful placement of Adam
and Eve in the natural hierarchy—their sex is "not equal" (4.296).
Shortly thereafter, Eve's "golden tresses" are described as "wanton
ringlets" and then as vinelike tendrils in a simile implying a more
even exchange of power between husband and wife:

As the Vine curls her tendrils, which impli'd
Subjection, but requir'd with gentle sway,
And by her yielded, by him best receiv'd,
Yielded with coy submission, modest pride,
And sweet reluctant amorous delay.   (4.307–11)

Eve may yield first place to Adam, but as she yields, she retains some
measure of control, a "gentle sway." The final line suggests the complexity of her yielding, a submission both amorous and reluctant, hesitant: each adjective breaks slightly the flow of the line and signals the
"delay" at the end of the sentence.

The simile thus provides a moment of hesitation in which one can
imagine another path for Eve, a different journey stemming from a
choice not to remain at Adam's side. Yet when Eve begins to create
her own garden, her wish to follow a single rill away from the "nether
Flood" takes her on a path much like the "Solid and slimy" bridge of
Sin and Death. As Satan leads her toward the tree, Eve is compared to
the "amaz'd Night-wanderer" who is misled in "Bogs and Mires, and
oft through Pond or Pool" (9.640–41). In Eve's fall, students may see a
continuation of the paradigm established by Sin and Death: new gardens in *Paradise Lost* will resemble less the Eden of book 4 than the

fixed and rigorous world of Sin and Death. And they may notice that any attempt to reenvision Eden leads to this same troubling repetition, a transformation of the garden into a satanic nightmare.

This bleak paradigm is further developed in book 11 when the garden becomes Michael's emblem for teaching Adam that "God attributes to place / No sanctity, if none be thither brought" (836–37). In the general account of the flood, Michael pointedly includes a narrative of the garden's desecration and uprooting by a flood larger than the "nether Flood" beneath its mountain:

> then shall this Mount
> Of Paradise by might of Waves be mov'd
> Out of his place, push'd by the horned flood,
> With all his verdure spoil'd, and Trees adrift
> Down the great River to the op'ning Gulf,
> And there take root an Island salt and bare,
> The haunt of Seals and Orcs, and Sea-mews' clang.
> (11.829–35)

Paradise floats away on one of the rivers mentioned in book 4. Sown with salt, Eden resumes its place in the imagination as rumor, a space haunted by echoes of generation. The account of Eden's destruction has been suspended for eleven books: we are promised a "loss of Eden" in line 4 of the poem but are not shown this loss until book 11. As narrative, *Paradise Lost* has itself developed from a moment of delay.

IV

In discussing Milton's description of Eden, I have suggested that we teach *Paradise Lost* as a process or activity that reflects its own growth as narrative. If students were asked to identify moments of delay and from these to construct an image of Eden—or of creation, heaven, and hell—they might learn not only how narrative emerges from figure but also, in Milton's terms, how the fall is always and only a step away from the wish to create an imaginative space. For at each moment of delay, with its choice between conflicting modes of thought, an old path will be followed or abandoned for a new one; a wall will be broken or retained as a shelter. Characters will choose to remain "in narrow room" or expand to create new worlds. Given the way *Paradise Lost* works, this choice will appear many times: in Raphael's ordering of paradise; in the funereal artwork of Sin and

Death; in the statuesque narration of Michael's history; in the lamen-
tation of the invocations. As students learn to identify these choices
and the paths they will follow, they may discover genuine connec-
tions between *Paradise Lost,* so foreign to them at first meeting, and
their own experience of "mazy error."

Our students will be delighted to learn that the road to and from
Eden, though well-worn by three centuries of critics, still has room for
new travelers. Moreover, in choosing an interpretation or constructing
their own narrative, they may reevaluate some of the great passages or
discover others that have escaped our notice; in any event, they will
continue our tradition of seriously interpreting the poem. To refer one
last time to water systems—and *Areopagitica*: "Truth is compared in
scripture to a streaming fountain; if her waters flow not in a perpetual
progression, they sicken into a muddy pool of conformity and tradition" (Hughes, *John Milton* 739). While it may appear that I am advocating a heresy of sorts—releasing the most canonical of texts into the
hands of novices—I wish only to apply the process chosen by Milton
in *Paradise Lost.* What makes the poem exciting for Miltonists, its
endless maze of interpretation, will also entrance our students and
train the next generation of the "fit audience." We can give them
space, and as Satan so wisely reminds us, "Space may produce new
Worlds."

NOTES

[1] For a more comprehensive discussion of this methodology—collaborative
learning—see Kenneth A. Bruffee, "Structure" and "Liberal Education."

[2] In using the term "moments of delay," I am recalling the line "And sweet
reluctant amorous delay" (4.311), which appears at the end of the simile
comparing Eve's "wanton ringlets" to a vine.

[3] Stanley Fish refers to this process as "surprised by sin," the reader's
inevitable choice of false paths. I would argue that the choice is less a manifestation of the reader's "fallenness" than a continual movement away from a
"providential" interpretation on the part of the figuration itself.

Mazes of Sound:
Toward the Metrics of *Paradise Lost*

Eugene D. Hill

There are reasons for avoiding consideration of metrics in teaching *Paradise Lost* to American students—not good or sufficient reasons, I believe, but reasons worth looking at. To begin with some obvious ones, there is so much to claim our time in the classroom: so much background to provide in political history and genre theory, so much paraphrasing and summarizing and interpreting to do. And teaching metrics is not easy; graduate students are rarely trained to give such instruction, and, alas, a good ear for English verse rhythm has never been a prerequisite for holding down a professorship of English. Whatever the difficulty of teaching metrics, it is not a highly regarded pedagogical task; there seems something schoolmasterish to it, as if attending to stress and accent could only reduce Milton's artistry from the sublime to the meticulous.

Some teachers will avoid discussing metrics out of fear of the student ignorance they would expose. "Oh no, I can't do *that*," said one of my pupils when asked to indicate the stresses in a phrase of simple English words, her intonation suggesting (with fine prosodic aptness) that I had asked her to perform some intricate calculation in quantum chromodynamics.

A less obvious reason for slighting metrics takes us into the realm of cultural politics. We grin lamely or grimace when we read Tennyson's characterization of Milton as a "mighty-mouth'd inventor of harmonies," the "God-gifted organ-voice of England." But T. S. Eliot—on this point, as on so many others, the last of the great Victorian critics—held a similar view of Milton, a view that may still influence our teaching of *Paradise Lost*. Writing after an alleged dissociation of sensibility, Milton separated (or so Eliot argues, in "Milton I") sound from sense; accordingly, his verse should be read "first solely for the sound," "the *noise*" (143, 142; of course the italics are Eliot's). Eliot reports: "I cannot feel that my appreciation of Milton leads anywhere outside of the mazes of sound," but he assures us that "for the pleasure of the ear the meaning is hardly necessary" (144, 143). This is not the place to speak of strategy for defending his own style that obliged Eliot to dispose of Milton's poetry, which "could *only* be an influence for the worse, upon any poet whatever" (139). Nor is this the place to take up the larger issue of the various evasions of Milton's masterwork over the centuries, Eliot being one of the prime evaders; a good start on this larger question of cultural politics has been made by Bernard

Sharratt in his recent essay "The Appropriation of Milton." The point here is that one of the best poet-critics of our century subtly down-graded Milton by separating sound from sense. And we, Milton's ad-mirers, carefully avoiding the trap Eliot has set for us, may unwit-tingly deprive our pupils of that splendid interplay of sound and sense that is *Paradise Lost*. We may teach the book, but not the poem.

The situation sounds bad enough, though I wonder if our pupils are that much worse off than many of their nineteenth-century counter-parts. In his standard monograph on Milton's prosody, Robert Bridges reports that he was encouraged to write on the topic by a scholar editing the opening book of *Paradise Lost* for a school text: "He be-sought me to contribute such an account of the versification as should knock out the prevalent usage of misreading the rhythm; for it was generally thought necessary and correct to mispronounce words so as to make them scan with regular alternate accent" (113). Modern slack-ness matches Victorian metrical pedantry of the sort Bridges describes in its inability to reveal the life of the rhythm, which lies in syncopa-tion, in variation—in short, in teasing. As an expert on the subject, Vladimir Nabokov writes, in his *Notes on Prosody*, that "the beauty" of variation in English iambic verse "lies in a certain teasing quality of rhythm, in the tentative emergence of an intonation that *seems* in total opposition to the dominant meter, but actually owes its subtle magic to the balance it tends to achieve between yielding and not yielding—yielding to the meter and still preserving its accentual voice" (20).

Milton was a master of such variations; like any good poet, he makes his words dance his meaning. And if our students have too much tin in their ears to attend to the sensuous music that is also the dance of sense, then we have to devote some part of our time to getting the tin out. In what follows I offer two quick suggestions; then, at greater length, I present (1) some theoretical points (with supporting authori-ties) that can help explain to students why metrical study is important and (2) examples of how to develop metrical exercises for classroom use.

My two quick points: the students will need to acquire what Dr. Johnson (in *Rambler* 88) calls "this petty knowledge" "of analysing lines into syllables," of deliberating "upon accents and pauses" (4: 99). While any of the standard manuals can do the trick, I send stu-dents (and novice teachers) to Paul Fussell's exemplary text *Poetic Meter and Poetic Form*. Second point: if I am teaching *Paradise Lost* as part of a course on Milton, and not in some course with a broader focus, I always come at the epic from Milton's prose. (And I devote almost as much time to the prose selections as I do to the epic, three weeks as against four.) My experience has been that if students have learned to hear the different voices in the argumentative prose—to recognize when (and how) Milton is sneering, insinuating, rollicking, provoking—they are well prepared to enter the epic's "mazes of sound" with the clue of Miltonic meaning firmly in their grasp. My pupils are encouraged, cajoled, and compelled (by a midterm examination devoted entirely to the prose) to attend to the expressive resources in what Milton once called the works of his left hand. Students catch on quickly when we work our way through passages like the one in *The Reason of Church Government* in which Milton condemns the desiccating sophistry of Oxbridge learning, noting the "scholastic burr in their throats" that has "cracked" the young scholars' "voices for ever with metaphysical gargarisms" (Hughes, *John Milton* 686).

I may be guilty of a gargarism or two myself in developing for my young scholars a brief theoretical account of what poetry does with words. I draw on the essay "Langage poétique, poétique du langage" (in *Figure II*), in which Gérard Genette appeals to that modern restatement of the biblical story of Babel, Saussure's doctrine of the arbitrariness of the linguistic sign. In the Adamic language (which some seventeenth-century scholars of repute were still seeking to reconstruct), the word had been (it was believed) the perfect mirror of the thing it named; sound and sense were inextricably bound, and linguistic forms and structures corresponded to their referents in the way that chemical formulas correspond to the compounds they specify. But all natural languages are characterized by a lack of fit between sound and sense—there is nothing necessarily doglike in the various words for dog in the hundreds of known languages. As Genette (following Mallarmé) notes, however, this very failing of our language is "the *raison d'être* of poetry"; for "if languages were perfect, *verse would not exist,* because every utterance would be poetry—and so none would." The task of verse is precisely to overcome—or pretend to overcome—the arbitrariness of the sign. The poet's function is "to motivate language," says Genette, who defines the poetic activity as "a revery of linguistic motivation" (144–145; trans. mine).

From this chunk of theory I turn to Adam's narrative (in *Paradise Lost* 8) of his earliest memories—a passage centrally concerned with the matching of word to thing and of reality to dream—and I try to speculate along with my students about the implications the passage may have for Milton's poetics. The multiple congruences that make up Adam's world ("I wak'd, and found / Before mine Eyes all real"

[309–10]) point up by way of contrast the arbitrary distinctions that structure natural languages. Our linguistic status reverses Adam's: his language *was* his world, was transparent to the contents and structure of that world; but our language, an arbitrary medium that functions by juggling differentia, can communicate, but not incarnate, meaning. Accordingly, as Genette's account indicates, our paradise can be no more than a revery of congruence, a revery within language. Only poetry can provoke such a revery—that is, only poetry can make words seem to dance their meaning. And poetry, which presupposes the fall into arbitrary language, derives from that very dispossession from the literal paradise (and from the paradise of literality) that the revery seeks to overcome. So the many little variations that felicitously enact the poet's dance of meaning have as their raison d'être the one great variation from felicity that was the source of "all our woe."

These speculations can take some interesting turns—I've been surprised to note how much students seem to enjoy this (to them) unfamiliar mode of thinking. We soon find ourselves bringing together the dialectic of a fallen (that is, an arbitrary) natural language recuperated through poetic force with Milton's parable (in *Areopagitica*) of restoring the body of truth. We also look closely at the prefatory note "The Verse," in the 1674 edition, in which a miniature captivity narrative of "ancient liberty" and "modern bondage" presents a differently encoded version of the same dialectic (Hughes, *John Milton* 210). This much literary theory can't harm the students. And it may alert them to some ways in which the nexus of sound and meaning is overloaded with significance in *Paradise Lost*, even beyond what is so in most poems. But the question remains of how to teach the interplay of sound and sense in specific passages.

Here, too, insight comes from dispossession, from enfeebling change. The French poet Théodore de Banville (in his *Petit traité de poésie française*), noting the derivation of *poetry* and *poem* from a Greek verb meaning "to make," "to fashion," deduced that "a poem is therefore something which is made and consequently no longer needs to be made—that is to say, it is a composition whose expression is so . . . perfect and definitive that no change can be made in it . . . without rendering it less fine and without weakening its sense" (7; trans. mine). It follows that the way to get students to hear what a good poet does with words is to change the words and consider what has been lost.

For example, take this pair of lines from book 4 of *Paradise Lost:*

> For contemplation hee and valor form'd,
> For softness shee and sweet attractive Grace. . . .   (297–98)

Thomas Newton, an eighteenth-century editor, wrote in his note on these verses:

> The curious reader may please to observe upon these two charming lines, how the numbers are varied, and how artfully *he* and *she* are placed in each verse, so as the tone [the stress] may fall upon them, and yet fall upon them differently. The author might have given both exactly the same tone, but every ear may judge this alteration to be much for the worse.

> For valor he and contemplation form'd,
> For softness she and sweet attractive grace.

Bishop Newton's revision enables us to pinpoint the fine ratiocinative hesitance of rhythm in line 297 as Milton's verses register the differences between the man and the woman, "Not equal, as thir sex not equal seem'd" (4. 296). The doctrine here may not satisfy us, but the poetic craftsmanship should.

To develop classroom exercises in metrical analysis one need only follow Newton's example: rewrite a passage from *Paradise Lost* in a manner that regularizes it and then see what has been lost. The procedure is a very simple one, and it may seem to fetishize the given text, but I don't know any substitute for ear training of this sort. And the teacher who would refrain from deliberately marring Milton's language can draw on some most instructive earlier efforts to render *Paradise Lost* into a different form.

Let me present three examples from different periods, the last from a book just published. The reader should have at hand that bravura passage late in *Paradise Lost*, book 1, in which Milton dares to challenge Homer to a comparison of artistry. Near the end of the first book of the *Iliad*, Homer wrote expressively of the fall of Hephaestus; Milton retells the story, using the less common name Mulciber, and then boldly cancels it ("thus they relate, / Erring . . ." [746–47]). To be sure, the passage is a rich one thematically—it provides a little model of how Milton revised ancient epic; but first one must *hear* it.

In 1756, A Gentlemen of Oxford (in fact, George Smith Green, an eccentric watchmaker with literary interests) published *A New Version of the* Paradise Lost, in which Milton's "Measure and Versification are *corrected* and *harmonized*." A verse paraphrase of the opening book of the epic, Green's *New Version* was designed for the reading public of his day, who, "used to smoother Productions, and shorter periods, disrelish [Milton's] Roughness, and the Length of his Sentences." Here is the Mulciber passage:

> In *Greece* long since, and in *Ausonia's* Land,
> Men call'd him *Mulciber,* the God of Fire;
> And fabled—that he fell from Heav'n's high Battlements,
> Thrown down by *Jove* for his enormous Make:
> From Morn to Noon, from Noon to Night, he fell,
> A Summer's Day before he reach'd the Earth,
> And falling upon *Lemnos* broke his Leg,
> And limping walk'd a Cripple ever after.
> Thus they relate, but erring—for he fell
> With this rebellious Rout long Time before;
> His Wickedness beyond his Art prevailing,
> His Heav'n-built Palaces avail'd him not,
> For he and all his Crew were headlong sent
> To try their structure-raising Skill in Hell.

Milton students can develop their meter-hearing skill by studying the manifold lamenesses of Green's verses, even apart from Green's exquisitely bathetic diction. The class will return to Milton's original with some purchase on its rhythms, and on the seriousness of its mockery.

My second example of Milton revised is rather more subtle. In 1831, one William Forde published *The True Spirit of Milton's Versification Developed in a New and Systematic Arrangement of the First Book of* Paradise Lost. Forde observed that "the perusal of the entire Poem entails a load of cumbrous and repulsive exertion on the reluctant patience of the general reader," who "is soon fatigued by the effort of attention which the nature of the style exacts" (viii–ix). Since the line breaks have, Forde asserts, no significance and no effect, Forde rearranges Milton's words to clarify the poet's grammatical constructions by making line breaks correspond to syntactic breaks. Here is what happens to Mulciber:

> · · Nor was his name unheard or unadored
> · · in ancient Greece;
> · · and in Ausonian land men call'd him Mulciber;
> · · and how he fell from Heaven they fabled,
> · · thrown by angry Jove

> · ·   sheer o'er the crystal battlements—
> · · ·   from Morn to Noon he fell
> · · ·   from Noon to dewy Eve
> · · · ·   a summer's day
> · · ·   and with the setting Sun
> · · ·   dropt from the Zenith like a falling star
> · · ·   on Lemnos, the Aegean Isle—
> · ·   thus they relate, erring;
> · ·   for he with this rebellious rout fell long before:
> · ·   Nor avail'd him now
> · ·   to have built in Heaven high Towers,
> · ·   nor did he 'scape by all his engines,
> · ·   but was headlong sent with his industrious crew
> · ·   to build in Hell.

Forde gives us Milton's words, virtually unaltered, but the rearrange-
ment of the words dislocates many of Milton's rhythmic effects. The
line breaks have especial importance in this passage: note how Milton
ends five successive lines with stressed monosyllabic nouns—nouns
that themselves enact the descent of Mulciber: "angry *Jove*," "from
Morn," "dewy Eve," "setting Sun," "falling Star." For all its clarity,
Forde's revision wonderfully misses the life of Milton's verse. The
booklet is a capital source of exercises for comparative study; no critic
establishes more firmly than Forde the integrity of the Miltonic verse
line.

   The verse line has entirely disappeared in another rich source of
Miltonic dislocations, a new version of *Paradise Lost* published by the
Seabury Press in 1983; it was prepared by Robert A. Shepherd, Jr., a
Houston lawyer. The back cover of the paperback edition promises
"an imposing and remarkable rendition" of Milton's poem, which it
calls "arguably one of the foremost epic poems in the English language." In his introduction Shepherd writes that his intention is "to
make *Paradise Lost* more readable than it is in Milton's blank verse,
but without destroying the beauty and vigor of his words." Shepherd
wishes to show us the rich human story "locked within the remorse-
less geometry of blank verse." Here is Shepherd's unlocking of lines
738–48 of the Mulciber passage:

> Nor was his name unheard or unadored in ancient Greece,
> and men called him Mulciber, and in fables they told
> how he fell from Heaven, thrown by angry Jove over the
> crystal battlements; but they are wrong, for he fell
> long before—with Satan's rebellious rout.

Clearly, this is a trot on the poem; and if Shepherd's pony wins any new readers for the original, we must be grateful to him. But his version enfeebles both sense and rhythm: "in fables they told" does not capture the force of "they fabl'd"; and even the neophyte reader must perceive the difference between Milton's "thus they relate, / Erring" and Shepherd's "but they are wrong." I look forward to introducing bits of the Shepherd rendition into my Milton classes.

These three examples, of course, are milk for babes, to be replaced (as soon as the class seems ready) by the real thing. Consider these verses from Satan's soliloquy in book 4:

> Be then his Love accurst, since love or hate,
> To me alike, it deals eternal woe.
> Nay curs'd be thou; since against his thy will
> Chose freely what it now so justly rues.
> Me miserable! which way shall I fly
> Infinite wrath and infinite despair?
> Which way I fly is Hell; myself am Hell;
> And in the lowest deep a lower deep
> Still threat'ning to devour me opens wide,
> To which the Hell I suffer seems a Heav'n.   (69–78)

Ask your pupils to account for the seemingly awkward bunching of consonants and of stresses in the second half of line 71. Ask them why, in the middle of line 72, Milton speeds up the line and diminishes his stresses. (Ask them how line 77 shows a similar effect, and ask how it differs.) Ask why, in line 74, "infinite" appears in two different stress contexts—first offbeat (that is, with its natural word stress placed on an odd-numbered syllable), then on beat. And ask why the finely Marlovian line 75 elevates its offbeats, so that the line can be read as having nine or even ten stresses, none perhaps stronger than the offbeat copulative verbs. Carry through the metrical analysis to its thematic issue—Nabokov's remark about the teasing effect of variation might well help here. And then get out of the students' way as they begin, at last, to read the *poem*.

"Proportion Due Giv'n and Receiv'd": Tailoring *Paradise Lost* to the Survey Course

Robert W. Halli, Jr.

Joshua Reynolds once noted that the supreme challenge for any biographer of Samuel Johnson would be "to proportion the eccentric parts of his character to the proportion of his book." He feared that most authors, constrained to select from a plethora of material even for the lengthiest of volumes, would be tempted to concentrate too heavily on Johnson's physical oddities and flashes of brilliant wit, at the expense of more important but less picturesque or pyrotechnic aspects of the man. The teacher of John Milton's great epic in a survey course encounters similar constraint and temptation.

At my institution, English Literature 1 is divided equally among four historical periods, stretching from *Beowulf* to Boswell. I can devote only about 150 minutes to *Paradise Lost,* far too little time to cover the entire poem. Because no popular anthology contains the complete text anyway, I must choose the passages for assignment from a preexisting selection. Most of my students enroll to fulfill a humanities requirement and will study no literature beyond this level. No matter how bright, they have neither the time nor the training to absorb all that is best in recent Milton scholarship.

Although format, textbook, and audience preclude our "doing justice" to *Paradise Lost* in the survey course, we should avoid doing more violence than necessary to the proportion, focus, and experience of the epic as a whole. Students believe that the passages and aspects on which we spend most time are those most important to the overall meaning of a given work. Thus we should initially avoid a treatment of Satan so lengthy that it distorts his importance in *Paradise Lost.* Likewise, a presentation that concludes with a detailed treatment of the fall and a glance at the expulsion from Eden is untrue to the total experience of the poem. It neglects our first parents' reconciliation with God, the promise of redemption, and the disposition of "Eternal Providence." I can appreciate the seductiveness of these approaches, because I succumbed to their temptations when I first taught the survey course. I wallowed in hell, wept over the fall, and generally ignored the comedic aspects of the epic because the tragic ones were so much more interesting. Only gradually did I realize that I was teaching very different poems in one week at the sophomore level and in half a semester in my advanced Milton course. Clearly I needed a proportion for the survey unit that would better reflect the whole of *Paradise Lost.* After many trials and much tinkering, I arrived at the following assignment: book 1.1–330; book 2.299–485, 629–1055; book 3.1–302; book 4.1–408; book 9.192–1189; book 10.452–577, 706–1104; book 12.466–649.

Establishing a focus that includes, orders, and explains these assigned passages is another exercise in constraint. As the essays in this volume suggest, there are many excellent and coherent approaches to *Paradise Lost*. Indeed, no single focus can include all important aspects of the epic, nor can all the issues raised by any sensible focus be treated in one week. Although we should tell our students that there are many legitimate points of view on *Paradise Lost*, we had best choose only one focus of reading in the survey course for nonmajors. If we do not, our presentations will lack unity, and students will take that as reflecting disunity in the poem itself. For my focus, I choose the unified duality of justice and mercy, a concept that informs all of *Paradise Lost* and one we encounter elsewhere in the survey course.

Beginning with the opening prologue, I ask the class to explain Milton's intention to "justify the ways of God to men." I usually have to guide discussion with another question: "If I assign you a grade of A for this course, do I have to 'justify' it?" The students realize immediately that justification is needed only for a grade lower than an A or for one lower than they think they deserve. They will also realize that, for justification to be accomplished, they must admit that they have earned the lower grade by failing to perform at the highest level. Transferring these ideas to Milton's subject, the students see that we must consider the perfect state from which we fell ("Eden"), the imperfect state to which we fell ("all our woe"), and the means by which that fall was justly earned ("man's first disobedience").

That is, of course, the tragic side of *Paradise Lost*, but the prologue gives equal weight to the comedic. "Man's first disobedience" is balanced by "one greater Man" who will "restore us"; "all our woe" in this world is poised against the possibility of regaining "the blissful seat" in the next. Milton announces not only that he will treat past deeds and their consequences, our justly earned mortality, but also that he will "assert Eternal Providence," God's infinite and unearnable mercy to be poured out upon his faithful.

But where does this approach leave Satan? To omit discussion of him is unthinkable: he is Milton's most fully developed character, and students find his scenes the most accessible and enjoyable. To stress Satan unduly, however, distorts the epic's proportion, and his story is only tangential to the focus of reading I have chosen. I portray Satan as a grand object lesson for humanity (both inside and outside *Paradise Lost*) on disobedience and divine justice. Essentially negative, he is the anarchic opponent whose career is marked by successive failures. The mainspring of his character is the tight intertwining of pride and hate, and I always need to explain why pride is considered bad. Hate, pride's external manifestation, drives Satan "out of good still to find means of evil" (1.165). That we find him attractive teaches us something about our own fallen nature, despite which, keeping our faith and wits about us, we can resist his temptations and see through his appeal.

Milton's pervasive irony, and occasional humor, mark Satan as neither irresistible nor heroic. For example, when Beelzebub says that Satan "endanger'd Heavn's perpetual King" (1.131) and when Satan exhorts his troops to "Awake, arise, or be for ever fall'n" (1.329), irony reigns in the truth of Beelzebub's adjective and in the falsity of Satan's conjunction. Two instances of humor at Satan's expense are his infernal hotfoot (1.295–97) and his difficulties with the air pocket and updraft (2.929–38). Lest the class underestimate him, however, I stress Satan's formidable size and dangerousness. An explication of the denotations and moral connotations of the Leviathan simile (1. 200–08) effectively establishes both qualities.

Satan's decline from Lucifer to serpent is really more a falling than a fall, and it clearly reveals the just rewards of sinning. His leadership, heretofore disastrous for the infernal horde, is challenged in the council scene and reaffirmed only by his acceptance of the mission against humanity. Before Sin and Death, Satan's language falls from boastful insult to groveling flattery. Like Spenser's, these monsters fascinate students with their ugliness (especially Sin's combination of woman, serpent, and dog kennel), which reflects the creatures' paternal heritage. Lastly, Satan appears "weather-beaten" and "torn" as he flies up out of "darkness visible." By the end of book 2, students should realize that it is possible to see Satan in a good light only in the absence of any light at all.

The prologue to book 3 engages students most strongly through its references to Milton's blindness, which establish the distinctive importance of inspiration. The prayer for illumination so "that I may see and tell / Of things invisible to mortal sight" (54–55) implies not that Milton will show us something we have not seen before but that God's essence cannot be visualized. I stress that precisely because Milton's depictions of God as light and as a speaking character are humanly apprehensible, they are not to be taken as perfect representations of the deity.

Although students will admit the truth of what God says, they respond to him much less favorably than to Christ, with whom they are familiar through the Gospels. I point out that just as Milton's stated purpose in *Paradise Lost* entails both tragic and comedic aspects, so too does the single Godhead comprehend both justice and mercy. We are naturally more attracted to the agent of mercy, and I stress Christ's role as the active principle, the "effectual might" of God who creates and re-creates for the benefit of the human race.

No passage is more crucial to my focus than the celestial conversation. Students need to understand that God's foreknowledge predestines neither sin nor salvation, that the praiseworthy or culpable choice of good or evil necessitates free will, that each man and woman was and is sufficient to resist temptation by reliance on faith, and that Christ's ultimate charity is completely voluntary and unselfish. To help students achieve definition of both good and evil, I point out many of the contrasts deliberately set up between heaven and hell.

At the beginning of book 4, Satan's soliloquy reveals that hell is a spiritual condition, not just a place, and also that he understands clearly the necessary consequences of his sinful actions. We listen in horror to his admissions that God is good, merits faithful service, has punished him justly, and that his own nature and free will exclude him from forgiveness and joy. His abandonment of hope, fear, and remorse, and his total commitment to evil, make Satan, like any terrorist, consummately dangerous.

Book 4 also depicts the environment that was made for us, that would still be ours if Adam and Eve had not transgressed, and that is a figure of the eternal bliss prepared for those who accept Christ's redemption. I stress Milton's detailing the multiplicity and variety of "Nature's whole wealth" as a reflection of the infinite goodnesses of the Creator, for which appropriate homage must be returned by faithful service. The perfection of Adam and Eve is conveyed less easily from the passages in my anthology. I note their noble appearance, pure "naked majesty," and reflection of God's image. I discuss their "true filial freedom" by contrasting justly hierarchical liberty with the anarchic license espoused by Satan. Although unavoidable, the discussion of woman's subordination to man is only rarely profitable. I point out that both Adam and Eve are perfect and sufficient to resist temptation and that Eve has qualities that will become particularly important as the two seek reconciliation with God after the fall.

Movement toward the tragic climax begins in book 9 as Eve correctly argues her sufficiency alone. The psychological groundwork for the fall is revealed in Adam's comments on their mental faculties, and he also correctly sees that, rather than confront, they should avoid temptation. Although he can argue persuasively that they should remain together, he cannot deny Eve the exercise of her free will, and no man can prevail against a woman's "sweet austere composure." Sinless Eve among her flowers embodies our last view of Eden's perfection. I note that the question of her ability to detect the fallacies in Satan's arguments is essentially irrelevant, because she understands the prohibition and should remain faithful to its benevolent Author. But her pride, stimulated perhaps by Adam's slights, leads Eve to persuade herself of the fruit's efficacy, and she eats. Her fallen state is immediately revealed in gluttony, selfish reasoning, worship of the tree of knowledge, and lies to her husband.

That both humans consider the possibility that God may create "another Eve" for sinless Adam is an important indication that her fall does not predestine his. With clear understanding of his action's consequences, and in violation of his own teachings on faculty psychology, Adam willingly exalts flesh over spirit. Because some students believe "man's disobedience" is a sexual sin, I distinguish carefully the *taking* pleasure of "foul concupiscence" from the *giving* joy of prelapsarian intercourse, noting that God's command to "increase and multiply" predates the fall. I stress Milton's psychological explanation of sin (9.1127–31) and note the incorrectness of "mutual accusation" instead of self-condemnation. Our feeling closer kinship with Adam and Eve after their fall teaches us much about ourselves.

Although we last see Satan ultimately degraded in book 10, Michael's prophetic narrative will reveal his continuing power of temptation. One consequence of the fall is the new disorder in nature, which is reflected and magnified in the "troubled sea of passion" within Adam. In his long soliloquy, he intellectually accepts responsibility for his actions and admits the justice of his punishment. But this conviction leaves Adam without hope or happiness, because he believes he has cut himself off from God's providence and because he foresees only geometrically expanding sin and mortality. Eve's emotions, meanwhile, lead her to reaccept subservience to Adam and to attempt reconciliation with him. Gaining his forgiveness through her tears, humility, and persistence, she exemplifies the approach they must make to God. Arguing against Eve's proposals of childlessness and suicide, Adam now leaves his tragic vision of the past for a glimpse of a hopeful future. Recalling Christ's mingling mercy with justice in their judgment and his prophecy that Eve's "seed shall bruise / The serpent's head" (1031–32), Adam realizes that perhaps they need not be excluded completely from providence. I stress the verbal repetition at the book's close, because it underlines the importance of contrition to reconciliation with God.

Following a brief summary of God's acceptance of the human couple's petitions and of the embassy of Michael, I pick up book 12 after the angel's narration of Christ's career, which banishes all tragic elements from the divine comedy of the epic's conclusion. In ecstasy, Adam understands that Christ's infinite love renders the fall paradoxically fortunate. Michael explains that earthly humanity will never be completely freed from sin or its consequences, but he stresses that God, in his mercy, will send the Spirit to his faithful, who shall inherit at judgment the glorious "New Heaven, new Earth" of "righteousness and peace and love."

The last three speeches in *Paradise Lost* merit careful treatment. Adam details his "learning," his correct religious attitude toward life, and his participation in God's providence. Michael urges an active witnessing of faith leading to the spiritual state of "A Paradise within" and reaffirms the celestial promise that "the Woman's Seed" will offset earthly sorrow. Eve exhibits perfect religious love for Adam and states their final peace. I stress heavily the last words of each: Adam's "ever blest," Michael's "the happy end," and Eve's "restore."

After reading aloud the magnificent concluding passage (624–49), I focus on Adam and Eve and keep my comments short. Sorrow for past sins yields place to faith and hope. Hand in hand, they turn their back on paradise lost to fare into the world as we know it. In their optimism and humble acceptance we see the fulfillment of Milton's purpose "to assert Eternal Providence / And justify the ways of God to men."

As I mentioned, one reason I choose this focus from among the many good ones available for reading *Paradise Lost* is that the class has seen a concern with justice and mercy reflected in literature studied earlier. I point out such relations, as I do those with other significant aspects of the writings we have covered. After all, the survey course is designed to present students with selected works of literature within the context of English literary history. I believe, however, that our primary emphasis should be on the works themselves rather than on their context. We should show our students that great writing can serve as a window offering vistas and perspectives on human beings, their situations in the world, and the ways they attempt to comprehend and deal with those situations. Without a good understanding of the individual texts, our students simply cannot come to any firsthand apprehension of literary trends or of their own cultural history. Continuity and change can be illustrated effectively through reference to works already studied and should be discussed primarily as they throw light on the texts at hand.

The survey course should have a sense of wholeness about it, reflecting a coherent experience of the disparate types and purposes of writing that make up our literary tradition. For those students who will take more English courses, it should also serve as a sort of menu of advanced offerings. Finally, for all students and for the teacher, the semester should be fun. The content of no other course is as wonderful as this, and the students quickly pick up their instructor's enthusiasm for reading great literature. Horace's prescription for good writing could be taken as our imperative in the survey course. Teach and delight. We do the former best by means of the latter.

A Guide for *Paradise Lost,* Book 9

George Klawitter

To assign a large section of *Paradise Lost* to undergraduates and to tell them to come to class prepared to discuss the poem without benefit of any guiding questions is to invite chaos. Working through so difficult a poem for the first time, many students are ill equipped to struggle with the convolutions of Milton's lines. To expect them to grasp argument, to trace the sinews of rhetorical emphases, to be undistracted by philosophical asides is to expect them to bring to a course the very skills the course is meant to develop. Milton is not easy to read. A tool highlighting those areas that we feel are most important to appreciating the poem helps minimize student frustration. A study guide is not too puerile to hand out before students tackle *Paradise Lost,* if we tell them it is a crutch that may be helpful to many but harmful to a few. Students should be warned that if a study guide distracts them from a text, they should not use it. All too often students read a study guide before reading a poem and never learn how to manage difficult texts. The poetry is primary: after that comes the study guide.

Sound teaching of *Paradise Lost* requires reading the narrative itself, explaining the critics, and analyzing the style. Criticism and analysis cannot be ignored. History and hundreds of critics have added to the poem dimensions Milton was never aware of. Although all facets of the poem are important to the modern student, at what point does a teacher use summarizing? At what point critical analysis? stylistic analysis? The art of teaching involves a sense of timing: a teacher may begin class by reading aloud from book 9, stopping now and then to ask for questions and opening discussion when the class shows particular interest in a passage. When interest dwindles in that question, the teacher may return to reading aloud until another question surfaces. Or the teacher may skip ahead in the study guide for a related question.

The study guide I have used for many years is the result of a summer seminar during which a guest lecturer so eloquently admired book 9 that I picked up a love for it myself. That love has never paled. I am more apt on a winter evening to turn to book 9 than to any other part of *Paradise Lost* because of the soundness of its drama of human frailty. Along with reading book 9 itself, my students read Genesis 1–3 and an excerpt from a medieval mystery play in order to receive maximum benefit from the guide. However well students think they know the Genesis narrative, they are advised to read it again carefully.

The study guide contains the following questions:

1. What reason does Milton offer for changing the tone at the outset of book 9? Does the anticipation of the fall heighten or undercut the suspense?
2. Why does Satan choose to enter the serpent? Where in Genesis 1–3 does it say that Satan took on the form of a serpent? In his apostrophe to the earth (99–179), does Satan seem more human than diabolical?
3. Why does Eve suggest that the pair "divide [their] labours"? This notion of the division of labor has suggested to some critics that the separation of the couple indicates Milton's belief in androgyny as an explanation for the fall. But does such an explanation merely reinforce accusations that Milton is antifeminine because he relegates woman to the emotional half of an androgynous creature while allowing Adam to enjoy the superior rational half?
4. What is curious about the serpent's approach to Eve? How does Satan get Eve to doubt God's word that anyone who eats of the tree will die? Which of the serpent's arguments does Eve review in her long speech beginning line 795? Is this speech as logically ordered as her exchanges with the serpent are? Marshall Grossman notes that this speech moves by "free association," indicating that Eve's reasoning is far from pristine (213). If the fall has thus darkened her powers, how will she be able to persuade Adam to taste the fruit?
5. Why does Adam finally eat the fruit? Why, in Milton's view, has he fallen before the fall?
6. The Puritan in Milton claims that lust as we know it is a primary effect of the eating. Could a more devastating effect be Adam's view of Eve? Or is their new relation to each other healthier? As C. S. Lewis points out, Adam and Eve hardly ever address each other before the fall without fancy titles, which make their relation more formal than human (115). Was the fall totally without good effects?

The first question in the guide can be answered by any student attentive to the first eight lines of book 9, but careful students will want to know how Milton came to choose his subject matter in the first place. In class discussion, it can be pointed out that early in his poetic career Milton had thought of writing an epic on King Arthur, a subject he seems to disdain in lines 25–44 of book 9. Students can be asked to link subject to tone: did Milton's choice of a religious subject limit his tonal possibilities? Students might also wonder about Milton's method of accepting inspiration (9.22–24): did that likewise limit the tonal range?

Question 2 requires students to read outside the text. We tend to assume that the biblical creation narrative is familiar to everyone, but students often express surprise that Genesis 1–3 does not mention Satan in conjunction with the serpent. We have grown accustomed to the notion that the devil engineered humankind's downfall, but Genesis simply says the serpent tempted Eve.

Although the question of Satan's choice for infiltration might be easily answered from this delightfully graphic section of the poem, the teacher might further challenge the students by raising the idea of metamorphosis. Milton would have been conversant with Ovid's work, but it might interest the class to know that Milton detested the Aquinian theory of transubstantiation. According to Michael Lieb, "Milton is uncompromising in his expression of disgust toward anything that profanes the holy" (*Poetics* 33). Do Satan's transformations profane the holy by transubstantiating matter? To appreciate the intricacies of the question, students should be familiarized with Aristotle's concepts of matter and form. They should also understand Aquinas's adaptation of Aristotle to explain medieval liturgical faith in the presence of Christ in ritual bread and wine. (They need not read, but the teacher should, Aquinas's *Summa*, pt. 3, question 75, arts. 3–6.)

The first reaction of students in the 1980s to question 3 concerning androgyny is that Milton is continuing the sexist line of biblical storytelling. Such a reaction often reflects a failure to grasp Milton's general development of Eve, the holistic Eve. Marilyn R. Farwell demonstrates that separation affords Eve an opportunity for growth, and it is this growth as a rational character that best shows Milton's concept of her. Farwell argues that the couple's strength is based on cooperation and support rather than on "androgynous, ontological fusion" (15). Eve is not weakened in her separation from Adam so much as she is given the chance to operate as a separate being. Students may point out, however, that whereas Eve falls "separately," Adam falls only in tandem with his mate, and they may raise the question all over again of Milton's belief in woman as a being of secondary strength. They may wonder too if Adam would have fallen had he faced Satan alone.

Item 4 should help students understand the first of the four dialogues that form the bulk of book 9. I use an exercise correlating drama with epic to enhance my students' awareness of the importance of dialogue in this book. They are to read an excerpt from a twelfth-century mystery play called *Le jeu d'Adam* (Legarde and Michard 154–56). I give them copies of both the original text (many of them may have studied French and will enjoy the simplicity of the archaic language) and a modern translation. Appended to the handouts are the following questions: How does the playwright's concept of Adam differ from Milton's? Although both the play and the epic can be considered drama, what technical advantages does the play have to catch the imagination of an audience? The point of this exercise is to show students that literary texts often take freedoms with basic materials. Milton, like the author of *Le jeu d'Adam,* reshapes basic biblical material to suit his purposes. If students encounter alternative forms of the Genesis story, they will be more apt to appreciate the magnificence of Milton's creative imagination. Milton may not have known the little twelfth-century play, but the exercise is not designed to show literary influences. It is used to expand students' awareness of varied narratives of the creation.

Another exercise I use for lines 205–384 involves simulation. To indicate mastery of a *Paradise Lost* dialogue, a student should be able to take the part of a character and "argue" with a second student who is role-playing another character. Since of the three dialogues in book 9 that benefit from this activity the first is much the easiest, I spring the experience on the class without previous notice. I have the students first block off the speeches between lines 205 and 384 so that they can recognize at what points to expect a change in speaker, and we begin. Good speech reductions approach the following:

> EVE: This work is getting to be too much for us. Anything we straighten turns back to wild in two days. We'd better split up today so our smiles and chitchat won't distract us from our work.
>
> ADAM: No. Our enemy wants us to separate so he can attack us single.
>
> EVE: I've heard about that enemy from you, and I overheard the angel talking about him. You have no faith in my strength.
>
> ADAM: You underestimate his cunning. Besides, I need you next to me because I would be ashamed to give in to him if you were near me. You should feel the same way.

And so on. Reduction of the speeches to modern idiom helps internalize the argument so that the students feel closer to the text. At some point in the dialogue experience, students should be made aware of C. S. Lewis's comments on the dialogue between Adam and Eve. It may be helpful to read aloud to the class the final paragraphs of chapter 16 ("Adam and Eve") from his *Preface.* (On simulation as teaching method, see Black; Cassel; Michels and Hatcher; Stanford.)

The sixth question on the study guide could very well lead students to wonder where Milton inherited his views of sexuality, at which time a teacher might introduce the class to Augustine. A thumbnail synopsis of the Augustinian dogmas is contained in C. S. Lewis, chapter 10. From Lewis, students could be led to consider more recent critics on the sexual psychology of Adam and Eve (see Aers and Hodges).

As a finale to our discussion of book 9, I like to let students consider a woman's rights in Eden. Item 6 takes them from a focus on sexuality to one on equality. Is there a feminist movement burgeoning in book 9? After all, the section ends with accusations and counteraccusations, the sexes beginning to share a ground (mutual lack of trust) on which Adam should not care to force his superiority. Students may conclude that woman is better off for the fall, but that suggestion ignores the view of Eve as a partner in a relation, not as a weaker element.

Ideally, students should read an entire book of *Paradise Lost* on their own before looking at a study guide. Even without the help of glosses, they should be able to follow the action of the poem, with many lines, perhaps whole segments, speaking to them clearly and directly. There remains, however, the matter of those segments that fail to register. Reading Milton, even for experts, requires intense concentration of a kind we do not associate with young people bred on the gadgets of Sesame Street pedagogy. A study guide can help keep their interest in the poem, but unless it is carefully prepared, it can be more of a hindrance than a help. A good study guide is sequential. The questions are ordered so that the first is answered before the second, and no question anticipates material that comes later. It makes no sense to ask students how Pandemonium contrasts with heaven until the students reach a description of heaven.

A study guide need not be a torturous tool for helping students inch their way through difficult epic poetry. It can be a creative adjunct to lecture and discussion if students realize the questions are meant to be open-ended, intended to foster their own reading of a poem that people have studied and argued about since its first publication. Most students appreciate knowing the direction a class discussion will take. They arrive better prepared to contribute because they have not only read the poem but feel in touch with its major ideas. As classes come and go, a teacher naturally will shift weight in the study guide: some questions will disappear as others take their place. Since discussions are creative, students will develop new insights that need inclusion in a future study guide.

Visualizing *Paradise Lost*: Classroom Use of Illustrations by Medina, Blake, and Doré[1]

Virginia Tufte

Although this article concerns teaching *Paradise Lost* at the under-graduate level, I want first to say a word about my graduate classes. For more than ten years my seminars in Milton have met in the beauti-ful north book room of the William Andrews Clark Memorial Library, our good neighbor a few blocks from the University of Southern Cali-fornia campus, and there each week I have spread on the table before us early editions from the Clark's rich collection. Students are in-trigued by the first illustrated edition of *Paradise Lost*, the splendid folio published in 1688 with a full-page illustration for each book, most of the plates the work of John Baptist de Medina. In the early years of the seminar, as we discussed each book, we found ourselves referring again and again to the 1688 illustrations. I encouraged stu-dents to regard them as "a form of non-verbal criticism," to borrow a phrase from Joseph A. Wittreich, Jr. (Hunter, Shawcross, and Stead-man 4: 56). One result of this infiltration of illustrations into the semi-nar was that students began to reread *Paradise Lost* with greater atten-tion to imagery. Another was that they became interested not only in Milton illustration but in iconographic traditions that preceded Milton and that influenced both the poet and his illustrators. Marcia R. Poin-ton's *Milton and English Art*, Roland M. Frye's *Milton's Imagery and the Visual Arts*, and Wittreich's essays on "Illustrators" and "Blake" in *A Milton Encyclopedia* (ed. Hunter, Shawcross, and Steadman) were added to the seminar reading list, along with Erwin Panofsky's *Studies in Iconology* and James Hall's *Dictionary of Subjects and Symbols in Art*.

My graduate courses usually influence my undergraduate teaching, and Milton is no exception. We rarely offer an undergraduate course devoted entirely to Milton, but I often teach an upper-division course in English literature of the seventeenth century that includes close reading of at least two books of *Paradise Lost*. After my experience at the Clark, I began introducing visual materials related to *Paradise Lost* into the undergraduate class, using slides, photographs, art books, and illustrated editions. It is, of course, expensive to make slides and photographs; it is also cumbersome to lug a slide projector, Martin Butlin's edition of Blake's paintings, and a Doré edition of *Paradise Lost* halfway across the campus to the room where my class meets. But I find myself refreshed by the visual materials. Often the illustrations enrich my perceptions of familiar lines of *Paradise Lost*, and at times they bring to the surface wonderful lines I hadn't much noticed before. For students, I believe these materials stimulate thought and careful rereading, heighten visualization, and stir the imagination (imagination at its root is imaging).

I have always found it frustrating to try to teach *Paradise Lost* piecemeal, but it is unrealistic to undertake close reading and discussion of the entire epic in the time we can allow to Milton, usually four weeks. In my typical class of twenty-five or thirty, about half have previously read books 1 and 2 in a sophomore course, perhaps six or seven have read the entire epic, and the rest little or none of it. I recommend that everyone read the entire epic, and I assign "close study" of two complete books, usually 4 and 9, plus the opening of book 1 and the close of book 12, along with Milton's "Arguments" to all the books. In two or three class periods I try to give an overview of the narrative. Then we discuss the text of books 4 and 9, moving through it in a conventional way, talking about selected passages, raising and exploring questions, sometimes casting volunteers as Eve, Adam, Satan, and the Epic Voice, and reading aloud sections of dialogue. Finally, after we have made our way through these pages, we pause for some reflections on major themes. Then we turn to the illustrations of the two books and examine them in relation to the passages they illustrate and the themes we have discussed. I ask a battery of questions. Sometimes I assign a short paper that requires students to discuss a selection from the text in relation to a designated illustration.

When I introduce the illustrations, I comment briefly on book illustration in general and Milton illustration in particular. I mention that in the twentieth century, book illustrators often try to create something decorative or original, and in any era some illustrators draw on earlier illustrations or paintings instead of reading the text. But, as Wittreich has remarked, most of Milton's illustrators assume an interdependence of text and design: "Their objective in illustrating a poem was to illuminate it; their designs, therefore, attempted a crystallization of the Miltonic vision, which the artist then criticized and might even try to correct" (Hunter, Shawcross, and Steadman 4: 56). Of more than a hundred illustrators of Milton listed in Wittreich's catalog, I have worked with seven or eight, but I most often choose Medina, Blake, and Doré. Each is a fairly careful reader of *Paradise Lost*; each has illustrated all or nearly all of the books; the illustrations are readily available; and the three represent a time span of nearly two hundred years—Medina in 1688, only fourteen years after Milton's death; Blake in 1807 and 1808; and Doré in 1866. One could explore certain cultural assumptions implicit in the illustrations from the different periods, as indeed one explores cultural assumptions of Milton's time—concepts of hierarchy, for example—in contrast to cultural assumptions of our own time. But my focus is on the illustrations themselves, although if such matters arise incidentally, we talk about them.

I have listed below, under three headings, the sorts of questions I raise as we examine the illustrations. The phrases quoted in a few of the questions in group 2 are borrowed from five critics whose comments I find helpful: Helen Gardner, "Milton's First Illustrator"; John T. Shawcross, "The First Illustrations for *Paradise Lost*"; Pamela Dunbar, *William Blake's Illustrations to the Poetry of Milton*; Stephen C. Behrendt, *The Moment of Explosion*; and Millicent Rose, *Gustave Doré*.

1. *Identifying characters, actions, and scenes in relation to the text.* Who are the characters, what are the actions, and what is the scene that the illustrator is portraying? What lines of Milton's text does the artist appear to be illustrating? Is the illustration accurate in relation to Milton's text? Is it clearly dependent on some source other than Milton? In choosing these characters, this action, this scene, what is the illustrator suggesting about them? Does the illustration indicate their relative importance? Does the illustrator ignore certain episodes usually deemed crucial?

2. *Examining the methods of the illustrators.* Has the illustrator designed one plate or more than one for each book? Does the illustration present only one action or episode? A series of episodes? Does the illustrator "choose to illustrate a single episode and to fill in as background subsidiary episodes" (Gardner 27)? Does the illustrator "attempt to epitomize the narrative sense of the whole book by focus on major events, by suggestion of their significance, and by iconographic details" (Shawcross 45)? In representing Milton's universe—heavenly, demonic, and human characters and settings—does the illustrator have "command of scale" (Rose 57)? Does the illustrator draw "single-episode plates" that "give undivided attention to the poem's crucial dramatic moments"? "Dual-reference plates" that attempt "visually to imitate the poem's elaborate pattern of cross-references"? Is there "a visual association between plates—a pictorial equivalent of narrative sequentiality"(Dunbar 36)? Is "concern with landscape" important in the illustration? Is landscape "a *central* and predominating feature"(Behrendt 95)?

3. *Meaning: the illustrations as interpretations of the poem.* In the figures, the actions, or the features of landscape, are there symbolic meanings in addition to the literal—images that carry iconographic values relevant in this context? Does the illustration suggest the char-

acters' states of mind, interior experience as well as exterior? Can you state some kind of thesis concerning the illustration: What kind of messages or meanings in *Paradise Lost* is this illustrator emphasizing? What kind of comments on, or criticisms of, *Paradise Lost* is this illustrator making?

In this essay I present a sampling of the kinds of observations that arise in the classroom, from both sides of the lectern, as we work inductively with the illustrations. Perhaps I can thus give some sense of the way these visual documents work as interpretations of the poem.

Considering Medina's plate for book 9 (fig. 1), we see a series of episodes that compares readily with Milton's narrative. We are immediately struck by the large dark figure of Satan in the foreground at lower right. Milton has not described Satan's looks explicitly, although in books 1 and 2 he has impressed us with Satan's majesty and might. Milton's archangel Satan is winged, and in size he compares to a tower and to the "hugest" of the creatures, "that sea-beast the Leviathan," which in turn is so large as to be mistaken by ship pilots for an island. Milton tells us as well that the tallest pine hewn on Norwegian hills to serve as the mast of a great ship is but a wand compared to Satan's spear. It is from this original loftiness that Milton portrays Satan's deterioration. As Satan enters Eden, Milton presents him in one disguise after another—a "stripling cherub," various animals, a toad, a cormorant, a black mist. But nowhere in Milton is he the satyrlike figure we see here—with horns, batwings, long tail, clawed fingers, furry legs, and cloven hoofs. Medina has simply borrowed an established iconographical convention, described by Mary D. Anderson: "What we might call 'the basic devil' was probably derived from the faun of classical mythology, for this creature, half goat, half human, was associated by the early Christians with the devils, elves, and fallen angels who all inhabited the wild woods" (138). Let us look at Milton's depiction:

> So saying, through each Thicket Dank or Dry,
> Like a black mist low creeping, he held on
> His midnight search, where soonest he might find
> The Serpent: him fast sleeping soon he found
> In Labyrinth of many a round self-roll'd
> His head the midst. . . .
>   . . . on the grassy Herb
> Fearless unfear'd he slept: in at his Mouth
> The Devil enter'd. . . .   (9.179–88)

In Medina's illustration, Satan's stare leads the viewer's eye toward the serpent Satan is about to enter. The serpent's head points diagonally upward toward the figures of the human couple, Adam seated, his right hand in a rhetorical gesture of explanation or persuasion, as Eve stands close to him, listening intently. What are they talking about? Adam is responding to Eve's proposal that they work separately. The garden is getting out of hand, she has said, because when they are together, looks and smiles and conversation distract them from their work. In the interests of efficiency she is urging a division of labor. Adam at first objects: working alone, each will be in greater danger. But Eve insists, "Frail is our happiness if this be so." And then Adam persuades himself. He explains to Eve that man is

> Secure from outward force; within himself
> The danger lies, yet lies within his power;
> Against his will man can receive no harm.
> But God left free the Will, for what obeys
> Reason is free, and Reason he made right.   (9.348–52)

Medina has illustrated here a key passage in Milton's attempt to justify God's ways to men. We can almost hear Adam speaking as he holds his right hand to his breast in Medina's sequence and the couple separate, pruning hooks in hand: "Go; for thy stay, not free, absents thee more . . . God towards thee hath done his part, do thine" (9. 372–75). The angle of Eve's body leads the eye to the tiny figures in the next episode, where the serpent coils acrobatically erect, balanced on the tip of his tail, taller than Eve as she stands in front of the tree of knowledge, passively holding the fruit. Milton has shown her actively reaching for and plucking the fruit:

> So saying, her rash hand in evil hour
> Forth reaching to the Fruit, she pluck'd, she eat:
> Earth felt the wound, and Nature from her seat
> Sighing through all her Works gave signs of woe.   (9.780–83)

In Medina's succeeding vignette, Eve hands the fruit to Adam. Next, upper left, we see the two clad in leaves, ashamed, Eve's head bent, with hand to her face and Adam's face turned from her. Above their heads nature reflects the fall, with dark rolling clouds and jagged shafts of lightning.

Medina's sequence shows reasonable fidelity to Milton's episodes. But the fall seems simply one event in a serpentine chain of events that winds from the bottom to the top of the page. By foregrounding Satan, Medina focuses on the external demonic force as the prime author of evil in the world rather than on the human pair.

Like Milton, however, Medina highlights the separation of the pair, thus perhaps stressing individual responsibility for decision, and individual vulnerability. The role of human beings as "choosers" is demonstrated by the linear simplicity of the events Medina selects. Readers of Milton's book 9 are likely to think of it as centering on a single wrong choice, Eve's eating the fruit. But Medina's synoptic method shows this act as merely one of a sequence of events, each involving decisions that bring immediate consequences. Medina's first scene of the human pair shows them in a conversation that results from Eve's decision to discuss with Adam her need to work separately. The following scenes reflect a series of choices: Adam's reluctant decision to acquiesce in the separation, a decision that gives Satan the opportunity to find Eve alone; Eve's decisions to eat the fruit and to offer it to Adam; Adam's decision to join Eve in the act of disobedience; the decisions of both to "gird thir waist . . . to hide / Thir guilt and dreaded shame" (9.1113–14). Human life is a sequence of choices with impact that goes beyond the chooser to society and nature.

The impact of the forbidden choice radiates at once not only to Adam but to the universe: "Sky lou'r'd, and muttering Thunder, some sad drops / Wept at completing of the mortal Sin / Original" (9. 1002–04). Lightning and thunder in both classical and Christian iconography represent celestial fire and force; they are emblems of heavenly sovereignty, judgment, and wrath. The arrows that Medina places on the shafts of lightning link this plate for book 9 with Aldrich's plate for book 1, published in the same volume, where similar arrows mark the paths of Satan's expulsion from heaven with his fellow rebels. In the book 9 plate, the two arrows presage the consequence of Adam's and Eve's wrong choices: their expulsion from the "Heaven on Earth" (4. 208). But behind Medina's dark cloud there is light, and the design does not leave the viewer with a total sense of loss. Thunderbolts can also represent spiritual illumination, the realization of truth, and the destruction of ignorance. And the "sad drops" of rain, mentioned by Milton and impending in Medina's clouds, hint at God's future mercy.

Like Medina, Gustave Doré portrays a sequence of episodes, although in separate plates, and he is also preoccupied with Satan. Appearing in five of Doré's six illustrations for book 9, Satan is the central figure in three and is in the foreground in two others. In only one plate do we see Adam and Eve alone; it is the final one, where they are sorrowing after the fall. Even before the fall, Doré's landscapes of Eden are ominous. His first design is awesome with its dark rocks and cascading waters, centered by the silhouette of Satan, who stands atop the huge rock projection (fig. 2). It is as if the rushing waters represent his surging thoughts. Certainly the illustration does not depict Satan "involv'd in rising Mist," as Milton's lines state. And the turbulence in Doré's design hardly represents Milton's words: "Tigris at the foot of Paradise / Into a Gulf shot under ground, till part / Rose up a Fountain by the Tree of Life" (9.71–73).

Doré draws Satan as a winged human figure. In the next two designs we see him clearly—well muscled, his deterioration indicated by snaky hair, cloven feet, and wings with sharp claws, their lines repeated by leafless tree limbs in stark landscapes. Doré's second design for book 9 highlights Satan against rocky prominences from which grow gnarled trees (fig. 3). Barely visible in the right background are Adam and Eve, in deep shade amid more luxuriant vegetation. The words beneath the design are the opening of Satan's long soliloquy:

> O Earth, how like to Heaven, if not preferr'd
> More justly, Seat worthier of Gods. . . .
>   . . . the more I see
> Pleasures about me, so much more I feel
> Torment within me, as from the hateful siege
> Of contraries; all good to me becomes
> Bane. . . .   (9.99–123)

Doré's third design, like the foreground of Medina's plate, shows Satan contemplating the serpent, whose body he is about to enter (fig. 4). Even if one were to block out the central figures of Satan and the serpent, Doré's grim setting with its prickly dead limbs and empty sky is as bleak and menacing as Satan's "relentless thoughts."

In the softer landscape of the fourth engraving, we see highlighted in the center the small figures of Adam and Eve, seated and relaxed, unconscious of the evil that approaches (fig. 5). In the foreground, head raised and pointing in their direction, Satan slithers toward them with extended fang. In Milton's epic the lines here illustrated mark Satan's approach to Eve alone, but the smallness of Doré's figures and their obliviousness to the danger suggest that even together they would be helpless against the intruder. In Milton, Satan approaches in a "delicious" garden, "Among thick-wov'n Arborets and Flow'rs" (9. 437–39). But Doré's garden is not Milton's, for here (upper right) bare tree limbs and distorted trunks echo the menace below.

Fig. 1. John Baptist Medina, illustration of book 9, *Paradise Lost*, 4th ed., London, 1688. Courtesy of William Andrews Clark Memorial Library, University of California, Los Angeles.

Fig. 2. Gustave Doré, illustration of 9.74–75, *Paradise Lost*, London, 1866.
By permission of the Huntington Library, San Marino, California.

Fig. 3. Gustave Doré, illustration of 9.99–100, *Paradise Lost*, London, 1866.
By permission of the Huntington Library, San Marino, California.

Fig. 4.   Gustave Doré, illustration of 9.182–83. *Paradise Lost*, London, 1866.
By permission of the Huntington Library, San Marino, California.

Fig. 5. Gustave Doré, illustration of 9.434–35, *Paradise Lost*, London, 1866.
By permission of the Huntington Library, San Marino, California.

Fig. 6.   Gustave Doré, illustration of 9.784–85, *Paradise Lost*, London, 1866.
By permission of the Huntington Library, San Marino, California.

Fig. 7.   Gustave Doré, illustration of 9.1121–23, *Paradise Lost*, London, 1866. By permission of the Huntington Library, San Marino, California.

Fig. 8.   William Blake, *The Temptation and Fall of Eve,* illustration of book 9, *Paradise Lost,* 1807. By permission of the Huntington Library, San Marino, California.

Fig. 9.   William Blake, *The Temptation and Fall of Eve,* illustration of book 9, *Paradise Lost,* 1808. Courtesy of the Museum of Fine Arts, Boston, Massachusetts.

In the next scene, the fifth engraving, even the limbs of the tree of knowledge are gnarled and writhing (fig. 6). The plate depicts not the instant of the fall but a moment after the fall: "Back to the Thicket slunk / The guilty Serpent" (784–85). In the foreground, the serpent turns his head, fangs still in motion as he looks back at Eve, who is highlighted in the center, clutching the fruit, her face bleak. Doré's Adam, seated quietly in the background in thoughtful posture, does not suggest the intuitive experience of Milton's Adam, who at the instant of Eve's fall sensed "something ill."

In Doré's last plate for book 9, barren rocks and a monstrous tree provide the background for the distraught Adam and Eve after the fall (fig. 7). Doré's plate reflects Milton:

> nor only Tears
> Rain'd at thir Eyes, but high Winds worse within
> Began to rise, high Passions, Anger, Hate,
> Mistrust, Suspicion, Discord, and shook sore
> Thir inward State of Mind, calm Region once
> And full of Peace, now toss't and turbulent:
> For Understanding rul'd not, and the Will
> Heard not her lore, both in subjection now
> To sensual Appetite, who from beneath
> Usurping over sovran Reason claim'd
> Superior sway. . . . (9.1121–31)

The leafless surroundings emphasize the leaves Adam and Eve wear to hide "The Parts of each from other, that seem most / To shame obnoxious" (9.1093–94).

Looking back over Doré's designs for book 9, we see that, like Medina, he has fastened attention on Satan. The landscapes augment the impression of ever present, powerful forces of evil, against which the human beings have no defense. And we must pause to note that Doré does not portray the instant of the fall itself. Instead of depicting Eve or Adam at the precise moment of decision, he shows us the moment when "Back to the Thicket slunk / The guilty Serpent." It is the serpent's guilt he stresses, not Eve's or Adam's.

In Doré's illustrations, states of mind are reflected—at times melo-dramatically—in postures, gestures, and facial expressions, but most vividly in landscape. Doré is concerned with the torment that evil brings, the terrible realization that evil is its own punishment. Milton had written in the *Doctrine and Discipline of Divorce II* that even the pagans recognized that sin is its own punishment, banishing the sinner into "a local hell" (Wolfe, *Complete* 2: 294; bk. 2, ch. 3). In book 9

Milton expresses a conventional view of revenge that also seems partly true of evil generally: "Revenge, at first though sweet / Bitter ere long back on itself recoils" (171–72). Evil doesn't seem sweet at all in Doré's portrayals of Satan or, in the final plate, of the fallen Adam and Eve but is from the beginning "bitter." The bleak environment mirrors their internal "local hell."

The peril that lurks in Milton's garden even before the fall in the person of Satan, variously disguised, brings a sinister cast to Eden's beauty and serves as an omen that "Paradise" will be "Lost." As A. Bartlett Giamatti tells us, the archetypal paradise is pictured as "a beautiful place because that is the best symbol for man's inner need and desire for peace and harmony." But the archetypal paradise is also "lost or far away or fortified or . . . false, because that is the only way to convey man's daily awareness of the impossibility of attaining his ideal" (84). Doré's dark forests convey the "lost" characteristic, emblematic of the feeling of aloneness and estrangement that modern existentialism sees as the nature of the human condition. Doré's final plate for book 9 reflects not only the lines Doré uses as its caption but the "alienated" state of postlapsarian human beings that Milton mentions in the book's prologue (9).

When I use the work of these three illustrators in the classroom, I save Blake until last, partly because I think he is the best artist and the best critic of Milton and also because his illustrations of the books of the epic are linked to one another to an extent that is not true of the Medina-Aldrich-Lens illustrations of 1688 or the Doré illustrations. Unlike Medina and Doré with their sequential designs for a single book, William Blake illustrates only one episode of book 9, and that is the one Doré left out, the exact moment of the fall. Blake also brings Satan to the foreground. In both versions of Blake's engraving, Satan as the serpent is nearest the viewer, his coils rising from center foreground upward about the body of Eve, his mouth placing the fruit in hers as she stands highlighted and facing us in front of and slightly to the right of the tree of knowledge, which rises massively in the center, from bottom to top of the pictures. At left background, his back to Eve and the viewer, Adam shows his awareness of "something ill," as bolts of lightning zigzag around him. Eve appears to be caressing the serpent, her right hand touching the diagonal of the serpent's body as it covers hers in what seems an erotic embrace, her left hand cradling the serpent's head as he extends the fruit. She does not pluck the fruit herself, as in Milton's book 9, but accepts it from the serpent. Blake's illustration for book 9 is closer to Milton's description of Eve's dream in book 5. Eve tells how in her dream Satan "to me held, / Even to my mouth of that same fruit held part / Which he had pluckt" (5.82–84). In Blake's illustration, especially in the second version, her eyes are vacant, and she seems mesmerized. She looks "beguil'd," to use the word Milton has her speak in book 10, borrowed from Genesis 3.13 (Authorized Version): "The serpent beguiled me; and I did eat."

Blake's figures of Adam and Eve are strikingly beautiful. They reflect accurately Milton's description: "Two of far nobler shape erect and tall / Godlike erect, with native Honor clad / In naked Majesty" (4. 288–90). In the perfection of Blake's statuelike figures, one can believe, with Milton, "The image of thir glorious Maker shone." And Blake's serpent, like Milton's, is seductive:

> Circular base of rising folds, that tow'r'd
> Fold above fold a surging Maze, his Head
> Crested aloft, and Carbuncle his Eyes;
> With burnisht Neck of verdant Gold, erect
> Amidst his circling Spires, that on the grass
> Floated redundant; pleasing was his shape
> And lovely. . . .   (9.498–504)

Blake's two versions of the fall come from two sets of illustrations for *Paradise Lost,* the 1807 set now in the Huntington Library and the 1808 set now in Boston's Museum of Fine Arts. In the 1807 design, Blake shows the instant when Eve touches her mouth to the fruit, as she leans to receive it (fig. 8). The face of the serpent is sly but not yet fully victorious, his body partly relaxed. Adam still holds the garland he was fashioning for Eve when his heart "misgave him." In the 1808 design, the time is a moment later (fig. 9). Eve is feeling the effects, her eyes hypnotized, her body no longer leaning as far toward the serpent. The serpent's expression has become triumphant and his posture more aggressive. Adam too is altered, his reaction more intense. His posture and demeanor are fairly close to Milton's description of Adam after he returns to Eve, his body taut before it turns slack with sadness:

> On th' other side, Adam, soon as he heard
> The fatal Trespass done by Eve, amaz'd,
> Astonied stood and Blank, while horror chill
> Ran through his veins, and all his joints relax'd;
> From his slack hand the Garland wreath'd for Eve
> Down dropp'd, and all the faded Roses shed:
> Speechless he stood and pale. . . .   (9.888–94)

The garland that trails over Adam's hands in the first version has fallen to the ground in the second and lies wilted near Adam's left foot. Iconographically, garlands suggest linkage, honor, a happy fate. The wilted flowers signify the fragility of earthly things, even the fragility of bonds between human beings.

In the later illustration, Blake has brought the scene closer to the viewer and intensified the colors. Thorns sprout from the trunk of the monstrous tree and from the surface roots that carpet the foreground on which the serpent rests. We are reminded that in Milton's prelapsarian Eden grew "Flow'rs of all hue, and without Thorn the Rose" (4. 256) and that one result of the fall is that "Thorns also and Thistles it shall bring thee forth / Unbid" (10.203–04). In the background of the 1807 design, the landscape is gentle; in the 1808 design, it has become harsh, and the shape of the rounded hill at the right has become volcanic. The lightning has become sharper and closer, and the flashes surround Adam and Eve. It has been remarked that the touches of the lightning on Adam's hands and right foot perhaps allude to the stigmata of the second Adam who will come as the Redeemer (Butlin, text vol., 387). And the idea that in the seeds of the fall lies the redemption is further suggested by the position of Eve's left foot atop the serpent in the 1808 design. "Her seed shall bruise thy head," Milton writes (10.181). Thus in the human fall as portrayed by Milton, and by Blake, are foretold God's mercy, Christ's coming, and the opportunity for redemption.

Blake and other careful readers of *Paradise Lost* are aware of Milton's essential sympathy for his human characters. In the effort to "justify the ways of God to men"—that is, to justify the existence of evil in the world—Milton must give heed to doctrine and to events of the biblical narrative. In the opening words of the epic, he indicates he must show "Man's first disobedience" as the bringer of "Death into the World, and all our woe." But Milton mitigates man's wrong decision by stressing that the fall contains within it the seeds of redemption and also by advancing in book 12 the idea of the fortunate fall— fortunate in that it offers opportunity for "a Paradise within thee, happier far." Urging right reason rather than passion as a guide, Milton focuses on the individual intellectual responsibility of each human being to make choices that can bring a paradise within rather than a hell within. Although *Paradise Lost* ostensibly conforms to conventional doctrine, Milton at times criticizes the very theology he postulates, as perceptive commentators have remarked. (Wittreich, for one; see Hunter, Shawcross, and Steadman 1: 178.) Milton's perceptive illustrators of book 9, sensing his sympathy with the human pair, have been moved to dramatize evil as something primarily not of human making. All three illustrators show the human pair as victims. If we reflect a moment on Blake's designs for book 9, we realize that with the powerful serpent wound about her, Eve does not have many options.

Blake was the first artist, so far as I can find, to show the serpent coiled about Eve. In Milton's poem the serpent did not touch her, though he "Curl'd many a wanton wreath in sight of Eve" (9.517). Conventionally the serpent had long been pictured coiled about the tree, or about the cross, or about the body of the crucified Christ. Coiled about the body of Eve, it suggests a sexuality that is associated with the fall by Milton and is expressed in various ways by a number of artists representing the biblical scene—Michelangelo, Titian, and Tintoretto among them. But Blake's portrayal in book 9 needs to be seen in the context of his portrayals of Satan and the serpent in his entire group of designs for the epic. In his illustrations for books 1 and 2, Blake shows Satan as a beautiful human figure, very like Adam and Eve. In his design for book 3, especially in the 1808 set, Blake's Satan, although winged and wearing a puzzled expression, is scarcely less beautiful than the graceful human figure of Christ on the cloud above him, and the two closely resemble each other and the human couple. In Blake's illustration of book 4, the serpent coils about the human figure of Satan in much the same way as the serpent coils about Eve in the illustration for book 9. In Blake's design for book 5, the serpent winds about the tree of knowledge, and in a design for book 12, around the base of the cross. The crucified Christ's foot is on the serpent's head, and the nail through Christ's feet also pins the serpent's head to the cross. Thus in the total pattern, as well as in book 9, Blake's symbolism of the serpent dramatizes a key theme of *Paradise Lost*: the human fall brought with it the opportunity for human redemption. As Stephen C. Behrendt concludes in his useful discussion of Blake's illustrations:

> We need to remember above all that for Blake, perhaps even more so than for Milton, the Son is finally the absolute hero of *Paradise Lost*. Blake came at last to reject the tradition of interpretation that had elevated Satan to heroic eminence by its failure to perceive the symbolic significance of the Son's offer to die for man within the total vision of Milton's epic.   (185)

Behrendt also suggests that the tree in Blake's illustrations for book 9 "is an iconographic reference to the cross, the symbol of the act by which the fall is reversed and eternal reintegration accomplished" (163). I would add that for the body of Christ that in traditional iconography appears on the cross-tree, sometimes encircled by the serpent, Blake has substituted Eve. Blake is anticipating the Eva-Ave idea expressed by Milton in later books. In book 10, Milton refers to "Jesus son of Mary second Eve" (183). In book 11, Adam hails Eve as "Mother of all Mankind, / Mother of all things living, since by thee / Man is to live, and all things live for Man" (159–61). And in book 12, the last words spoken by any character in the epic are Eve's: "By mee the Promis'd Seed shall all restore" (623). But Blake's illustrations, like Milton's epic, stress that evil continues. In Blake's design for the expulsion in book 12, the serpent accompanies Adam and Eve out of Eden and into the world where human beings have always "to choose." Blake's depiction of the serpent, like Milton's, makes plain that the choices are not simple.

The serpent is one of the most frequent and elaborate symbols in Blake's illustrations of the Bible and of his own works. His illustrations of Milton remind us that for Milton also the serpent has centuries-old multiple connotations—sexuality, energy, knowledge, immortality, as well as evil. One of Blake's designs for the Book of Job seems pertinent. Illustrating Job's evil dreams, Blake draws God the Father as a human figure but cloven-hoofed, with the serpent coiled about him much as it is coiled about the human figures of Satan and Eve in the illustrations of *Paradise Lost*. One cannot help being reminded of Milton's *Areopagitica*:

> Good and evill we know in the field of this World grow up together almost inseparably; and the knowledge of good is so involv'd and interwoven with the knowledge of evil, and in so many cunning resemblances hardly to be discern'd that those confused seeds which were impos'd on *Psyche* as an incessant labor to cull out, and sort asunder, were not more intermixt.

Blake's illustrations for *Paradise Lost* intimate that he sees God and Satan as metaphors for potentials of human personality. In Blake's system, what are conventionally thought of as good and evil are sometimes both good, and "the clash of contraries is part of a process of human transformation." (See Morton D. Paley 11–13.) For Milton, God does not bind the human being "under a perpetuall childhood of prescription, but trusts him with the gift of reason to be his own chooser" (Wolfe, *Complete* 2: 514).

We have seen that these illustrators have in common an accurate sense of Milton's sympathy for his human characters, and all display the exteriority of evil by presenting Satan as villain and the human beings as victims. But the interiority of emotion and choice, the human responsibility for decision, the subtleties of human motivation are all central to Milton's epic. And these illustrators respond in varying ways to the challenge of portraying the fall as a psychological event.

At the beginning of book 9, Milton announces "I now must change / Those Notes to Tragic." The epic is "tragic" in the medieval sense of tragedy as a fall. The "fallen" human condition is "tragic" in that the world and human beings are not perfect. Evil exists; human beings at times make mistakes; pain and loss are substantial and inevitable. The sad note on which book 9 ends—with human beings alienated from each other, from nature, and from God—is well represented by the three illustrators. But book 9 is not the whole story. One must read it in context, and remember the promises of book 3 and of the epic's close: the error of human beings is redeemable, the world is all before them, and Providence is their guide.

To conclude, I must mention that working with visual materials in a literature course takes a good deal of time and fresh study. A busy teacher, successful with more traditional approaches, may be inclined to forgo the approach, in the belief that a word by Milton is worth a thousand pictures. I would not disagree. But visual materials, like good critical essays and footnotes, can aid one's reading of *Paradise Lost*. Illustrations, with the special virtues of aesthetic and emotional appeal as well as intellectual, linger vividly in the memory. Often they invite us to ponder meanings we and our students might otherwise miss in Milton's complex and subtle poem.

NOTE

[1] The title of this essay is drawn in part from the forthcoming book by Virginia Tufte and Wendy Furman, *Visualizing* Paradise Lost: *The Illustrations of 1688 and of Blake, Doré, and Groom as Aids in Reading Milton*. The book reproduces 119 illustrations, including all those discussed in this essay.

We Ribs Crooked by Nature:
Gender and Teaching *Paradise Lost*

Joan E. Hartman

Paradise Lost is a daunting and remote poem for undergraduates, and when I teach it, I lecture more than I like to; trying to provide routes of access, I extensively mediate their experience of it. My activity, though I take it to be necessary and useful, produces in them dependent passivity. Our relation to each other and to the poem alters, however, when we consider Adam and Eve, or, as I refer to them hereafter with conscious feminist intent, Eve and Adam. The sections of *Paradise Lost* in which they appear are relatively accessible. They are also profitably problematic in that the politics of gender students and I encounter outside the classroom command our attention inside. While I celebrate and sustain feminist consciousness for reasons unrelated to *Paradise Lost*, teaching the poem as a feminist enables me more collaboratively to engage a class in issues important to them and to me. We are implicated in Eve and Adam and in the sexual division of labor that Milton presents in *Paradise Lost*. Joan Webber observes that Milton is modern in that his is the first Western epic to put domestic relations rather than heroic adventures at the human center of a cosmic plot. Moreover, I argue, in his depiction of those relations he imaginatively renders the sexual polarities of patriarchy still present to us more powerfully than the hierarchical order that was their seventeenth-century concomitant.

Teaching *Paradise Lost*, I focus on patriarchy in its seventeenth- and twentieth-century manifestations. That we are twentieth-century readers of a seventeenth-century poem goes without saying; that we are female and male readers of a poem in which gender figures prominently often remains unspoken. To pretend that in *Paradise Lost* Milton transcends the politics of gender in his time or ours is to distort the poem, to make it blander and less engaging than it is. Milton inherited patriarchal ideology; grappled with it intellectually, emotionally, and imaginatively; and by choosing to tell the story of man's (and woman's) disobedience chose a text basic to patriarchal thinking. He may have lived amicably with Katherine Woodcock and Elizabeth Minshull, though not with Mary Powell and his daughters, Anne, Mary, and Deborah; he may have respected and admired Lady Margaret Hobson and Lady Katherine Ranelagh—these are aspects of his life that make some critics anxiously defensive. But Eve is the woman present to us. I hope students will see her and Adam as remarkable creations, creations that Milton did not freely imagine but grandly

126

realized. In what follows I indicate the issues of gender I call attention to, the passages we look at in class, and the readings they sustain.
Paradise Lost is a multivalent poem, dramatic as well as narrative in
presentation, and Milton, in his imaginative rendering of the relation
between Eve and Adam, partially subverts patriarchy by his valuing of
Eve, his capacity to realize her experience, and his perception that
female virtue is active as well as passive.

The workings of patriarchy in what I call its benign and harsh forms
are both exemplified in *Paradise Lost*, the benign form before the fall,
the harsh form after. Both are predicated on difference and degree:
man the superior rules and woman the inferior obeys. When Milton
introduces Eve and Adam in book 4 (291–311), he acknowledges that
"in thir looks Divine / The image of thir glorious Maker shone." Nevertheless, the difference between Adam's contemplative and valorous
nature and Eve's soft, attractive, and graceful one is a difference both
in kind and in degree. They are "Not equal, as thir sex not equal
seem'd" (as in that emphatic and unlovely line "Hee for God only,
shee for God in Him"), and to Adam is assigned "Absolute rule." What
makes prelapsarian patriarchy benign is that Eve obeys him "with coy
submission, modest pride, / And sweet reluctant amorous delay," thus
enabling him to govern her with "gentle" and pleasurable "sway."
Benign patriarchy is the perfect, literally the paradisal relation between woman and man.

With the fall the image of God is partially effaced in both Eve and
Adam, and in Adam we see the misogynistic potential of a system that
exalts men and devalues women (Rogers ix–xvi). He not only vilifies
Eve as a crooked rib, a fair defect of nature, and a novelty on earth but
also predicts her daughters yet unborn, that is, all women, will be
cause of infinite calamity and confounders of household peace (10.
884–908). "He really lets us have it," one of the women in my class
recently observed, and the rest of the students, both female and male,
assented to the force of what she said. I did not hurry over the bitter
particulars of Adam's accusations or his irresistible tendency, anachronistic in Eden, to generalize from woman to women, to include us all.
Of course Adam is rebuked by more authoritative voices for shifting
the blame for his disobedience to Eve and for arraigning her creation
as defective. But God (in the person of the Son) also reminds him that
he, Adam, "whose perfection far excell'd / Hers in all real dignity,"
has doubly sinned, first by eating of the tree and second by abdicating
his rule (9.150–56). This rule, no less absolute after the fall than
before, is exercised benignly when Eve's obedience is willing,
harshly when it is not. Consequently the shift from one form of patri-

archy to the other is presented as woman's peculiar responsibility, the result of her fallen condition, not his. She is the one who destroys the paradisal relation.

Milton first interpreted the Genesis narrative of the creation that sanctions patriarchy in the divorce tracts of 1643–45. As I teach *Paradise Lost* now, in a course in seventeenth-century literature, I lecture on them; in a Milton course I should assign either *The Doctrine and Discipline of Divorce* or *Tetrachordon*. Critics from Gilbert in 1920 ("Milton") to Webber in 1980 ("Politics") have underplayed the sour and compelling power of Milton's androcentrism in the divorce tracts, the cumulative effect of his explanations of difference and degree and their consequences. Whatever happened during the weeks Mary Powell and John Milton lived together and the years of their separation, it is evident that Milton was disappointed in his wife; nevertheless, arguing for divorce as a relief necessary for the distresses inflicted on a husband by an unhappy marriage, he vividly imagines many more distresses than Mary Powell could possibly have inflicted on him during their brief cohabitation. He has no corresponding imagination for the distresses a wife might experience: to think of divorce as a remedy for women is "Palpably uxorious!," a mistaking of the end of their creation, which is to be a helpmeet for man (*Doctrine* 324). While he gives extensive play to varieties of natural and temperamental incompatibility in marriage—charitable love can be willed but conjugal love "requires not only moral but natural causes to the making and maintayning" (*Tetrachordon* 680)—he does so exclusively with respect to husbands. Wives he expects naturally to shape themselves to their condition, to fit and to please their husbands by what, given the end of their creation, amounts to natural inclination. Women's virtues are thus presented as passive rather than active; only their failures as wives are active, and perversely so, as against their natures.

Had Milton written the divorce tracts primarily to justify a divorce from Mary Powell, he could have limited his arguments to desertion, thereby causing less scandal, since divorce was allowed on such grounds in Protestant countries on the Continent. Instead, characteristically, he enlarged his predicament and chose to argue that marriage is preeminently a mental and emotional rather than a physical union. Critics, male critics uncomfortable with his devaluing of women, are apt to argue that this choice demonstrates his high-minded vision of marriage and his respect for women as creatures more of mind than of body: to quote from Parker's life, "he exalts, in fervent language, the glories of true love and successful marriage; he is indestructible in his idealism" (1: 240). I find Milton's vision of marriage unusually oppressive to women. True, we are not sex objects, liable to divorce only for our failure to be faithful. But we are liable to divorce for failure to please—and by the decision of husbands alone, since Milton also argues for reviving the Mosaic law that a man may write his wife a bill of divorcement and send her out of his house. The distresses inflicted on women by this condition of emotional servitude Milton is incapable of imagining; they wait for Henry James, in his portrait of the marriage of Isabel Archer and Gilbert Osmond. If Milton, unlike his contemporaries, is modern in grounding marriage on personal satisfaction (Halkett 25–26), he nevertheless grounds it exclusively on the personal satisfaction of the husband, or, as he puts it: "in Gods intention a meet and happy conversation is the chiefest and noblest end of marriage; for we find here [in the Genesis account of Eve's creation] no expression so necessarily implying carnall knowledg, as this prevention of loneliness to the mind and spirit of man" (*Doctrine* 246). *Man* does not include *woman*.

"Conversation," as Milton uses it here and elsewhere, signifies in its seventeenth-century sense the nonverbal as well as the verbal intimacy of married life. He did not expect Mary Powell to be fit for the conversation—in our sense of the word—of what his nephew Edward Phillips described as the "philosophical life" of his household (316). Marital conversation was not a meeting of minds: none of Milton's wives were educated for such companionship, nor were his daughters. In the divorce tracts, Milton describes marital conversation as a holiday respite from the serious masculine business of life: "We [i.e., we men] cannot therefore alwayes be contemplative, or pragmaticall abroad, but have need of som delightful intermissions, wherin the enlarg'd soul may leav off a while her severe schooling" (*Tetrachordon* 597)—"delightful intermissions" echoes in my head when I turn from my desk to play with my dog. Of women's pragmatical work at home—household management and the rearing of children—there is no mention, nor is there any sense that women and men together might be engaged in serious work, including maintaining the relation of marriage. In *Paradise Lost* this is the work that Milton assigns to Eve: after the fall she creates love and peace, recreates paradise in the relation of marriage. In the divorce tracts love and peace are, by definition, simply there: marriage, Milton writes, is "a covnant the very beeing whereof consists, not in a forc't cohabitation, and counterfeit performance of duties, but in unfained love and peace" (*Doctrine* 254).

In *Paradise Lost* Milton has a more resonant view of marriage than he has in the divorce tracts and, notably, a more generous and responsible view of women in the person of Eve. Nothing in the tracts prepares us for his imaginative realization of her sexual, mental, and emotional attributes. I have only the most obvious conjectures to account for the change: distance from the unhappy beginning of his first marriage, experience, maturity, commitment to rendering his great story, imaginative power—all these seem likely to have figured in his creation of the world's first marriage and the satisfaction both Eve and Adam find in it. If we hear more of Adam's satisfaction, Eve also has her turn, in the elaborately interlaced lyrical passage that begins "Sweet is the breath of morn" (4.639–56). In this blank-verse adaptation of a Renaissance love lyric she expatiates on her pleasure in marital conversation ("With thee conversing I forget all time") by an extended comparison of her delight in Adam with her delight in the natural world. My students, reading *Paradise Lost* in the context of the seventeenth-century lyric, see the analogy as conventional, which it is. The role reversal is not, nor is the paradox of Eve in paradise declaring herself emparadised in Adam.

Eve's expression of her satisfaction in marriage is not explicitly sexual, except as her language echoes Milton's charged and multilayered celebration of sexuality, which I trace in book 7 as well, in his praise of material creation. We read these passages as evidence not only of God's wisdom and generative power but also of his delight. Eve and Adam are part of this creation as well as its possessors, and their pleasure in it as well as in each other is divinely sanctioned. Adam's satisfaction in marriage includes the explicitly sexual. In the divorce tracts, Milton had coolly dismissed desire, male desire: "strict life and labour with the abatement of a full diet may keep that low anough" (*Doctrine* 251). In *Paradise Lost* the satisfaction of desire figures prominently but problematically in the unfallen world.

Milton tried in a variety of ways to extricate sexuality from its association with our fallen condition: the passages I look at are "Hail wedded Love" in book 4 (736–75) and the dialogue between Adam and Raphael at the end of book 8 (500–629). In realizing the quality and texture of the unfallen world, Milton had other imaginings of earthly paradises at his disposal, except with respect to sexuality. Genesis suggested indirection: of Eve and Adam in their unfallen state it says, "they were both naked, the man and his wife, and were not ashamed." Shame—their covering themselves with fig leaves—is a consequence of the fall. Hence the paradox of unfallen sexuality: while the unfallen world is like the best we know, only better, unfallen sexuality is quite unlike fallen sexuality. Milton employs both indirection and negation to describe it in book 4. When Eve and Adam enter their bower hand in hand for "the Rites mysterious of connubial Love," they have no clothes to remove, for, as Milton rather coyly reminds us, they are naked already. Their bed is "undefiled and chaste pronounc't"; their coming together in it is not like an encounter with a harlot, a sexual intrigue at court, or the serenade of a lover to a disdainful lady, examples of both fallen sexuality and its repression.

Milton's more original and arresting presentation of unfallen sexuality occurs at the end of book 8. Adam, describing human love to Raphael, begins by likening his delight in Eve to his delight in the natural world, much as she did in her love lyric. His delight is also, he owns, greater and different: in the consummation of their love after her creation "here passion first I felt" and here "transported I behold, / Transported touch." Speculating on the nature of this experience, he finds his male superiority diminished,

> so absolute she seems
> And in herself complete, so well to know
> Her own, that what she wills to do or say,
> Seems wisest, vertuousest, discreetest, best.

Raphael responds immediately to what he takes to be Adam's confusion of Eve's sexual power with mental and moral power and reads him a lecture on passion and its dangers. Passion, even in paradise, subverts the hierarchical order on which patriarchy rests: in the sexual act, Raphael admonishes, Adam is seen by Eve as "least wise," least in control of himself and deserving to rule her, and the sense of touch it engages he shares with "Cattle and each Beast." Adam, though "half-abash't," is not silenced, and the burden of his response is that Raphael has misunderstood him. Human love includes passion, transport, and more,

> those graceful acts,
> Those thousand decencies that daily flow
> From all her words and actions, mixt with Love
> And sweet compliance, which declare unfeign'd
> Union of Mind, or in us both one Soul.

Adam in effect domesticates passion and, by speaking of Eve's "sweet compliance," attempts to subsume it under patriarchal rule. Then, before Raphael can respond, he rather aggressively inquires how celestial beings express their love, to which Raphael, blushing, acknowledges that angels, though incorporeal, also unite. Raphael's— and Adam's—strategy of accommodating great things to small is strained to its utmost in Raphael's explanation of how angelic union takes place, but his awkward admission that it does evidences Milton's insistence on the possibility of unfallen sexuality and shameless innocence; their potential for subverting the patriarchal order he elides.

If the divorce tracts do not prepare us for Milton's celebration of sexuality in *Paradise Lost,* neither do they prepare us for the serious work performed by Eve after the fall. To Adam is assigned the work of intellect, to Eve the work of emotion, and in theory at least it is the difference in degree between their characteristic faculties that legitimates not only the sexual division of labor but also the patriarchal order. But in working out the fall and its consequences, Milton represents Eve as surprisingly capable in both intellect and emotion. In the divorce tracts he roughly distinguished between contemplative and pragmatical thought ("we cannot therefore alwayes be contemplative, or pragmaticall abroad"), and in *Paradise Lost,* in two obvious instances, he exempts Eve from the work of contemplation, when she leaves of her own volition during Adam's and Raphael's discussion of celestial motion and when Michael puts her to sleep to introduce Adam to the study of history, that is, the visionary history of the consequences of the fall in books 11 and 12. In the first, however, Milton specifies that Eve leaves neither out of boredom nor out of incapacity to understand but rather because she prefers contemplative thought mixed with "Grateful digressions" and "conjugal Caresses" (8.55–56). It is a repellent model for women's education, though one I am sure Milton thought charming, as he did other instances in which he presents Eve as the busy housewife in Eden. The politics of housework aside, I find them jarring in the poem's terms, for they are incommensurate with the gravity of her other actions.

Eve's fall is grave indeed. Both she and Adam fall because they mistake a lesser good for a greater and choose it: Eve prefers knowledge, or what seems like knowledge, to obedience, and Adam, Eve to God. It is Eve's mistake, however, that Milton expands, her mental processes that engage him and that he richly develops, and I read her fall as one of two significant varieties of human disobedience rather than as a characteristically female variety: Milton, with only two characters available to him to represent the range of human experience, does not have her fall as a result of female muddleheadedness. How to take her aspiration to become (in Satan's words) "as Gods, / Knowing good and evil as they know" (9.708–09) is problematic, as is her impulse, after the fall, to keep the apple with its magic properties to herself, in order to be "more equal" to Adam "and perhaps, / A thing not undesirable, some time / Superior: for inferior who is free?" (9.

823–25). She repeats in a human dimension elements of Satan's rebellion against God, and the repetition can be used either to diminish or to enlarge her. I choose to enlarge her, to see her aspiration as Faustian, as noble folly, and to see her rebellion against the patriarchal order of Eden as a startling recognition, on Milton's part, of how, even in the benign patriarchy of Eden, it galls a capable spirit always to be second.

If Eve is not notably inferior to Adam in mental power, she is, after the fall, notably superior to him in emotional power. In the jangling exchanges between them we see her take the blame for both herself and him and offer to ask God to exempt him and punish her alone; we watch her kneel to him and ask forgiveness and, in her submissive distress, move him to respond lovingly, so that his anger is dissipated and the harmony between them restored. She makes herself responsible for repairing the ravages of sin by reestablishing love and peace. I think it is accurate to say that after the fall Eve comes into her own, that in her sphere, the work of emotion, she is stronger than Adam, whose feelings are disordered and incapacitating. What we see in postlapsarian Eden is their complementarity, as Eve provides what Adam lacks. She is actively engaged in serious work, the work of maintaining the relation of marriage. Yet this work is also self-abnegating and self-denying: Eve provides the first great example of female heroism that will be reenacted by her daughters, a heroism of self-effacement rather than self-assertion.

When Adam and Eve leave paradise at the end of book 12, they go hand in hand into the world, as earlier they went hand in hand into the bower to consummate their love; both are suggestively egalitarian images, but images whose import *Paradise Lost* does not sustain. Milton mutes but does not obliterate the difference in degree between Eve and Adam in valuing Eve, realizing her experience, and rendering her virtue as active; that is to say, he mutes elements of patriarchy that are also muted for us. What he does not mute is the difference in kind between them and the sexual divison of labor that follows from it, the assigning of emotional work to women, contemplative and pragmatic work to men. These are elements of patriarchy that persist. Eden, in *Paradise Lost*, is literally a place that cannot be recovered, though, as Michael enjoins Adam, by the exercise of virtue he may hope to possess "A paradise within thee, happier far" (12. 587). Few paradisal states are solitary, and their closest approximation may well be a loving relation. If women's work is to maintain love and peace in such relations, then when these qualities vanish, as they are bound to from time to time, women are peculiarly to blame for their loss and peculiarly responsible for re-creating them. The fall of Eve and Adam thus prefigures more of our domestic history than Milton includes in the vision of books 11 and 12.

All of which is to say no more than and no less than that in *Paradise Lost* Milton represents the sexual polarities of patriarchy still present to us, represents them more powerfully than the hierarchical order that was their seventeenth-century concomitant. His is not an androgynous vision, but to say so is not to belittle his achievement. Feminist scrutiny shows the epic to be a remarkable representation of the enduring elements of patriarchy.

Paradise Lost and the Novel

Herman Rapaport

Like many instructors, I am aware that Milton's *Paradise Lost* is taught according to certain givens: ideally, every teacher of the poem should attempt to examine Milton's biblical and classical sources, his intellectual heritage, his historical significance as poet and politician, his great influence on English poetry, and his critical reception. Those of us who teach *Paradise Lost* regularly also like to explore some specific topics that appear with some frequency in the Milton criticism, such as Eve's fall, Milton's misogyny, Adam's uxoriousness, the status of the trinity, the speeches of God, and the heroism of Satan. These issues allow us to raise stimulating discussions as well as prepare students to engage directly the Milton criticism, that vast apparatus necessary for a proper appreciation of Milton's great epic. Lastly, teachers need to discuss Milton's craftsmanship as a poet and read aloud passages to demonstrate what Joseph Addison called the "many beauties" of *Paradise Lost*. After all, we want students to recognize that literary critics not only analyse and interpret poetry; they also celebrate and teach others to appreciate its compelling charms.

These aspects constitute a fairly standard approach to Milton and one that is most valuable for students unfamiliar with Milton's oeuvre. Yet, there is always some room for departure. I like to stress that *Paradise Lost* marks not so much the end of the Renaissance as the optimistic anticipation of the Enlightenment and what followed.[1] There is a sense in which the poem ought to be studied alongside works such as Daniel Defoe's *Robinson Crusoe*, Montesquieu's *Persian Letters*, Jonathan Swift's *Gulliver's Travels*, Denis Diderot's *La religieuse*, J. W. Goethe's *Elective Affinities*, Nathaniel Hawthorne's *The Scarlet Letter*, Herman Melville's *Moby-Dick*, Fyodor Dostoevsky's *The Brothers Karamazov*, Gustave Flaubert's *Madame Bovary*, Henry James's *The American*, and James Joyce's *Ulysses*. I try to show my students that this epic not only foreshadows prose of the eighteenth century but adumbrates works written in later periods as well. In particular, *Paradise Lost* has strong affinities with the novel, and I like to make the case for heuristic purposes that the poem is a novel with the facade of an epic. This is the thesis, then, that I develop in my approach to *Paradise Lost*.

I begin with Georg Lukács's well-known study *Theory of the Novel*, written in 1914–15. It helps us directly assault the notion that *Paradise Lost* is a Renaissance work anachronistically written during the Restoration. In *English Literature in the Earlier Seventeenth Cen-*

tury, Douglas Bush remarks that Milton had grown thoroughly out of tune with his epoch and had become a "noble anachronism" (378)— an evaluation, Bush says, that is accepted by the Milton establishment as a whole. Although not all Miltonists may want to be so represented, Milton criticism largely supports Bush's contention that Milton's Restoration writings belong to a Renaissance culture and milieu, not a neoclassic or Enlightenment society. And certainly the criticism often implies that Milton was a sort of "poet in exile," as Louis Martz has called him. Yet, with Lukács in hand, it is tempting to counter this "anachronistic fallacy" and, moreover, expose a motive for placing Milton in the earlier part of the seventeenth century rather than in the time of Charles ii. The desire may be to protect *Paradise Lost* from criticisms that call its authenticity as a genre into question and that therefore problematize the usual uncritical assumptions concerning Milton's relation to his appropriation of texts from the epic tradition. With healthy skepticism Lukács suggests that *Paradise Lost* has much more in common with the novel than we might ordinarily expect and that this affinity discloses an important truth about the relation of genre to historical epoch: that genres are not transcendental forms but articulations of particular historical and class consciousnesses as they are constituted within a specific political network of productive and social relations.

Lukács draws heavily from Friedrich Schiller's *On the Aesthetic Education of Man,* which those who want to avoid Lukács's Marxist resonances can turn to for a less politically charged argument. What Lukács noticed in Schiller was that the ancient Greek epic reflects a culture in which the individual had not yet emerged as someone isolated from modes of economic and cultural production. As Schiller notes, a character like Achilles may have felt melancholy or tragedy, but he did not think about those feelings in such a way that a self or cogito emerged. He did not, that is, see himself as essentially estranged from all human relations, nor did he come to speculate in the poignant and self-satisfying gap between "me" and "you." Action was considered not from the standpoint of the individual but as part of a polis. The greatness of ancient epics lies in their ability to open onto a totality of social relations while still representing individuals at once typical and unique. These were public figures whose privacy refrained from overwhelming the bonds between the individual and the collective. Only in bourgeois society would this privacy rearticulate the relations between individual and collective consciousness, a rearticulation motivated by industry and capital and characterized by obsessive narcissism and depression. The novel, then, is a genre specific to the emergence of a Cartesian self, specific to an age in which economy passes from the control of the nobility to the control of the middle class. Whereas the hero in the epic typifies the whole of social relations, the hero in the novel exemplifies middle-class individualism, consciousness isolated from the totality of human relations. Epic and novel, then, are not transcendental literary forms but specific articulations that reflect particular social consciousnesses at particular historical moments.

Adam Smith's *The Wealth of Nations* (1776) is well known for its theory about the division of labor. Smith argued that fracturing and alienating labor relations would increase productivity and give the worker more leisure to develop as an individual whose essence transcends the toil of everyday laboring. In large part, the nineteenth-century novel considers this view. For example, in Henry James's *The American*, Christopher Newman is not only wealthy and free because of his labor, but he is also isolated, self-conscious, and subject to intensive introspection that savors the tragic gap between self and other. Newman's marriage plans are only a tasteless diversion arising out of idleness and cultural estrangement. As the diversion develops, Newman's loneliness, distance, class difference, irony, and miscalculations show how the freedom of the American laborer or entrepreneur represents its source, the relations of work, which are themselves alienated. Indeed, Newman's pursuit of Mme de Cintré ensures that capitalist leisure replicates or mirrors capitalist labor. If, however, we can consider James's novel in relation to Adam Smith, we have also to recognize that a division of labor has its effects in *Paradise Lost*. Here a fall facilitated by the dividing of tasks and the rupturing of a collective consciousness results in the increased isolation of Adam and Eve. After the fall, the couple will always be divided—hence the purpose of the quarrel between Adam and Eve in book 10—and the couple or family will itself appear as autonomous. But, of course, in Milton the pair is saved by God's grace. In James there is also metaphysical reparation. Mme de Cintré turns her back on Newman and joins the harshest nunnery she can find.

Like Milton's epic, the bourgeois novel concentrates on the couple as an estranged pair of lovers who must combat an insensitive community. The love between persons is irrational, subjective, and incomprehensible. And the couple itself is often ostracized or persecuted for its individualism. Some common antagonisms the bourgeois couple faces are sensitive lovers versus callous world, intuitive and private pair versus rational and public society, honest lovers versus hypocritical milieu, and permissive love versus unyielding laws. The bond between self and community is fragmented and replaced by the couple or family. These antagonisms typify novels like Charlotte Brontë's *Jane Eyre* and Margaret Mitchell's *Gone with the Wind*. But again, consider *Paradise Lost*. Adam willingly falls after Eve has eaten the forbidden fruit, not because he is duped by her, but because already in the prelapsarian state Adam views Eve as half of an individual couple whose love is irrational ("commotion strange") and whose bond is inherently antagonistic to the totality of relations that God's law has revealed. The division of labor thematized in book 9 does not separate the couple so much as it strengthens their relation, for through the separation, Adam and Eve learn of their need for each other and the power of the family or loving couple as a unit that can withstand worldly misfortune. Here we see a strong current of bourgeois influence on Milton: the definition of the couple as two individuals whose love for each other is strengthened by a division or alienation of labor.

At times it is helpful to read students passages from Lukács. For example, "The novel is the epic of an age in which the extensive totality of life is no longer directly given, in which the immanence of meaning in life has become a problem, yet which still thinks in terms of totality" (56). In Lukács's view, what unifies the fragmented consciousness of the novelistic temperament is both the novel's style and the dominance of the hero's presence. What replaces the totality of social and historical relations is the artistry or organicism of the novel's stylistic features. Thus, through a novel like *Madame Bovary* a new perspective of life is established,

> that of the indissoluble connection between the relative independence of the parts and their attachment to the whole. But the parts, despite this attachment, can never lose their inexorable abstract self-dependence and their relationship to the totality, although it appears as closely as possible an organic one, is nevertheless not a true born organic relationship but a conceptual one which is abolished again and again.   (75–76)

A false and arbitrary conceptualization of the totality of the represented world results from alienated thinking, and this occlusion of the real, Lukács argues during the 1930s, reaches its apogee in James Joyce's *Ulysses*, in which Leopold Bloom's estranged consciousness is expressed through a strident medley of contorted and cryptic styles. The details belong temporally to a single day, and yet this time frame is but an alibi, Lukács thinks, for arbitrary juxtapositions whose stylis-

tic interplays rest finally on a bourgeois sentimentalism wholly igno-
rant of true historical relations. Only under the humanistic excuse of
aestheticism can this monstrosity be rehabilitated for the so-called
serious reader. Harsh as this evaluation of Joyce may seem, it contains
useful ideas for the history of genres.

Lukács, curiously enough, treats the novel as a fallen form of consciousness, one that strongly resembles the fall and the estrangement
of Adam and Eve from God and Eden. It is therefore helpful to suggest to students that *Paradise Lost* ought to be read metapoetically as
an epic that discovers its own novelistic understructure, or what Fredric Jameson has called literature's "political unconscious."[2] Joseph
Addison, whose *Spectator* essays on *Paradise Lost* are a good reference for students, considers Milton's ending in book 12 imperfect.
The description of Adam and Eve's expulsion concludes this way:

> Some natural tears they dropp'd but wip'd them soon;
> The World was all before them, where to choose
> Thir place of rest, and Providence thir guide;
> They hand in hand with wand'ring steps and slow,
> Through Eden took thir solitary way.   (645–49)

Addison's complaint, not surprising for an eighteenth-century reader,
is that the closing line should have been "Thir place of rest, and
Providence thir guide" (*Spectator* 369, 3 May 1712). He apparently
preferred the bourgeois resonances of an ending in which Adam and
Eve optimistically look toward the wilderness and the future like
bourgeois adventurers or like their real-life counterparts in New England, the pioneers. Addison likes to think of Providence not as a lost
topos but as the historization of spirit exemplified in the figure of the
pioneer couple who will, through toil, learn to master the wilderness
and produce order out of chaos. When Adam and Eve leave paradise,
they fulfill an ontological destiny that is conceptualized within the
framework of middle-class ideology: to know and do good by way of
inevitable evil. One may have failings, but one must carry on, since it
is the will of Providence and the legacy of a happy fall, or *felix culpa*.
Addison would place Adam and Eve in the role of a novelistic hero
like Robinson Crusoe, a figure who is similarly homeless or stranded
in a remote wilderness but who nevertheless overcomes savagery and
the wild. Even if such figures cannot read the divine portents of God
but have only utilitarian signs—for example, Crusoe's utilitarian recognition of footprints or Adam and Eve's utilitarian reading of natural
signs after the fall—they can, through right reason and pragmatics,

make order out of chaos, good from evil. Given this clue from Addison, we can say that the end of *Paradise Lost* can be read as a text about the death of the epic and the birth of the novel, that what Addison felt toward the end of Milton's poem was not so much the imitation of classical poets as the writing of a fiction closer to Defoe. In this sense, Milton appears less a Renaissance figure than an Enlightenment one, a point of view contrary to what Bush had in mind when he said Milton was out of tune with his epoch.

By now, the shape of the lecture material becomes clear, I think, and much more can be filled in. One has the option of stressing rather heavily a social theory inspired by Marx and can even turn to passages in the *Grundrisse* that support the analysis above. One can also turn to less politically charged sources like Addison to make similar points. In more advanced classes one can expand on Lukács and study Jameson's *The Political Unconscious*, thereby supplementing the discussion with psychological, ideological, and structuralist analysis. In a survey course covering *Paradise Lost* as well as prose in later periods, this analysis can be conducted by way of a comparative study of, say, *Paradise Lost* and *Moby-Dick*. This is a fruitful tactic, because Melville's novel is, of course, an epic in prose, and it concerns many of the same issues that Milton treats. Needless to say, *Paradise Lost* with its satanic leviathan strongly influenced Melville, yet that influence in itself points out how compatible Milton is with a nineteenth-century historical condition, more compatible in some ways than with many of the Renaissance models that have been located as sources for Milton's epic vision. I would go so far as to suggest that a close reading of *Paradise Lost, Moby-Dick,* and Joyce's *Ulysses* would show that all these works concern the impossibility of epic at a historical time when consciousness is "novelistic." And yet, all these works strongly resist the novelistic consciousness. In this sense, Milton is reacting against the eighteenth century, and we see why, for example, his ending would clash with Addison's preferences. Similarly, *Moby-Dick* and *Ulysses* struggle against the normative use of everyday language, incorporating poetic devices. This tendency is strong in Melville, but it is overwhelming in Joyce, particularly in sections of *Ulysses* like "Hades," "Sirens," or "Penelope." In this context, then, we can appreciate genre in terms of a dialectic between epic and novel that discloses a collision of the formations of consciousnesses within a historical perspective.

A helpful assignment for students is the composition of a paper or an essay examination response that outlines the ways in which *Paradise*

Lost could be said to be novelistic. From this base other extrapolations can be made. A few of the responses to this question are outlined here, though they are not exhaustive. Note that some are necessarily more sophisticated than others.

1. *Paradise Lost* stresses Cartesianism in at least a couple of key instances. First, in book 1, Satan's remark that he can make a heaven of hell and a hell of heaven suggests that the mind is its own place (as Satan says) and that with the fall into individuality comes a new and radical subjectivity. This advent is the power of positive thinking that has been traditionally at the heart of middle-class attitudes. Witness, for example, the writings of Benjamin Franklin, or, on a much more vulgar level, the thoughts of Dale Carnegie and J. W. Marriott. Second, Cartesianism marks the destiny of Adam and Eve. Their fall through satanic temptation results in their position as masters of a wilderness they have to tame. It is through Satan that the bourgeois adventurer, indeed the bourgeois order, is born. The pioneer looks out at a brave new world.

2. *Paradise Lost* stresses the homelessness and nostalgia for origins Lukács feels are central to the novel tradition. Already in Eden, the parents of humankind have formulated questions for which the answers seem inadequate. If Adam and Eve pray to God in an unconsidered and spontaneous manner, their words are dogmatic and loaded with theological doubt and wonder. Good examples are found in books 4 and 5. Adam's words to Eve concerning the meaning of her nightmare raise more questions in her mind than they can resolve. Similarly, Raphael's instruction serves mainly to perplex and estrange Adam by developing a speculative thought process that isolates the individual. Also, in book 8, Adam tells Raphael that he finds Eve most beautiful but not interesting to talk to, because she is intellectually inferior. In this instance, Adam reminds one of Michel in André Gide's *The Immoralist*.

Another key issue concerning homelessness is the ontology of woman in Milton's epic. Eve is the "dangerous supplement" in Jacques Derrida's deconstructive sense: the belated completer or addition that signifies a lack or impoverishment. In *Of Grammatology*, Derrida explains by way of Jean-Jacques Rousseau that the supplement is at once necessary and yet superfluous to any system, that the supplement is at once greater and lesser than the sum it makes up with respect to a whole or totality (144–52). That Eve is taken from the side of Adam already points out the supplementarity of woman in Genesis, and for Milton this is problematized by a radical ambiguity: that onto-

logically woman is within and not within the normal order or system-
ization of things. It is not so much that woman is secondary—if she
were, there would be no problem, because she would belong to a
natural station in a hierarchy—as that she is occupying neither Adam's
station nor one secondary to it even while she must function as if she
were. Woman is, therefore, ex-centric to God's order and not logically
recuperable within a hierarchy. She is, in a word, deconstructing the
patriarchal relations of *Paradise Lost*. In discussing this idea, students
may want to take a feminist approach that considers the alienation of
woman within the bourgeois couple or family as itself a function of a
middle-class ideology, which logically irrationalizes not only the
place of woman but her ontology as well. In nineteenth-century literature we have an opportunity to study this condition from other angles:
consider Hester Prynne in *The Scarlet Letter* or Ottilie in *The Elective Affinities*.

3. One can stress the use of style in *Paradise Lost* as curiously at
odds with classical practice. A usual argument is that Milton's epic is
baroque in its use of heterogeneous styles, an effect not found in
Homer, Vergil, or Dante. Yet this merely reinforces the view that
Milton's epic is novelistic, since the novel is baroque in precisely this
sense, as is evident in Swift, Sterne, Fielding, Flaubert, and, again,
Joyce. One can also argue that an aesthetic category devised to resolve
the problem of Milton's clashing styles really begs the question. Particularly odd is the relation of book 6 to the opening two books. While
the war in heaven is very neoclassical—reminiscent of the rococo—
the opening books are Vergilian and Dantesque. In the epics of
Homer and Vergil, not to mention the *Commedia* of Dante, various
styles cooperate to focus and integrate the work even as its stylistic
range is extended. But in Milton's epic, the styles clash, fracture, and
break apart our perception of an integral whole. For example, the
styles function to disintegrate a coherent vision of Satan's fall and
raise more questions than they resolve. The reader, far from being
initiated into an overall vision, is estranged.

A more challenging point students may develop is that book 9 of
Paradise Lost is a condensation of the whole poem. I sometimes stress
in my lecture that instructors in survey courses often teach only this
book, a practice that is not merely encouraged by anthologists. Perhaps it is stimulated by the poem itself, since Milton may have considered the value of providing the practical middle-class reader with a
little "reader's digest." Given the explosion of printed matter during
the seventeenth century and the increased drive to read for informa-

tion, there may be reason to think that *Paradise Lost* was composed with readerly efficiency in mind. This kind of cultural speculation aside, one can note that there are no such condensations in Homer, Vergil, and Dante. The *Inferno* from Dante's *Divine Comedy* does indeed reflect the *Purgatorio* and *Paradiso*, but one has to read the whole to understand even this large part. In fact, *Inferno* remains largely a mystery without an understanding of the whole poem. But in *Paradise Lost*, we have to read the part to understand the whole. That is, it is preferable to begin with book 9 as a sort of transcendental clue to the rest.

To put matters another way, a student with a background in linguistics could point out that book 9 of *Paradise Lost* is not just a condensation but a metonymical structure. Roman Jakobson, in the celebrated "The Metaphoric and Metonymic Poles," suggests that "for poetry, metaphor, and for prose, metonymy is the line of least resistance" (96). That is, poetry is generally characterized by metaphorical features and prose by metonymical ones. Since Milton's epic is structurally skewed in favor of metonymic relations with respect to the significance of book 9, it seems that Jakobson gives us a stylistic hint that the epic genre is not authentically embodied in *Paradise Lost*, that Milton's epic is compromised by novelistic features, and that the epic conventions are something of a facade for what is a text curiously allied with prose. That is, *Paradise Lost* appears once more as a novel camouflaged to appear as poetry.

Thus we arrive linguistically at a perception implied by Lukács in *Theory of the Novel*: that the domestic epic is necessarily a contradiction in whose form we see the opposition not only of two genres, epic and novel, but also of two social tendencies, the stress on individualism as well as cultural identification through neoclassical aestheticism. Milton's epic, in part, suggests that it belongs to an authentic classical heritage recovered from a belated historical position. But as the culture of the bourgeoisie matures, this kind of deception becomes less and less convincing. The art of Joshua Reynolds, Dominique Ingres, and Gustave Moreau reveals rather clearly the degree to which the consciousness of classicism is but a symptom of a modernist consciousness of radical estrangement and even terror. Again, the contradiction between the materials of classicism and the forces of bourgeois modernism is extremely evident in the *Cantos* of Ezra Pound, in which the classical erudition is almost entirely indebted to a political context that is as remote from classical values and attitudes as one might possibly imagine.

NOTES

[1] I am grateful to Roy Roussel of the State University of New York, Buffalo, for having pointed this out to me after I had read a paper on Milton and Descartes.

[2] The political unconscious is composed of submerged narrative structures called ideologemes "upon which the novel as a process works and which it transforms into texts of a different order" (Jameson 185). I am arguing that *Paradise Lost* is novelistic in process and that its epic features are a result of a transformation onto the level of a different order from the genre of the novel.

TEACHING THE BACKGROUNDS AND CONTEXTS

Milton Contexts

Hugh M. Richmond

All too often the anticipation of Milton's supposed defects must be transcended before students can respond creatively to the verve and sophistication of his verse. For the catalog of his limitations has been a principal subject of discussion and investigation among many of his critics in the twentieth century. In his own time his aggressive republicanism and defense of regicide led him close to execution at the Restoration, and they have scandalized many traditionalists, such as Samuel Johnson in his "Milton." Now, however, Milton's supposedly harsh theology offends many progressives, including William Empson in his attack on the poet's beliefs in *Milton's God*. Milton's view of women is savagely censured from a feminist perspective in Robert Graves's novel *Wife to Mr. Milton*. His poetic worth was lowered by T. S. Eliot and Dr. Leavis; his intellectual sufficiency has been questioned by John Carey; and even his artistic goals as currently expounded by a supporter, Stanley Fish, in *Surprised by Sin*, appear to have the end of humiliating the reader who gullibly succumbs to Satan's fascination.

By confronting these problems openly, we can provide a lively and informative introduction to any Milton course, which validates the investigation of Milton's context. It is crucial for students' understanding and positive involvement that we establish the domestic, political, and cultural contexts of his verse, so students can grasp why Milton is the epitome of the European tradition and can be called "the last Elizabethan" yet nevertheless proves in many ways to be the first modern writer in English.

The first major step in overcoming the alienating impressions of Milton's genius is to demonstrate that just as Shakespeare is often creatively aware of the dangers of his empathy and verbal wit (in *Love's Labour's Lost,* for instance), so Milton consciously transcends his defects and those of his time in ways that remain exemplary and attractive. For example, taking his domestic experience into account, we discover that his hasty and naive marriage soon generated a frustrated sense of the need for true mutuality between the sexes, which led to the writing of the provocatively radical pamphlets advocating divorce between incompatible spouses, prefiguring modern views. These publications in turn generated his classic defense of free speech in *Areopagitica,* when the Presbyterian Parliament banned the pamphlets. And the whole issue was unpredictably resolved by the abrupt but permanent reconciliation of Milton and Mary Powell, described so vividly by Milton's nephew and pupil Edward Phillips. Knowledge of these experiences of the author surely helps us to recognize the authority and insight reflected in the evocation of the fluctuating relations between Adam and Eve in *Paradise Lost,* which are its central and most subtle creations. Such a bizarre and instructive cycle—from costly experience to the illumination of literary tradition—is the model I propose to teachers of Milton, and of *Paradise Lost* in particular. Not only may it transmute Milton's supposed defects into something more creative and salutary, it revalidates literary history as a catalyst of critical awareness. The purpose remains heightened alertness to the actual text and its nuances, to which a less informed response may be insensitive. In Milton's poetry we may perceive the enrichment of tradition through discovery of its limitations and of its failures to match up with the author's idealistic expectations—a very modern theme.

As described by my mentor E. M. W. Tillyard (in only latently Freudian terms), the relevant aspects of Milton's upbringing fascinate students and illuminate the concerns, emphases, and insights of his work. In terms of education, Tillyard's *Milton* displays the ongoing results of Milton's father fixation, which reinforced his adherence to Old Testament values and achievement and risked making him conventionally ambitious and outer-directed throughout his career. Such considerations draw our attention in *Paradise Lost* to its stress on patriarchal figures like Noah and Moses, with their apotheosis in the presiding deity of God the Father. Admirably enough Milton's energies and awareness not only survived this compulsion to aim at conventional achievements but found an alternative model for action, in his own father's rebellious reaction against his Catholic family. When the family disinherited the elder Milton, he developed the desire for vicarious triumph through his son's achievement (the complex web of familial tensions may be disentangled from Milton's Latin poem *Ad patrem*). Milton's career and writings offer students a reassuring wavelike progression of surge toward high, classic achievement, followed by failure, withdrawal, and repudiation, and ultimately succeeded by a spontaneous flow of reconciliation and humble recommitment, leading to a new high-water mark of distinctive creativity. Not only is this a salutary model for education, it is a clue to the intrinsic structures of very different works, such as the progression in the sonnet "How soon hath Time, the subtle thief of youth / Stol'n on his wing my three and twentieth year!" or the recovery by the end of "Lycidas," and above all the remarkable transcendence of his own blindness in the great lyric opening of book 9 of *Paradise Lost*. This introduction to the narrative of the original sin affirms Providence's cooperation in transmuting seeming ruin into deeper awareness. In all these cases the threat of failure to meet a Father's magisterial requirements evolves to the discovery of a new resilient humanity favored by a less partriarchal authority, epitomized in the Son. Initially inspired by the Old Testament, Milton continually rediscovers the need for and meaning of the new one.

For students, Milton's formal intellectual training also illustrates helpfully the less biblical model of Renaissance humanism, as outlined by Roger Ascham in *The Schoolmaster*. Raised in the tradition of classical studies, Milton's ambition at Cambridge is to rival the achievements of pagan Latin and Greek epic, as he asserts in "At a Vacation Exercise in College" (Hughes, *John Milton* 31; lines 47–52). In *Epitaphium Damonis* he explains how he will expand patriotically on the Arthurian "Matter of Britain" in the Reformation spirit of Spenser (Hughes, *John Milton* 137–38; lines 161–78). Milton's treatise *Of Education* provides students with an unnerving extreme of intellectual ambition in the tradition of Plato's *Republic*, only slightly tempered by Reformation thinkers like Comenius and much nearer to the Renaissance ideals of nationalist, aristocratic, and elitist minds such as Bembo, Castiglione, and Bacon. Yet at this moment of extreme pretension, Milton's own academic career shows many symptoms of failure to achieve such goals, as his defensive autobiographical allusions indicate in the extracts from his prose writings (such as *An Apology for Smectymnuus*) in Merritt Hughes's classic anthology. In them we perceive the creative use of the artist's persona in ways prefigured in Dante and Chaucer, but sophisticated in Milton's age by artists such as Velázquez and Rembrandt. The Dutch painter's ultimately pessimistic account resembles Milton's early career, which found him rusticated for challenging his tutor, often alienated from his peers, failing to secure a fellowship, and unable to pursue his ecclesiastical vocation because of Archbishop Laud's new High Anglicanism. As a graduate student of sorts at Horton, Milton finds himself isolated, not to say ostracized, in rural England. Yet such a setting encourages in him a pastoral vein that is always one of his happiest, and it offsets his supposed severity, as we see in his Epicurean sonnet inviting Edward Lawrence to a rural feast. In such moods Milton recalls the spirit of Theocritus's seventh idyll about a country festival, or Horace's epode 2 about the satisfactions of rural life, or Vergil's nostalgia for the countryside in the *Georgics*. These precedents inspire Milton to two of his most enticing and deservedly popular poems: "L'Allegro" and "Il Penseroso." Milton could never have so convincingly evoked the seductive invitations of Comus and Satan if he had not savored the pleasures of this world, as William Haller has very precisely shown us in works such as *The Rise of Puritanism,* which help to correct our students' impression that all puritans were repressed ascetics. While the idyllic mood of unfallen Eden in *Paradise Lost* superimposes details of Ovid's Age of Gold from book 1 of the *Metamorphoses* on the spare narrative of Genesis, it gains depth, intensity, and pathos from Milton's reminiscences of earlier, simpler phases of his career, which climaxed in the social triumph of the performances of his two masques before aristocratic audiences and the publication of his juvenile poems, which earned him social and intellectual prestige in his Italian travels.

Yet this success in turn was broken off by another "modern" experience: the dislocation of English life by the turmoil induced by the patriarchal tyranny of the Stuart regime. This unrest deflected Milton from his literary goals to a career of advocacy and polemic, which proved increasingly frustrating and ineffective, as it led him beyond confrontation with royalists to the censure of his allies. In the end his pamphlet *The Ready and Easy Way to Establish a Free Commonwealth* (Hughes, *John Milton* 880–899) belies its title by a repressiveness equal to that of Plato's latest treatise, the *Laws,* and by a misanthropy worthy of Shakespeare's Timon (Hughes, *John Milton* 891).

Unlike Timon, however, Milton provides in his last years a climactic example of human resilience and powers of recovery. *Paradise Lost* is a powerful sublimation of the intense involvements and crises to which Milton had been a party in such employment as that of Cromwell's Latin secretary. These challenges are transposed and transcended through a consolidation of relevant European literary traditions for which only the earlier epic precedents of Homer, Vergil, and Dante are adequate comparisons, as epitomes of their ages' experience. To his mastery of orthodox intellectual tradition Milton brings the fusing intensity of Reformation trauma. To meet his need for reassurance in the face of outward defeat, he creates a fresh synthesis that orders all earlier resources in a personal perspective prefiguring our modern, primarily subjective consciousness. Dante had achieved as much for the more objective Aquinian worldview, refracted almost as drastically in his autobiographical narrative mode. Though Milton's authorial intrusions are more incidental, they ensure the contemporary relevance of his vast horizons, adjusting them to the perspective of the isolated individual who seems so archetypal to our modern view.

To study *Paradise Lost* is thus the best way for students to perceive how individual awareness is affected by the whole context, content, and positive implications of Western civilization. As archetypes for all humanity, Adam and Eve provide the focus for application of the full range of resources: epistemology, science, social hierarchy, artistic narrative, domestic relations, sexuality, and the gamut of choices and feelings. The epic's central act is a figure for each significant human choice and for the extraordinary complex of forces of which it is the resultant—including both cosmic and immediate personal factors and elements that many would still wish to call providential. *Paradise Lost* provides a perfect medium for education in the major cultural themes and issues of Western literature: the classic assertive hero with all his egotistical limitations, as in Achilles, Roland, and Satan; the self-deluding amatory idealism of Petrarch, in Adam's misguided cult of Eve; the nostalgic myth of Ovid's Golden Age in Eden; the prosaic but powerful encyclopedic tradition of such surveys as those of Hesiod and Lucretius in the narrative of the creation; and even such ideological issues as the affirmation of the superiority of dramatic to epic modes of Aristotle's *Poetics,* in the progression from the early scenes to the central dialogues of Adam and Eve (which my students have staged with great effectiveness in conditions analogous to scenes from Marlowe and Shakespeare).

Thus the poem must invite sophisticated psychological and moral judgments of a kind intrinsic to all valid education. For example, the myth of Milton's antifeminism can only truly be laid to rest by a sensitive exploration of the psychologies of Adam and Eve. Indeed, Milton's dependence on his wives and daughters cannot be exaggerated. And in Eve's central role in *Paradise Lost* we must see Milton's recognition of women's primary role in human affairs and in the evolution of the human condition, whether for good or ill. Eve is the most dynamic, flexible figure in the epic, initiating the fall and the subsequent reconciliation, which anticipates the final grace bestowed on both of them. Without her companionship Eden had proved static, narcissistic, and lacking in personal feeling and true mutuality. The pristine absoluteness of heaven leaves no scope for adjustment to the invincible egotism of Satan. While the more finite dependence of Eden increases the likelihood of failure, its admitted limitations make error pardonable and permit pragmatic adjustments. In placing woman at the center of his action, Milton does not merely follow the scanty data of Genesis, he invests the relations of Adam and Eve with all the subtle awareness of love and sexuality accumulated by poets as various as Ovid, Dante, Petrarch, and Shakespeare. In this he transcends the largely incidental sexuality of Achilles and Odysseus in Homer, the curious asexuality of medieval figures like Beowulf and Roland, and even the more developed roles of Dido and Aeneas in the early books of Vergil's epic. Anticipating modern values of Freud and others, Milton insists that sexual relations are at the core of human decisions, and they are such not just in the medieval sense of dogmatic misogyny. For Milton demonstrates that sexuality involves complex issues of intellectual and social hierarchy and interdependence, which are not easily or rationally resolved. As a result of his own doomed rebellious ambitions, Milton's empathy for the desire for self-assertion in both Eve and Satan is memorably and authentically realized, as every thoughtful reader agrees. But to fully savor his work, our students need to see that, when measured against the norms of European culture, *Paradise Lost* demonstrates the necessary chastening of heroic egotism by a spirit of empathy, reconciliation, and creativity for which his best human example is the repeated efforts for recovery by Eve in books 10–12 of the epic.

The question remains of how exactly this broad cultural perspective can be evoked in the classroom for beginning students of *Paradise Lost*, without intimidation or confusion. One simple way to highlight the classical precedents and their reworking in the Renaissance is to show visual expressions of those to which Milton himself was exposed in his European travels. Some of my students have even made a film travelogue based on pictures of sites, buildings, and other artifacts that Milton could have seen. A less ambitious approach uses slides of Florence, Venice, Rome, and Naples (among others), displaying their classical and baroque resources, reinforced by appropriate music. I find students readily assimilate classical values in surviving Greek and Roman architecture and in the reworking of such themes by artists like Raphael (say in *The School of Athens*) or Michelangelo. Equally revealing are the complex scenes and perspectives of Bosch, Brueghel, Rubens, and Rembrandt—or the more formal works of Bernini, Palladio, Poussin, and Inigo Jones. Even a single hour devoted to the readily accessible slides covering such work makes Milton's scenes and emphases much more intelligible, as we may expect from the arguments of such books as John Arthos's *Milton and the Italian Cities*, Robert Cawley's *Milton and the Literature of Travel*, Roy Daniells's *Milton, Mannerism and Baroque*, and surveys like Don Wolfe's *Milton and His England* or Roland Mushat Frye's comprehensive work on Milton's inconography.

Similarly, very succinct samples of literary precedents for key episodes in *Paradise Lost* can be effectively presented in class. At various points I read or distribute relevant passages: for example, the opening of book 1 of Ovid's *Metamorphoses* to supplement Genesis, in connection with Eden in the fourth book of the epic, or Petrarchan extravagancies from *Romeo and Juliet* (1.2; 3.5), to parallel Adam's flatteries of Eve and her responses in the same book. Obviously Satan's various roles can be illuminated by excerpts from the *Iliad* (the list of ships in book 2 of the *Iliad* is parodied in Milton's list of fallen angels in book 1 of *Paradise Lost*), and from the relevant playlets in the York or Chester cycles, as well as Renaissance precedents such as Mephistopheles in Marlowe's *Doctor Faustus* (compare lines 553–55 in Marlowe with Satan at the start of book 4). To demonstrate fully the dependence of Milton on Elizabethan dramatic precedents, one has only to read aloud the lively exchanges between Adam, Eve, and Satan in books 9 and 10 with such analogues as Richard of Gloucester's seduction of Lady Anne (*Richard III* 1.2).

Such re-creation and performance of the epic's dramatic contexts necessarily evoke its vitality of expression and readily refute the assertion of its supposed diffuseness and cold artifice by critics such as Arnold, Eliot, and Leavis. They validate the defense in Christopher Ricks's *Milton's Grand Style*. No doubts of Milton's verve, dramatic sophistication, and immediacy can survive a properly rehearsed rendering of Eve's self-debate over whether to conserve her newly acquired "superiority" to Adam and of the couple's subsequent exchanges (9.795–1186). The epic abounds in such masterly dramatic episodes, and perhaps their vitality and immediacy provide a better approach to the purposes of the epic as an "affective" work than too laborious a disentangling of its theological niceties. In fact, Milton seems consciously to skirt matters of theology in favor of dramatic, psychological issues that are more appropriate to poetry and that he considers as necessarily "more simple, sensuous, and passionate" (*Of Education*).

We may, nevertheless, still wish to stress the central dichotomy between humanist faith in the redemptive power of reason and education (epitomized in Raphael's virtuoso expositions, before the fall that reveals their futility) and the fact of what Protestants would consider the innate fallibility of humanity, at least as it is known to followers of Luther and Calvin. It is surely more effective to evoke these issues by setting the psychological force of the characterization free than it is to overrefine them by dwelling on such niceties as whether Milton consciously follows Socinian precedents in excessively subordinating the Son to the Father in *Paradise Lost*. In practice, the Son reflects the universally recognized cosmic principles of creativity and of the paradoxical love of the inferior thing created, even when that love conflicts with other seemingly irresistible absolutes of existence epitomized in the Father: justice, consistency, and logic. The point may be clarified by anticipation of the issue in similarly dramatic terms in Langland's *Piers Plowman* (passus 18). But even such broad and simple theological approaches may need careful introduction because of a modern loss of training in abstract thinking or unexamined reflexes and conditioning at odds with Milton's ideas of religious consensus. Even this challenge to understand possibly alien thought processes makes Milton a salutary educational resource, particularly since he usually proves to be still in advance of modern commonplaces favoring naive confidence in reason and reform as immediate and accessible goals.

From his vantage point at the start of modern, revolutionary history, Milton invites us to look at our assumed values in a more comprehensive intellectual and artistic perspective than most authors. For this reason he is central to the historical outlining of humanistic studies (for example, he remains a required author in English and comparative literature majors at the University of California at Berkeley). He restores vitality to concepts like the *felix culpa* by the force of his literary imagination, and in this renewal the epic is the very opposite of what the scholar Walter Raleigh dubbed it: "a monument to dead ideas." Milton gives modern psychological validity to the anonymous medieval poet's quaint exclamation: "Blessed be the time / That Appil také was." Once our students perceive this unique modulating function in the epic, Milton's interest proves irresistible to them, as I found even at the height of the cult of "relevance" in the sixties. Yet the rigor and comprehensiveness of Milton's resources ensures that we cannot merely assimilate him to some fashionable contemporary cult. Just as he himself was forced to reevaluate his commitment to the values of both the Renaissance and the Reformation, so he requires us to question our commitments in the light of the broadest cultural context. To ignore the nature of that context is to misread and minimize Milton's educational potential.

Methods and Muses

Sanford Golding

I have taught *Paradise Lost* over the years at various levels in many formats. In a two-quarter graduate course, for example, I offered traditional readings in *Paradise Lost* and *Paradise Regained* in the first quarter and, in the second, had students read Dryden's translation of the *Aeneid* (noticing along the way the influences of Vergil on Milton and those of Milton on Dryden), Dante's *Commedia*, Harington's translation of the *Orlando furioso*, and selections from *The Faerie Queene*. We then returned to *Paradise Lost* for further discussions of the poem as epic. Most of the students were familiar with Homer; those who were not were advised to become so. The course went well, and the students learned almost as much as their teacher, who got to teach some great works for the first time at this level.

In the present essay, however, I should like to discuss the method I am now using in teaching the two-quarter undergraduate Milton course. I have altered the first quarter considerably so as to provide students with more of a Milton milieu. My initial motive was to make the course more diverse and interesting, as I believe I have, but I also realized that expanding the material would help me better to present the context of Milton's ideas. My major text is Merritt Hughes's *Complete Poetry and Major Prose*. I begin by assigning the early lives of Milton and various chapters of Christopher Hill's *The World Turned Upside Down*, which is an excellent treatment of the religious and political movements of the period. We then read some of Milton's early poetry as far as "Lycidas." I next assign Bunyan's *Pilgrim's Progress*, with the intent of familiarizing students with Puritan covenant theology. I once used *Grace Abounding*, thinking it a more direct treatment, but the fictional work engages the students more. Since they are almost entirely without knowledge of this once universally read masterpiece, it is especially gratifying to introduce them to the book while simultaneously building up some important background knowledge of Calvinism and defining such terms as grace, reprobation, election, and justification, all of which are indispensable to an understanding of Milton. With covenant theology out of the way and Calvinism in its full glory, we turn to Samuel Butler's *Hudibras* and a view of the politics of the interregnum, this time from the Anglican side. Both these books are well worth reading in their own right, of course, but my experience has been that those undergraduate students who previously had some difficulty in absorbing the religious subtleties and political niceties of the period from my lectures now find the issues and ideas vivid and immediate. When we return to

Milton and his *Areopagitica* and sonnets, students read them with considerably more interest and understanding. I leave Milton for the last time to read some of Andrew Marvell's political poems ("An Horatian Ode upon Cromwell's Return from Ireland," "Upon Appleton House," "The First Anniversary of the Government under His Highness the Lord Protector," "A Poem upon the Death of His Late Highness the Lord Protector"). The political context is obvious, and again the material is valuable in its own right. I finish the term with *Samson Agonistes*, partly because of the exigencies of the quarter system, which leaves me no time in the next quarter to teach anything but the two epics. (Many scholars feel that the poem belongs to Milton's middle period anyway.)

The students are now well equipped to begin the study of *Paradise Lost*. I have them buy Joseph Addison's *Critical Essays from the Spectator*, because I have found that his eighteen essays on *Paradise Lost* are more effective as critical commentary and more accessible to undergraduate students than most modern collections of critical essays. Excellent collections, like A. E. Barker's *Milton: Modern Essays in Criticism* and C. A. Patrides's *Milton's Epic Poetry*, work well in graduate courses, but the articles tend to be too technical or narrowly scholarly for undergraduates. On the other hand, Addison, himself an important literary figure, writes clearly, for a general if somewhat sophisticated audience. While the quality of his mind makes his critical comments timeless, he also reflects many of the critical strictures of Milton's contemporaries and, indeed, of Milton himself. Milton's epic, we must remember, appeared in the age of Dryden, and Addison's strictures as well as his praises of the poem were not generally unconventional. His comparisons of *Paradise Lost* to the classical epics—which Milton demands by his use of form, allusions, and even direct challenge—are more germane than ever, because few modern readers are trained in the classics. Moreover, Addison's skills in close reading and his sensitivity to language are valuable models for the student. In particular his singling out of certain passages for their beauty or special merit, not often practiced today, helps direct students' attention to aesthetic considerations of the poem. So, too, some of Addison's censures of specific passages are worth notice. For example, his objection to the image of Uriel sliding down a sunbeam is perfectly valid and allows me to say a few words about the concept of "decorum," a word not much used today but one that Milton would surely want his reader to know. Perhaps Addison's most famous (and most significant) objection is his attack on Milton's use of allegory. Not surprisingly, my students either do not realize that Milton is being allegorical in his passages about Sin, Death, and Chaos or do not know that he is not being allegorical in his accounts of Satan and the angels. While most modern critics no longer find fault with the allegory, Addison's point has merit. Even more important is the students' understanding of the attributes and roles of the characters in the poem, and a discussion of Addison's argument helps to clarify Milton's methods.

In teaching *Paradise Lost* itself, I usually begin with the epic as genre. I distribute handouts of pertinent material from Aristotle and a list of twenty-two epic conventions. While I fill in the backgrounds, the students are asked to read book 1 of the poem and the first six essays from Addison, which deal with the epic in general. In this way, I can use the first book to discuss form, as well as metrics, background, and the like, and Addison makes his contributions as well. By the fourth meeting or so, I once again assign book 1 and ask students to consider Addison's seventh essay, which specifically comments on that book. From here on, I assign the *Spectator* essay that corresponds with the book of the poem. A number of important issues of modern Miltonic criticism have their origin in these essays, including the character of Satan, Milton's use of similes, the narrative voice, the personal digressions, and the war in heaven. The question of the "true hero" of the poem is also an old one, already mentioned by Dryden and taken up by Addison. It creates an excellent entry into the subject of the structure of *Paradise Lost,* as we, in turn, consider the roles of Adam, Satan, and the Son and how they fit into the whole. We generally turn to the structure after we have read the entire epic, and it is then we discuss Milton's revision of the poem from ten to twelve books and the various possibilities of ordering the books—whether in twos, threes, fours, or sixes and how the ordering reinforces theme and meaning.

Addison's essays are not my sole guide to an understanding of the poem, nor are the students being taught the poem as Addison understood it. Addison serves as an introduction, a catalyst, and a historical focus to stimulate ideas and discussion. Recent studies, theories, and critical approaches need not be excluded or slighted. But at an undergraduate level, my emphasis must be on reading the epics, and Addison helps students read Milton with a degree of understanding and appreciation that few other introductions afford them.

Naming and Caring:
The Theme of Stewardship in *Paradise Lost*

Anne Lake Prescott

For some years I have taught *Paradise Lost* in a colloquium on Renaissance literature and in a seminar on literary treatments of heaven, hell, purgatory, and the earthly paradise. Particularly in the latter course students are intrigued by the seductive ambiguity of an imagined natural perfection. What are some common motifs in descriptions of paradise? I ask. Why the recurrent longing for a garden, for structured space? Above all, what is our species' role there and how does it change if we leave?[1] Students enjoy considering the archetypal aspects of Adam's garden kingdom: the images of our naked parents enclosed in an irradiated green space, regally erect or solicitously bending, surrounded by a multiplicity of obedient plants and animals and placed near trees whose high verticals contrast with the curves of serpent and flowing water.[2] Pictures further invigorate this preliminary discussion, and if there is time I play the opening of Handel's music for Dryden's "Song for St. Cecilia's Day." While "Nature underneath a heap / Of jarring Atomes lay," the harmonies themselves lack clear direction; but as the Creator's "tuneful Voice" is "heard from high," the music pulls itself together and both words and music celebrate "The Diapason closing full in Man."

Most students find all this fairly touching, but some wonder if a true paradise should be so anthropocentric and anthropocratic. Yes, according to the Bible: "God said unto them, Be fruitful, and multiply, and replenish the earth, and subdue it: and have dominion over the fish of the sea, and over the fowl of the air, and over every living thing that moveth upon the earth" (Genesis 1.28), words Milton paraphrases (7.531–34). Is this arrogant self-delusion? In recent years when teaching Milton I have raised the issue myself, briefly explaining why some people are irritated with Jehovah for giving us lordship or with Western civilization for fantasizing such an arrangement.

Recent discussion of human dominion has been given impetus by Lynn White's article "The Historical Roots of Our Ecological Crisis," first published in 1967 and often reprinted. White says that "By destroying pagan animism, Christianity made it possible to exploit nature in a mood of indifference to the feelings of natural objects" (1205). Secure in de jure as well as de facto dominion over the earth and believing that the God in whose image humanity was made had planned matters so that "no item in the physical creation had any purpose save to serve man's purposes," Western Christianity "bears a

157

huge burden of guilt" (1206). Others disagree. White certainly over-simplifies, and statements such as his assertion that Greek intellectuals could not conceive of a beginning to the world are simply wrong. His critics also point to ecological disasters in older and non-Western cultures, suggest he exaggerates religion's impact on technology, remind us that Greeks and Romans could also think the world designed for ourselves (stirring arguments to this effect appear in Cicero, *De natura deorum*, bk. 2), and cite passages in the Bible that promote not tyranny but stewardship.[3]

Even White's critics, however, agree we must further abandon power hunger and technological pride, unthinking belief in endless progress, and an exclusively mechanistic and atomistic view of the cosmos as unrelated particles of inert matter in motion. To exercise our by-now-unavoidable power more wisely, we need both holism and humility, a recognition that the world's constituent parts, including people, are both interrelated and significant in themselves and that all—to those with a religious sensibility—share in God's presence. Modern physics, in fact, suggests that nature is not made of tiny bits of material but, at its subatomic level, is as much event and energetic relation as it is substance (Schilling). True, such views alarm English majors, who often resist post-Newtonian science, but they have an uncanny kinship with some older scientific attitudes. Conceptual difficulties remain, of course, for while modern zoology has become less anthropomorphic, our popular culture has developed more fellow feeling for animals and even vegetation (in "Doonesbury" Zonker talks to his houseplants, and they talk back in studentese). So some of us will be better stewards from a renewed religious sense of creaturely relatedness, others from agnostic prudence. In any case, I tell my students, Milton's own treatment of stewardship can inspire them to further thought, whether by sympathetic or contrary motion.

After the class has mulled over the issue of stewardship for a while, I remind them of some late Renaissance attitudes. To be sure, there was no one view of "nature" and consequently no one view of humanity's position in it (Tayler). Nevertheless, it is clear, for example, that most people believed our dominion is over created nature, *natura naturata*, not over Mother Nature herself, *natura naturans*. Furthermore, although technology was developing rapidly and sometimes irresponsibly, some, like Bacon himself, chief promoter of human "empire," warned that we should extend our power with charity and reverence (McCutcheon). And many people were still convinced that animals, plants, and stars mean something: "From the highest Angell to the lowest worme, all teach us somewhat" (Nehemiah Rogers, qtd.

in Prescott 223). Milton's Raphael thus anticipates a long tradition when he tells Adam the sky is "the Book of God before thee set" (8. 67). Yes, the concept is anthropocentric, but those who express it usually do so with love and gratitude. A little silkworm, for instance, signifies the Resurrection when "by a prodigious metamorphosis it is born anew a Butterfly": those who study such tiny creatures will think of God and "cry out, O the depth!" (Thomas Moffett, in Topsell 1039). Whatever this silkworm's practical utility, it is not a mere morsel of desacralized matter awaiting exploitation.

This nature is hierarchal, a chain of being, not the democracy of creatures Lynn White calls for. But the cosmologies and aesthetics associated with it were changing and in fact had never been as stable as some moderns believe. I discuss several different Renaissance cosmological designs from Heninger (*Cosmological Glass* and *Touches of Sweet Harmony*), asking what sorts of feeling or imagination they might encourage; I recall that Milton committed himself to no one structure. Nor was Earth's central position a cause for pride, since in pre-Copernican cosmologies the power and the glory are *up* (Lovejoy, *Great Chain of Being* 101–02). The point is worth making because unless otherwise instructed, and despite Milton's cosmological agnosticism, students are likely to tie Adam's dominion too tightly to geocentricity.

Humanity's superior place in this hierarchy is due in part to speech and intellectual understanding, yet Eden's animals "reason not contemptibly" (8.374). Montaigne's "Apology for Raymond Sebond" is a good source for humbling stories of reasonable and even religious animals (note the sun-worshiping elephants). Particularly destabilizing of modern assumptions about past attitudes are Renaissance anecdotes, sometimes not always serious, concerning articulate beasts. Henry VIII's parrot, they say, fell in the Thames and squawked "A boat! a boat! twenty pounds for a boat!" but once restored to the king ungenerously said of the waterman who rescued him, "Give the knave a groat" (Thomas 128). Another talkative if shady animal is the ape shipwrecked in the Aegean. A passing rustic can't identify his species and before helping him ashore asks him what he is. A man, lies the ape. What sort? An Athenian. Still dubious, the man asks if he knows Piraeus (the port near Athens). Oh yes, says the ape smoothly, and his wife, friends, and children. Understandably irritated, the rustic tries to drown him (Topsell 4; the story derives ultimately from Aesop).

Milton's views of animals and stewardship were partly shaped by scripture. My students sometimes assume that Milton could simply rely on what "the Bible says," so I stress the extent to which scripture was subjected to commentary, debate, exegesis, paraphrase, and allegorizing (Corcoran; Evans). I tell them Philo Judaeus's reading of Adam as reason and the animals as passions, although I admit *Paradise Lost* is not an allegory, and as an example of commentary I bring in a facsimile of the heavily annotated 1560 Geneva translation, explaining that many English readers preferred it to the King James. I focus on Genesis and Psalms. In both text and marginalia students will find, certainly, that creation was made for human beings, but the Puritan translators respond thankfully to a living world that God cares for. Do we have blessing, dominion, and all plants for food? Then "Gods great liberalitie to man taketh away all excuse for his ingratitude" (Gen. 1.29 n.). God tells Noah to avoid meat with blood (Gen. 9.4), which the note says means that we must not strangle beasts in order to retain their fluids: "and hereby all crueltie is forbidden."

Similarly, when Psalm 96 tells trees to rejoice in the Lord, the margin remarks that if they can do so, so should we. In Psalm 104 "The lions roare after their praie, and seke their mete at God," the notes explaining that God "careth even for the brute beastes" as "a most nourishing Father." Nor is the world utterly desacralized, for a note to Psalm 147 says "His secret working in all creatures is as a commandement to kepe them in ordre, and to give them moving and force." Compare *Paradise Lost* 11.336–38. Furthermore, psalms and marginal comments sometimes move from delighted amazement at God as Lord of nature to awed fear of him as judge of history (see esp. Ps. 96), exactly the direction Milton takes in Michael's speech of instruction and consolation. All the more reason, then, for men and women to be careful stewards; unlike animals they are accountable (cf. *Paradise Lost* 4.622, for I think that is what Milton means here; see the *OED*).

One scriptural text, however, seems to offer a harsher view. Paul asks "doeth God take care for oxen?" (1 Cor. 9.9). He is interpreting the Mosaic law forbidding muzzles on working oxen, and the Geneva note paraphrases: "Had God respect properly to the oxen them selves when he made this Law, and not rather unto men?" Some in Milton's day did read this as license to act without regard for animals' well-being (Thomas 24), but the Genevan editors are interested primarily in the still-disputed question of whether laws, divine laws in this case, apply to an animal qua animal and not to an animal as property or as the object of human concern. Would even God make a law for beasts other than the laws he has implanted in them as instincts? So, too, my town's law against roaming dogs is directed to the dog's owners, not "with respect properly to the [dogs] them selves," and laws protecting dolphins are read by tuna fishermen, not by the dolphins—indeed some argue that such laws eventually are for our own sake: they protect us from the brutalizing immorality of committing delphinicide. In any case it is clear that the Genevan editors thought God "cared" for oxen in the usual sense; after all, Jesus says his father notes the sparrow's fall. And Milton's God says explicitly he loves all his creatures (3.276–77).

There is no space here to explore all passages in *Paradise Lost* relevant to a discussion of stewardship. I mention only a few essential points. First, Milton's world is indeed hierarchal and anthropocentric, ruled by a pair made in God's image (4.288–95), although like others Milton sees this "image" as referring primarily to moral understanding, not to creativity or mere power. Like classical writers, Milton emphasizes the first man's erect posture, but for Milton this dignity was expressed in stewardly work, not in golden-age indolence (see also the Genevan notes to Gen. 2.15). Like a good ruler, Adam also understands his subjects and gives them the right names. Lynn White sees this naming as another arrogance (interestingly, Vergil says in *Georgics* 1.137 that the golden age was before the sailor learned to number the stars and "nomina fecit" 'give them names'). But the matter is indeed very complex, touching on the relation of word to thing. Milton's Adam does not arbitrarily impose human sounds, whatever his descendants do; rather, he works from an illuminated understanding granted by God (8.338–54). Edenic naming is thus the act not of a *dict*ator but of one who apprehends the nature of the things named.

Adam and Eve, who also gives names, are rulers but not despots. For Adam, as for so many others, our cosmos is not merely an empire to be manipulated but a sign-bearing text whose study leads to wisdom and celebration. That it is made for humanity inspires only gratitude, humility, and perspective. True, Adam's rule is "absolute" (4. 301), for his position cannot be limited or conditioned (see the *OED*) by negotiations with his subjects—one cannot make a contract with an animal (although, to be sure, many of us sense an unspoken contract with certain beasts of our acquaintance and, in fact, God tells Noah the rainbow is a sign of covenant with the whole earth). Yet this same passage says that Adam derives his "authority" from "filial" freedom. Unlike future tyrants such as Charles i, Adam has a living father he must obey, one who loves the creation, animating it from within as well as ordering it from above. Nor does Milton allow Adam a sharply defined centrality, for the poet suggests there are possibly populated expanses of the universe with uses unknown to us and having their own relations with God.

Also illuminating, and suited to encouraging students to talk, is a close look at what unfallen stewardship in the garden was like. In space orderly enough to be rescued from wilderness yet in which nature "wanton'd as in her prime" (5.295), even boughs are "compliant" (4.331–32) and animals happy. Gardening is directed toward a restraint that encourages nature to fulfill herself more truly; binding and pruning promote not Versailles-like formality but fertile sinuosity as the feminine fruit-bearing vine is coiled around the vertical masculine elm. Of course such harmonious stewardship is now lost, and another good topic for discussion is the specific impact on it of the fall. Milton is explicit that all the world "felt the wound" (9.782), but to press further into the matter one can ask how the fall changes the first pair's perception of nature and the behavior of their now recalcitrant subjects. What is wrong with Eve's worship of the forbidden tree? What function do groves now serve? What does Adam call Eden after Eve's fall? Earth once fed us gladly; what will she do to us now? How does the curse on Adam enforce a new relation to the soil and what feelings does this change produce?

Because of our own anxieties about technology it is also instructive to see how Milton treats lapsed *homo faber*. In Eden there is minimal technology, Adam and Eve merely using melon rinds as simple biodegradable dippers. Once expelled, however, humankind must invent (God himself makes clothes for his sorrowing children). Good people struggling in a now less generous world know God's "works / Not hid, nor those things last which might preserve / Freedom and Peace to men" (11.578–80). But Michael roundly condemns those who abuse technology through vanity, who seek "Arts that polish Life, Inventors rare, / Unmindful of thir Maker" (11.610–11). Even worse is Nimrod, who wields "Dominion undeserv'd / Over his brethren" and erects the tower of Babel. Having earlier considered issues of stewardship and language, students are equipped to examine Milton's treatment of Nimrod (12.24–78) in terms of false dominion, dispossession, and prideful technology for the sake of "a name." God's punishment involves yet further division in humankind, a confusion of tongues. Here the theme of stewardship connects importantly with that of words and names and also with questions of political justice. The Nimrod passage is a model of complex negative redefinition (e.g., "name") and parodic irony (e.g., we see what "dominion" can become).

We are left, of course, with the paradise within, though this paradise too needs gardening by good and faithful internal stewards, for we have internal Nimrods as well, to say nothing of internal Babels, and perhaps even a serpent or two. Stewardship, as I hope my students discover, is not only a pressing social and ecological issue for fallen humanity; there is an analogous, or perhaps preliminary, need to restrain and redirect within the self those same impulses that now degrade our external environment and lead us to betray the role that God or chance has given us. Milton's perceptions of that role would not please all modern ecologists, but his insights into how our stewardship can go wrong are strikingly relevant to our condition.[4]

NOTES

[1] Many have written on such matters. I have been particularly helped by Stewart (good on the religious connotations of gardens); Giamatti; Strong; and Comito, who has some lovely and relevant quotations (e.g., Ambrose says, "We cannot fully know ourselves without first knowing the nature of all living creatures" [38], and Augustine asks, "Can reason speak more intimately with nature than when setting out seeds, planting slips, or trimming shrubs?" [37]).

[2] Even if such writers are inebriating, I sometimes expound a little on Jung, *Man and His Symbols* (an aerial view of Eden would show a mandala), and Eliade, *The Sacred and the Profane* (as Comito says, although Milton claims God "Attributes to place / No sanctitie," his Eden has all the flavor of sacred space [36]). See also Armstrong; and Duncan, "Archetypes."

[3] Hamilton; Scoby; Barbour, *Earth Might Be Fair* and *Western Man and Environmental Ethics*; Blackstone; Spring and Spring; and Passmore. These authors are not always trustworthy on literary or cultural history. The essential work on what Milton's generation felt is Keith Thomas, who traces a general tendency away from confidence in our right to rule while also showing that the late Renaissance held contradictory attitudes. The early modern period saw an *increased* anthropocentricity, Thomas says, but he quotes Philip Stubbes as saying that although carnivores "be evil to us and thirst after our blood, yet are they good creatures in their own nature and kind" (157), and during the Civil War a certain sectary claimed that "God loves the creatures that creep on the ground as well as the best saints, and there is no difference between the flesh of a man and the flesh of a toad" (166). Thomas points to the biblical origins of some such attitudes and to the surprisingly large role of the Protestant clergy in advancing them; one preacher called man's dominion "subordinate and stewardly, not absolutely to do what he list to do with God's creatures" (155).

[4] Throughout this discussion students work on papers on such topics as the impact of the fall on Adam's and Eve's views of nature; a study of Ovid's version of the creation and the transition from the golden to the iron age, with its increasing differentiation, its change from soft to hard metals and from the curved lines of wandering at will to the straight lines of agriculture and

written law (cf. modern laments as the Army Corps of Engineers straightens out our rivers and as paper companies plant firs in rows); a comparison with a radically different culture's creation myth, such as the splendid Polynesian story of the trickery and violence by which humanity established its dominion over all the rest of creation except hurricanes (Long). Milton's Eden can also be compared to other Renaissance *loci amoeni* (see Knott), or to modern paradises like C. S. Lewis's *Perelandra*, or to negative creations with distorted dominion like William Golding's *Pincher Martin*. Sometimes I ask students to write a brief description of their own imaginary perfect garden; the results are endearing and provide a basis for a few remarks on archetypal persistence and modern shifts in style.

Dancing around Milton's Allusions

William Malin Porter

In the two centuries following Milton's death, no dimension of *Paradise Lost* was more thoroughly and persistently investigated than its allusiveness to prior literary and scriptural tradition. Patrick Hume's commentary of 1695, the first in the field, set the example for its epigones—including the great editions of Newton, Todd, and Verity—in spending the major part of its effort on the identification of Milton's allusive targets (see Oras). The topic was generally regarded as of major consequence, and the poem's readers as well as its editors were capable of appreciating it in some detail.

Today, however, almost no dimension of the poetry is more inaccessible—not only for undergraduates but, I dare say, for contemporary scholars as well, even classicists such as myself. At its best, contemporary American education does not bring students to Milton already in thorough and confident possession of Western literature's foundational texts, the Homeric epics, the *Aeneid*, and the Bible—not even in translation. And yet what is wanted is not what we call "familiarity," the product of Lit Trad 100 in freshman year, or what we call "intimacy," the ability to find one's way around these books (aided by a massive commentative apparatus and bibliographical digests), such as one seldom achieves nowadays before the master's thesis stage. What is wanted—what Milton had to a supreme degree and not too fancifully expected from his contemporary readers—is a minute verbal recollection of these books, that is, the knowledge of tremendous amounts of both the Bible and secular literature by heart, preferably in the original:

> . . . and ere this time the Hebrew tongue at a set hour might have been gained, that the Scriptures may be read in their own original; whereto it would be no impossibility to add the Chaldee and the Syrian dialect. When all these employments are well conquered, then will the choice histories, heroic poems, and Attic tragedies of stateliest and most regal argument, with all the famous political orations, offer themselves; which, if they were not only read, but some of them got by memory, would endue them even with the spirit and vigor of Demosthenes or Cicero, Euripides or Sophocles.

Thus Milton in the letter to Mr. Hartlib, *Of Education*, describes in passing how a pupil might pick up what today would be the requirement of at least two PhDs. I grant that *Of Education* describes an ideal, not common reality, and that in Milton's day as in our own there was variety in intellectual attainments. Good Greek was not the property of every educated person; still fewer knew Hebrew. But tolerably good Latin—including thorough knowledge of the *Aeneid* and Ovid's *Metamorphoses*—and an even more thorough knowledge of the Bible, albeit in English, would have been universal among Milton's readers. It is a discouraging prospect.

Quae cum ita sint, some teachers no doubt despair and either ignore the topic of intertextuality altogether or, what is almost worse, relegate it (no matter with what private regret) to the "background." I am not unsympathetic to these difficult decisions. But to decide either way is to give a "primary" reading to a supremely "secondary" text. To treat the allusions as "background" is willy-nilly to suggest to today's students that the knowledge this material demands is an accident of the poem's historical provenance, part of the queer lore of the seventeenth century and not clearly a different kind of thing from a taste for Sylvester's DuBartas or such quaint notions as the Ptolemaic cosmology, witches, demons, and the virtue of chastity. To ignore the allusions altogether can make for a somewhat more efficient reading of the poem, perhaps even a more immediately satisfying one. Strictly in itself, *Paradise Lost* is undeniably a fascinating document of the English seventeenth century, offering advantageous perspectives on the political and religious history of the time. Constrained in such a context, however, it tends to become a poem about John Milton and in so doing allows us to reduce its vast erudition to data in the poet's psychological profile. These are grave sacrifices. Only if one is willing to let the poem or, if need be, to *help* the poem resonate throughout the literary tradition—ideally forward to the Romantics as well as backward to the ancients—does it reveal itself in its full majesty as epic, that is, as a comprehensive representation of the violent and fundamental antinomies that continually threaten to rend Western civilization asunder and yet animate it as well: Bible against classics, ancients against moderns, humankind against God.

What then are we poor pedagogues to do? Let us treat the pre-texts as seriously as our knowledge and the finitude of our syllabuses will permit, never conceding for a moment to the students (or to ourselves) 'that they might be able to read the poem "simply for the story." Some supplementary reading is necessary; not that reading a few pages from Milton's library of pre-texts has tremendous intrinsic value, but it does give the student someplace to stand and listen for at least one or two of the voices in Milton's strange, polyphonic argument with antiquity. And in view of the disadvantage at which we find ourselves with respect to the subtleties of verbal allusion, it is well to remember that there are other aspects to Milton's engagement of the pre-texts: generic conventions, structure, portrayal of character, the similes, classical and biblical style, and the handling of major biblical sources. Let us look closely at these macrophenomena while dancing suggestively around the allusions.

But I must turn to the example of my own imperfect application of the imperfect solution I have described. Now, as a scholiast I have been concerned with these matters for the last half dozen years or so; but unlike most contributors to this volume, I do not teach Milton regularly, so I cannot speak about how I "usually" deal with his allusiveness in my classes. Although my lower degrees are in English, my doctorate is in classics, and it is in a classics program that I presently make my home; my teaching of *Paradise Lost* is limited to books 9–12 in a course titled Homer and the Bible. The course on Milton I give an account of here was one I offered in spring of 1982 at the gracious invitation of the English department of Brandeis University, where I was doing research on a Mellon fellowship. It had a deliberately conventional reading list (major poetry except *Paradise Regained*; much of the minor poetry; *Areopagitica* and other selected prose), but because of the high quality of the students (upperclassmen and graduate students) and the peculiarity of my position as an outsider, I enjoyed considerable latitude in approach. Naturally, my focus throughout the semester was on the dimension of intertextuality (see the final examination appended to this essay).

Before coming to *Paradise Lost,* the students became well acquainted with certain basic problems of intertextuality through the Nativity ode, "Lycidas," and the *Epitaphium Damonis*, on which we spent a long time. (I pass over much not pertinent here.) I paid special attention to the conventions of pastoral (both as a genre and as a "mode"), as matters of interest in themselves but also as exemplary of the problem of intertextuality. The students read *Eclogues* 4, 5, and 10 of Vergil and Spenser's "November" from the *Shepheardes Calender.* Vergil was at the center of my lectures, which explored how he gave pastoral its "secondary" character; his introduction of the autobiographical allegory; pastoral as the training ground for epic (cf. Spenser); the Messianic eclogue; and the ease with which Vergilian allegory of the poet became in Christian hands an allegory of the Church (rumination on shepherding as symbol of more exalted vocations). I met privately with those students who could read some Latin, to do a little Vergil and some of Milton's *Epitaphium.* Through discussion of the odd fact that Milton chose Latin rather than English for his more heartfelt lament, we wondered about the status of Latin in his day. Those with no Latin read one of a couple of good essays on reserve and wrote one-page reports. In class discussion the two groups learned from each other. It was also possible to examine a few strong verbal allusions. The detailed attention we gave these poems was crucial to my semester's plan. Here in small students were able to see Milton's allusiveness at work and even to appreciate it to some extent. Later when we got to *Paradise Lost,* whose allusiveness is of quite unmanageable proportions and forced me to become increasingly sketchy, they were prepared at least to consider that its meaning might be as bound up with the Bible and the *Aeneid* as I claimed and were capable of thinking about what it meant if it was.

Even when we reached *Paradise Lost* itself, I spent extra time at first preparing the scene. To suggest something about the poem's original audience, I distributed a translation of the Latin elegiacs prefixed to the poem (by "S.B.") and commented particularly on the allusion to Propertius's reception of the *Aeneid,* "cedite Romani scriptores, cedite Graii" (cf. Propertius 2.34.65). (This invites incidental reference to Pound's *Homage,* pt. 12, and perhaps a digression on the modernists' reception of Milton.) Certain programmatic implications in Milton's note "The Verse" ("ancient liberty recover'd to Heroic Poem") were also unraveled.

The opening to book 1, roughly the first hundred lines but of course the invocation especially, received the most careful comment. My principal aims at this point regarding intertextuality were relatively simple: first, to observe the grammatical, rhetorical, and thematic resemblances and differences between Milton's opening and those of his most authoritative classical models and, second, to demonstrate that those models are present even after the first thirty lines or so when Milton's allusions become less concentrated. I distributed to the students translations of the openings of the Homeric epics, Hesiod's *Theogony,* and the *Aeneid.* We used Lattimore for Homer and Hesiod, but Dryden for Vergil; the contrast between the translations themselves enabled the students to get some sense of the peculiarly classical resonance of Milton's opening. The Bible was mentioned only briefly at this point, to explain why *Paradise Lost* begins with a preposition (cf. "In the beginning . . .") rather than a thematic keyword (cf. Homer's *mēnin* 'wrath' and *andra* 'man,' Hesiod's *Mousaōn* 'the Muses,' and Vergil's *arma virumque cano*) and to gloss one or two references ("that shepherd," "Siloa's brook," etc.). Then we looked briefly at two particular verbal allusions, line 74 ("As from the Center thrice to th' utmost Pole"), alluding to *Theogony* 722–25 and *Aeneid* 6.

577–79, and line 84 ("If thou beest hee; But O how fall'n! how chang'd"), alluding to *Aeneid* 2.275–76. The first of these is important because it ironically typifies the one-upmanship of many of the allusions ("thrice") and warns the reader, that is, the student, not to interpret Milton's intertextual arguments simplemindedly; the second typifies what I call the ethical allusions, in which a Miltonic figure derives credit or discredit by association with a classical hero (here Aeneas, to the enhancement rather than the discredit of Satan's character). All in all we spent a week in class on these preliminaries, which constituted the first phase of my treatment of the poem. Meanwhile the students were reading ahead.

During the second phase, the next three weeks or so, we worked our way through the poem largely on the "primary" level; the few divagations from the strict construction of the narrative I permitted concerned matters such as Milton's biography, theology, and politics. Not that I let the pre-texts be forgotten. I came to class each day with a short list of particulars deserving notice for their exemplary value, such as Latinisms in diction and syntax (e.g., the differences in the prelapsarian and postlapsarian meanings of several words, such as "error," 4.239 and 9.1181), striking instances of biblical or classical style, the similes, and, not least important, the allusions, a few of which were remarked on at this point, but briefly. I spent a businesslike minute on these before beginning each lecture. I should admit that, while I made these observations as succinctly as possibly in order not to strain the student's patience, even this brief handling of disconnected particulars would not have been possible, or at least would not have been advisable, with less advanced students than I was fortunate to have.

Supplementary readings were deliberately deferred until we had worked through most of *Paradise Lost*'s narrative, the "primary" argument. From the Bible, I assigned what is obviously indispensable: Genesis 1–3, James 1.12–15, and Revelation 12. From the classics, in addition to the various epic invocations already mentioned, I chose *Aeneid* 6 (in Mandelbaum's poetically inferior but grammatically more accurate translation, rather than Dryden's; I would now prefer Robert Fitzgerald's superb new version). The *Aeneid* is the single classical work most frequently alluded to both verbally and structurally; and book 6, which is nodal not only for Vergil's poem but for the entire tradition, is the single most important for Milton. The few sentences from James's Epistle were read early, but the passage from Revelation was deferred until after we had read *Paradise Lost* 6; Genesis 1–3 was assigned after book 10, and *Aeneid* 6, only after we had completed our initial reading of the entire poem. The consideration of the poem, in part or in whole, in relation to these pre-texts constituted phase three of my presentation. (Of course, phases two and three overlapped here and there.)

I recommend this reversal of what seems the logical order of reading as the single most important aspect of a successful classroom approach to Milton's intertextuality. Reading the pre-texts first is in fact much less effective, for several reasons. First, the immediate motive for reading them will be less clear, so the student's attention will inevitably be somewhat hesitant. Second, memory of the details—important matters often—of the relatively brief pre-texts will be obliterated as the student reads Milton's expansive epic. Third, the pre-texts will inevitably appear to be background only in the literary-historical sense; that is to say, the putative present relevance of the pre-texts to *Paradise Lost*, which motivated reading them in the first place, is, in the end, subtly called into question or at least diminished. On the other hand, if the excerpts are deferred as I suggest, Milton himself will seem to direct and stimulate the student's reading of them, and the questions that arise then will naturally reflect back on *Paradise Lost*.

Deferring these assignments will also raise the large thematic questions at the most appropriate time: near the end of one's study of *Paradise Lost*. The issues these readings raise are as various as one could want. I began by asking how Milton's account of the fall differs from that in Genesis and what the differences might mean; Basil Willey (234–58) has provocative things to say in this regard. I lectured on Milton's structural allusions to the *Aeneid* and argued that Vergil's presentation of the human condition, including fate and the problem of evil, is to an extent bound up with the formal character of epic as he fixed it for later tradition. How, I then asked, does Milton's choice of the Vergilian form compel him to reconsider the same problems in similar terms? Reference to the different attainments enabled by Dante's un-Vergilian form helps here greatly.

It was in this context, that is, in the course of a thematic summation, that I finally dealt at some length with a few critical allusions. I give here only one example and that but partially. In reference to the problem of evil, I spent an entire lecture on a single allusion—or perhaps it should be called an allusive complex. In *Paradise Lost* the serpent asks:

> What can your knowledge hurt him, or this Tree
> Impart against his will if all be his?

> Or is it envy, and can envy dwell
> In heav'nly breasts?   (9.727–30)

Milton is alluding to Vergil's great thematic question, "tantaene animis caelestibus irae?," literally, "Are there such great angers in heavenly spirits?" (*Aeneid* 1.11). Although Milton's English does not translate the Latin line exactly (as a rule his critical allusions deliberately alter the terms of the target line in some significant way), the allusion, nevertheless, is easy to recognize, because the tag from the *Aeneid* is famous and conspicuously placed in its own context; the students recalled it—at least they did once I reminded them—because they had some weeks earlier studied Vergil's proem carefully:

> Can heav'nly minds such high resentment show,
> Or exercise their spite in human woe?   (trans. John Dryden)

Of course, Dryden overtranslates, but his departure from the original, like Milton's, is deliberate. The rhetorical effect of this keynote line's placement at the end of the first part of Vergil's proem (not entirely forgetting its counterpoise at line 33, "tantae molis erat Romanam condere gentem" 'Such a great enterprise it was to found the Roman race' [trans. mine]) is analogous to the effect of Milton's ambitious "And justify the ways of God to Men." Both lines seem fundamentally to be hinting at the same thing: the problem of suffering in human experience. When asked to compare these opening lines, my students readily observed that Vergil's sentence is interrogative and Milton's declarative. With a little coaxing, however, they discovered that these grammatical differences, characteristic though they are of the two poets, nevertheless mask a surprising degree of synonymity or at least similarity of motive: for Vergil's question, which appears rhetorical, turns out to be genuine, while Milton's confident declaration implies that God's ways are in need of justification, perhaps even that to supply this justification is a bold and difficult labor ("tantae molis . . ." may echo here, too). But to return to the allusion in book 9. Space does not permit me here to pursue the ramifications of this strong allusion much further, but let me note that many lines of inquiry suggested themselves. I observed that Vergil's question is answered, chillingly, by Jupiter at *Aeneid* 12.831 ("irarum tantos . . . fluctūs" 'such great torrents of anger'), as he and Juno conclude their peace negotiation. Why, I then asked, does Milton call to mind just at this crucial juncture in his poem a line that virtually emblematizes the entire *Aeneid*? Does he mean to discredit Satan by associating him with the desperation of Vergil's vision (or vice versa)? But what are we then to make of the fact that here in book 9 Milton is alluding not only to Vergil but to himself as well, in a line earlier in the poem: "In heav'nly Spirits could such perverseness dwell?" (*Paradise Lost* 6.788). This is Raphael's question, not Satan's, and the "heav'nly Spirits" are angels. Now we are getting closer to the purport of Vergil's line. Raphael describes the rebellious angels as "proud" and "obdurate" and says they "took envy" at the sight of the Son's exaltation (line 793). Here I summarized the pertinent results of a little work with both the Miltonic and Vergilian concordances, s.vv. "envy" and "ira." (Patrick Hume, *Paradise Lost*'s first scholiast, needed only his memory.) Among other things, it was now possible to comment on Milton's "mistranslation" at 9.729: Vergil had changed Homer's "wrath" to "anger," and Milton in turn transformed "anger" into "envy" as the prime motive of epic destruction. We had traced a circuitous path, but at the end of the hour the unpretentious line we began with, "and can envy dwell / In heav'nly breasts?," rang with meanings like a bell choir, and the students had the sense that some of the greatest poets of the tradition were witnesses to the fall.

I hope this very restrained example will suffice to make clear why I recommend "dancing around" most of Milton's allusions, why I myself in the month and a half we spent on *Paradise Lost* examined with such care only a few. A critical allusion such as the one above is a trapdoor to the great tradition; once through it, one must be prepared to wander. The curious, of course, will want to consult some of what has been published on the subject. My recommendations for starters: on the Bible, J. H. Sims; on the classical allusions, Blessington; and one of my own essays.

On the other hand, I would not wish to give the impression that everything commonly called allusion can endure such probing. The mythological allusions, for example, are not such a problem. If students do not know who "Proserpin" or Pomona is and feel Hughes's note is inadequate, they go to the library to consult the *Milton Encyclopedia*. Most even of the verbal allusions that Hughes or other editors have caught in their nets are small fry, weak references, simple borrowings or thefts, mere echoes or reminiscences. None of these is very significant in itself; their effect is cumulative and is suggested well enough for our purposes by their ubiquity in the notes.

My task in this brief essay has demanded more exclusive attention to allusion than I actually gave in my class. I should affirm, then, appearances to the contrary notwithstanding, that in general I did not segregate the consideration of intertextuality and allusion from any of the other topics that were raised in the semester, such as the poet's biography; the Puritan revolution and the poet's role in the Commonwealth; his private theology and the theology of the late Reformation; his opinions on science, free speech, divorce, and the general relations between the sexes. Quite the contrary, I tried on the one hand never to treat the ancient books without clear motive of present interest, whether ours or Milton's; and on the other I thought it only right for me to permit the ancients to assert themselves whenever Milton himself seemed to, which is to say constantly and apropos of every sort of issue.

Such were my procedures. I have used them, *mutatis mutandis*, in other classes as well: in modern poetry, in pastoral, and in The Renaissance Ovid in England, not to mention my classes in Latin literature. The effect is double: first, the students achieve a remarkable degree of understanding of the nature of "secondary" poetry such as Milton's; and second, from that understanding it follows that to take Milton's poetry seriously means to take his pre-texts seriously as well—not all his sources, but those few ancient books of greatest authority or self-assertive power.

This essay argues along the same lines. It might be worth saying, as I conclude, that taking the ancients seriously means being willing to admit and to live with the fact that interpreting *them* is a tricky business, too. This is both a burden and a liberation. Wrestling with the books yourself, as Milton did line by line, is harder but infinitely more enjoyable and rewarding than stealing an interpretation from Milton's age that can be presented in a brief class lecture. For one thing, the approach does Milton no credit, not to mention the disservice done to the Bible or the classics. A good deal of superficially historical scholarship has saddled Milton with readings of the great books whose naïveté or wrongheadedness is apparent even to a moderately bright sophomore, that is, a student who has (as yet) no stake in upholding Milton's preeminence as a conqueror of the Tradition. Perhaps it is advisable to stand back from the details of Milton's work, life, and times, to survey the whole and reflect on the evidence that Milton was also a great reader.

In any case, the truth is that the attempt to distill the essence of Milton's beliefs about his pre-texts is not literary historical science but critical alchemy. Its results are sometimes interesting; nonetheless, it yields no gold. There was certainly no coherent or unified seventeenth-century view of the classics, and if Milton had a particular view, he kept it to himself. (*Paradise Regained* 4 is hardly unambiguous evidence.) Indeed, the *De doctrina christiana* notwithstanding, we scarcely have a more coherent view of Milton's interpretation of the Bible. The cardinal principle of his biblical hermeneutics as expressed in *De doctrina christiana,* chapter 30, appears to have been, "We are expressly forbidden to pay attention to any traditions whatsoever" (Bohn Library translation). This is his echo of Luther's *sola scriptura.* It means: read the original texts and make up your own mind. So one should feel free to judge more or less directly the comparison of the Bible or the classical epics to Milton's poem. This liberty is essential to the pedagogical consideration of Milton's allusions. Prudence constrains scholarship a bit more narrowly, but only a bit, and in the classroom one can and must take a few more risks.

APPENDIX
Final Examination for English 153b

Category A (early poems). Choose one.

Before answering one of the following questions, recollect briefly the various aspects that Milton's *mature* poetry presents to us: e.g., prosody, thought, literary and scriptural allusion, genre, understanding of history and politics, etc. So far as you can tell, what is conventional in Milton's poetry and what is peculiarly Miltonic?

Question 1 (pastoral). Many Renaissance poets followed Vergil's example, preparing for epic by writing pastoral (e.g., Petrarch, Tasso, Spenser). List and describe some of the advantages *Milton* may have derived from this progress. You may refer to any of the early poems, but I would like you to think especially of "Lycidas" and the *Epitaphium Damonis.* [Hints: What is it about pastoral that makes it an appropriate mode for the apprentice poet and, moreover, conduces to epic? In what ways was it even more advantageous to Milton than to Vergil? You will need to reconsider the nature of pastoral both as genre and as "mode." You might *briefly* consider, chiefly by way of contrast to Milton, the benefits got by those many twentieth-century authors who, aspiring to write novels, train themselves preliminarily in the short story (e.g., Joyce).]

Question 2 (sonnets). In what various ways did Milton's occasional labor at sonnets advance him toward *Paradise Lost?* You should make reference to these sonnets, at least: nos. 8, 10, 12, 15, 18, 19, and 23. [Keep in mind that Milton continued to write sonnets, although only infrequently, well after he had given up pastoral, masque, and the larger early forms he had experimented in. Consider, if you are able, the formal developments—or regressions—Milton effected in the tradition of the English sonnet.]

Category B (*Samson Agonistes*). Choose one.

Question 1 (Chorus). Describe the Chorus's interpretation of the action, internal and external, in *Samson Agonistes*, from the *parodos* (where they enter), through the five *stasima* (choral odes between dramatic episodes), to their final words. Relate the Chorus's understanding of what happens to Samson's and your understanding. What is the point of having a Chorus at all? Shakespeare seems to have done perfectly well without one. [Incidental matter: What do you make, if anything, of the prosodic peculiarities of the choral odes? Obviously, they set the odes apart from the dramatic dialogue as a distinct poetic medium, but how, and why? Critics have disagreed about the quality of the choral writing in *Samson Agonistes*, especially with respect to rhyming. Some regard the odes as sublimely beautiful, while others consider them deliberate doggerel. Are you inclined to either judgment?]

Question 2 (episode 5). Give a reading of the fifth episode (lines 1301 to 1659), demonstrating its contribution to the meaning of the drama. [Among other things, consider the following: the motive of Samson's peripety; the significance of Manoa's return to the scene: the effect of the fact that the catastrophe is not presented *dramatically*—as we would say—but reported (cf. Raphael's narrative in *PL*).]

Category C. One topic, everyone must treat.

How should we describe the relation between Milton's later *magna opera, Paradise Lost* and *Samson Agonistes,* and the biblical stories on which they are based? [Hints: Compare and contrast Milton's poems to other works adapted from originals in different media, e.g., modern movies based on short stories or novels, novels based on history. How are we to interpret Milton's claims to divine inspiration? Is it possible to discern some intrinsic distinction between literature and Scripture? Does it matter to how we read Milton's poetry? Try to refer your theoretical argument to specific parts of the poems that give rise to interpretative problems.]

PARTICIPANTS IN SURVEY
OF MILTON INSTRUCTORS

The following scholars and teachers of Milton generously agreed to participate in the survey of approaches to teaching *Paradise Lost* that preceded the preparation of this volume. Without their invaluable assistance and support, the volume simply would not have been possible.

Howard C. Adams, Frostburg State College; John M. Aden, Vanderbilt University; Judith H. Anderson, Indiana University; Stanley Archer, Texas A&M University; J. M. Armistad, University of Tennessee, Knoxville; Marc Arnold, University of Arkansas, Little Rock; Ann G. Ashworth, Texas Christian University; Lee Baier, University of Southern Maine; Steven L. Bates, Northwestern University; Donald R. Benson, Iowa State University; Samuel N. Bogorad, University of Vermont; J. N. Brown, MacQuarie University; Jean-François Camé, Université Paul Valéry, Montpellier, France; Georgia B. Christopher, Emory University; Martin K. Doudna, University of Hawaii, Hilo; Roman R. Dubinski, University of Waterloo, Ontario; Joseph E. Duncan, University of Minnesota; Robert L. Entzminger, Virginia Polytechnic Institute and State University; Andrew V. Ettin, Wake Forest University; Barbara C. Ewell, University of Mississippi; Stanley Fish, Johns Hopkins University; Alastair Fowler, Edinburgh University, Scotland; Philip J. Gallagher, University of Texas, El Paso; Jeffrey M. Gamso, Texas Tech University; R. B. Gill, Elon College; Joan F. Gilliland, Marshall University; Sanford Golding, University of Cincinnati; James M. Hall, University of Cincinnati; Michael L. Hall, Centenary College of Louisiana; Robert W. Halli, Jr., University of Alabama; Violet Beryl Halpert, Fairleigh Dickinson University; Joan E. Hartman, College of Staten Island, City University of New York; Eugene D. Hill, Mount Holyoke College; John G. Hotchkiss, Los Angeles Baptist College; James Hoyle, Oakland University; William B. Hunter, Jr., University of Houston; Lawrence W. Hyman, Brooklyn College, City University of New York; Myrl Guy Jones, Radford University; Arthur F. Kinney, University of Massachusetts; George Klawitter, Viterbo College; Michael M. Levy, University of Wisconsin, Stout; Mark Lidman, University of South Carolina, Sumter; Michael

Lieb, University of Illinois, Chicago; Anthony Low, New York University; Gerald MacLean, Queen's University, Kingston; Ellen Mankoff, Kenyon College; Diane K. McColley, Rutgers University, Camden; Elizabeth McCutcheon, University of Hawaii, Manoa; Phillip J. Miller, University of Tennessee, Martin; Earl Miner, Princeton University; Leslie Ellen Moore, Yale University; Anna K. Nardo, Louisiana State University; George W. Nitchie, Simmons College; Douglas A. Northrop, Ripon College; James Obertino, Central Missouri State University; Michael O'Loughlin, State University of New York, Purchase; Lois W. Parker, Southwestern University; C. A. Patrides, University of Michigan; Robert B. Pierce, Oberlin College; Melvin L. Plotinsky, Indiana University; Marilyn Pogue, University of Missouri, Rolla; William Malin Porter, University of Houston; Anne L. Prescott, Barnard College; Mary H. Pritchard, King's College, University of Western Ontario; Herman Rapaport, University of Iowa; A. E. Reiff, Bishop College, Dallas; Hugh M. Richmond, University of California, Berkeley; Clark Rodewald, Bard College; Roger B. Rollin, Clemson University; Philip Rollinson, University of Southern California; Karen E. Rowe, University of California, Los Angeles; Arnold Stein, University of Illinois; Joseph H. Summers, University of Rochester; Kathleen M. Swaim, University of Massachusetts; Gordon Tesky, Cornell University; Leonard Tourney, University of Tulsa; Virginia Tufte, University of Southern California; Thomas Willard, University of Arizona; Franklin Williams, Georgetown University; John Wooten, United States Naval Academy; Yeong Yoo, Yonsei University, Korea; Bruce W. Young, Harvard University

WORKS CITED

Books and Articles

Abrams, M. H., gen. ed. *The Norton Anthology of English Literature.* 5th ed. 2 vols. New York: Norton, 1985.

Adams, Robert M. *Ikon: John Milton and the Modern Critics.* 1955. Ithaca: Cornell UP, 1966.

Addison, Joseph. *Critical Essays from the* Spectator. Ed. Donald F. Bond. New York: Oxford UP, 1970.

Aers, David, and Bob Hodges. " 'Rational Burning': Milton on Sex and Marriage." *Milton Studies* 13 (1979): 3–33.

Allen, Beverly Sprague. *Tides of English Taste (1619–1800): A Background for the Study of Literature.* 2 vols. 1937. New York: Pageant, 1958.

Allen, Don Cameron. *Doubt's Boundless Sea: Skepticism and Faith in the Renaissance.* Baltimore: Johns Hopkins UP, 1964.

———. *The Harmonious Vision: Studies in Milton's Poetry.* Baltimore: Johns Hopkins UP, 1954.

———. *The Legend of Noah: Renaissance Rationalism in Art, Science and Letters.* 1949. Urbana: U of Illinois P, 1963.

———. *Mysteriously Meant: The Rediscovery of Pagan Symbolism and Allegorical Interpretation in the Renaissance.* Baltimore: Johns Hopkins UP, 1970.

Anderson, George K., and William E. Buckler. *The Literature of England.* 3rd ed. 2 vols. Glenview: Scott, 1979.

Anderson, Mary D. *The Imagery of British Churches.* London: Murray, 1955.

Aquinas, Saint Thomas. *Summa theologica.* Trans. the English Dominicans. 22 vols. 2nd ed. London: Burns and Oates, 1920–32.

Armstrong, John. *The Paradise Myth*. London: Oxford UP, 1969.

Arthos, John. *Milton and the Italian Cities*. London: Bowes, 1968.

Baker, Herschel. *The Dignity of Man*. 1947. Rpt. as *The Image of Man: A Study of the Idea of Human Dignity in Classical Antiquity, the Middle Ages, and the Renaissance*. New York: Harper, 1961.

———. *The Wars of Truth: Studies in the Decay of Humanism in the Earlier Seventeenth Century*. Cambridge: Harvard UP, 1952.

Bamborough, J. B. *The Little World of Man*. London: Longman, 1952.

Banks, Theodore. *Milton's Imagery*. New York: Columbia UP, 1950.

Banville, Théodore de. *Petit traité de poésie française*. Paris, 1871.

Barbour, Ian G., ed. *Earth Might Be Fair: Reflections on Ethics, Religion and Ecology*. Englewood Cliffs: Prentice, 1972.

———, ed. *Western Man and Environmental Ethics: Attitudes toward Nature and Technology*. Reading: Addison, 1973.

Barker, Arthur. *Milton and the Puritan Dilemma, 1641–1660*. 1942. Toronto: U of Toronto, 1955.

———, ed. *Milton: Modern Essays in Criticism*. New York: Oxford UP, 1965.

Behrendt, Stephen C. *The Moment of Explosion: Blake and the Illustration of Milton*. Lincoln: U of Nebraska P, 1983.

Berne, Eric. *Transactional Analysis in Psychotherapy: A Systematic Individual and Social Psychiatry*. New York: Grove, [1961].

Berry, Boyd M. *Process of Speech: Puritan Religious Writing and Paradise Lost*. Baltimore: Johns Hopkins UP, 1976.

Black, Ronald A. "Psychodrama in Classroom Teaching." *Improving College and University Teaching* 20 (1972): 118–20.

Blackstone, William, ed. *Philosophy and Environmental Crisis*. Athens: U of Georgia P, 1974.

Blau, J. L. *The Christian Interpretation of the Cabala in the Renaissance*. New York: Columbia UP, 1944.

Blessington, Francis C. Paradise Lost *and the Classical Epic*. London: Routledge, 1979.

Bodkin, Maud. *Archetypal Patterns in Poetry: Psychological Studies in Imagination*. London: Oxford UP, 1934.

Boswell, Jackson C. *Milton's Library: A Catalogue of the Remains of John Milton's Library and an Annotated Reconstruction of Milton's Library and Ancillary Readings*. London: Garland, 1975.

Bowra, C. M. *From Virgil to Milton*. London: Macmillan, 1945.

Bradshaw, John. *A Concordance to the Poetical Works of John Milton*. 1894. Hamden: Archon, 1965.

Brennecke, E. *John Milton the Elder and His Music*. New York: Columbia UP, 1938.

Bridges, Robert. *Milton's Prosody, with a Chapter on Accentual Verse*. Oxford: Oxford UP, 1921.

Broadbent, John B., ed. *John Milton: Introductions*. Milton for Schools and Colleges. Cambridge: Cambridge UP, 1973.

———. *Paradise Lost: Introduction*. Milton for Schools and Colleges. Cambridge: Cambridge UP, 1972.

———. *Some Graver Subject: An Essay on* Paradise Lost. 1960. London: Schocken, 1967.

Brown, Calvin S. *Music and Literature: A Comparison of the Arts*. Athens: U of Georgia P, 1948.

Bruffee, Kenneth A. "Liberal Education and the Social Justification of Belief." *Liberal Education* 68 (1982): 95–114.

———. "The Structure of Knowledge and the Future of Liberal Education." *Liberal Education* 67 (1981): 177–86.

Burden, Dennis H. *The Logical Epic: A Study of the Argument of* Paradise Lost. London: Routledge, 1967.

Burtt, E. A. *The Metaphysical Foundations of Modern Physical Science*. 1925. London: Routledge, 1967.

Bush, Douglas. *The Complete Poetical Works of John Milton*. Cambridge: Cambridge UP; Boston: Houghton, 1965.

———. *English Literature in the Earlier Seventeenth Century, 1600–1660*. Vol. 5 of the Oxford History of English Literature. Ed. F. P. Wilson and Bonamy Dobrée. Oxford: Clarendon, 1962.

———. *John Milton: A Sketch of His Life and Works*. New York: Macmillan, 1964.

———. *Paradise Lost in Our Time: Some Comments*. 1945. New York: Smith, 1957.

———. *The Portable Milton*. New York: Viking, 1949.

———. *The Renaissance and English Humanism*. Toronto: U of Toronto P, 1939.

Butlin, Martin. *The Paintings and Drawings of William Blake*. 2 vols. New Haven: Yale UP, 1981.

Buttrick, George Arthur, et al. *The Interpreter's Dictionary of the Bible*. 4 vols. New York: Abingdon, 1962.

Byard, Margaret M. "Poetic Responses to the Copernican Revolution." *Scientific American* 236 (1977): 120–29.

Campbell, Joseph. *The Masks of God: Occidental Mythology*. 1955. New York: Viking, 1964.

Carey, John, and Alastair Fowler, eds. *The Poems of John Milton*. London: Longman, 1968. (Fowler's edition of *Paradise Lost* is also available separately.)

Carsten, F. L., ed. *The Ascendancy of France, 1648–88*. Vol. 5 of the New Cambridge Modern History. Cambridge: Cambridge UP, 1961.

Cassel, Russell. "Instructional Gaming and Simulation." *Contemporary Education* 45.2 (1974): 100–05.

Cassirer, Ernst. *The Platonic Renaissance in England*. Trans. J. P. Pettegrove. Austin: U of Texas P, 1953.

Cawley, Robert. *Milton and the Literature of Travel*. Princeton: Princeton UP, 1951.

Cicero. *De natura deorum*. Trans. H. Rackham. Cambridge: Harvard UP, 1933.

Clark, Donald L. *John Milton at St. Paul's School*. 1948. Hamden: Shoe String, 1964.

Clark, George N. *The Later Stuarts, 1660–1714*. Vol. 10 of the Oxford History of England. Gen. ed. G. N. Clark. 2nd ed. Oxford: Oxford UP, 1951.

Colie, Rosalie L. *Paradoxia Epidemica: The Renaissance Tradition of Paradox*. Princeton: Princeton UP, 1966.

———. *The Resources of Kind: Genre-Theory in the Renaissance*. Ed. Barbara K. Lewalski. Berkeley: U of California P, 1973.

Collier, John. *Milton's* Paradise Lost: *Screenplay for the Cinema of the Mind*. New York: Knopf, 1973.

Comito, Terry. *The Idea of the Garden in the Renaissance*. New Brunswick: Rutgers UP, 1978.

Cooper, J. P., ed. *The Decline of Spain and the Thirty Years War, 1609–59*. Vol. 4 of the New Cambridge Modern History. Cambridge: Cambridge UP, 1970

Cope, Jackson I. *The Metaphoric Structure of* Paradise Lost. Baltimore: Johns Hopkins UP, 1962.

Corcoran, Mary Irma. *Milton's Paradise with Reference to the Hexameral Background*. Washington: Catholic U of America P, 1945.

"The Corpus Laid Out: English Literature for the Container Age." *Times Literary Supplement* 2 Nov. 1973: 1337–38.

Coward, Barry. *The Stuart Age: A History of England, 1603–1714*. London: Longman, 1980.

Craig, Hardin. *The Enchanted Glass: The Renaissance Mind in English Literature*. New York: Oxford UP, 1936.

———. *New Lamps for Old: A Sequel to* The Enchanted Glass. Oxford: Blackwell, 1960.

Crombie, A. C. *Augustine to Galileo: The History of Science, A.D. 400–1650*. London: Falcon, 1952.

Crosman, Robert. *Reading* Paradise Lost. Bloomington: Indiana UP, 1980.

Crump, Galbraith M. *The Mystical Design of* Paradise Lost. Lewisburg: Bucknell UP, 1975.

Curry, Walter C. *Milton's Ontology, Cosmology, and Physics*. Lexington: U of Kentucky P, 1957.

Curtius, Ernst Robert. *European Literature and the Latin Middle Ages*. Trans. Willard Trask. Princeton: Princeton UP, 1953.

Daiches, David. *Milton*. New York: Norton, 1957.

Daniells, Roy. *Milton, Mannerism, and Baroque.* Toronto: U of Toronto P, 1963.

Darbishire, Helen, ed. *The Early Lives of Milton.* London: Constable, 1932.

———, ed. *The Poetical Works of John Milton.* 2 vols. Oxford: Clarendon, 1952, 1955.

Davis, Godfrey. *Bibliography of British History: The Stuart Period, 1603–1714.* Oxford: Clarendon, 1920.

———. *The Early Stuarts, 1603–1660.* Vol. 9 of the Oxford History of England. Gen. ed. G. N. Clark. 2nd ed. Oxford: Oxford UP, 1959.

Derrida, Jacques. *Of Grammatology.* Trans. Gayatri C. Spivak. Baltimore: Johns Hopkins UP, 1976.

Diekhoff, John S., ed. *Milton on Himself: Milton's Utterances upon Himself and His Works.* 1939. New York: Humanities, 1965.

———. *Milton's* Paradise Lost: *A Commentary on the Argument.* 1946. New York: Humanities, 1958.

Dobbins, Austin C. *Milton and the Book of Revelation: The Heavenly Cycle.* University: U of Alabama P, 1975.

Dunbar, Pamela. *William Blake's Illustrations to the Poetry of Milton.* Oxford: Clarendon, 1980.

Duncan, Joseph E. "Archetypes in Milton's Earthly Paradise." *Milton Studies* 14 (1980): 25–58.

———. *Milton's Earthly Paradise: A Historical Study of Eden.* Minneapolis: Minnesota UP, 1972.

Dyson, A. E., ed. *English Poetry: Selected Bibliographical Guides.* London: Oxford UP, 1971.

Eisenstein, Sergei. *The Film Sense.* Trans. and ed. Jay Leyda. London: Faber, 1943.

Eliade, Mircea. *Images and Symbols: Studies in Religious Symbolism.* New York: Sheed, 1961.

———. *The Myth of the Eternal Return.* Trans. Willard Trask. London: Routledge, 1954.

———. *The Sacred and the Profane.* Trans. Willard Trask. New York: Harper, 1961.

Eliot, T. S. "Milton I." *On Poetry and Poets.* London: Faber, 1957. 138–45.

Elledge, Scott, ed. *Paradise Lost.* Norton Critical Edition. New York: Norton, 1975.

Emma, Ronald D., and John T. Shawcross, eds. *Language and Style in Milton: A Symposium in Honor of the Tercentenary of* Paradise Lost. New York: Ungar, 1967.

Empson, William. *Milton's God.* 1961. London: Chatto, 1965.

Evans, J. M. Paradise Lost *and the Genesis Tradition.* London: Oxford UP, 1968.

Farwell, Marilyn R. "Eve, the Separation Scene, and the Renaissance Idea of Androgyny." *Milton Studies* 14 (1981): 3–20.

Feaver, William. *The Art of John Martin.* Oxford: Clarendon, 1975.

Ferry, Anne Davidson. *Milton's Epic Voice: The Narrator in* Paradise Lost. Cambridge: Harvard UP, 1963.

Finney, Gretchen Ludke. *Musical Backgrounds for English Literature: 1580–1650.* New Brunswick: Rutgers UP, 1962.

Fisch, Harold. *Jerusalem and Albion: The Hebraic Factor in Seventeenth-Century Literature.* London: Kegan Paul, 1964.

Fish, Stanley. "Interpreting the Variorum." *Critical Inquiry* 2 (1976): 465–85.

———. *Surprised by Sin: The Reader in* Paradise Lost. New York: Macmillan, 1967.

Fixler, Michael. *Milton and the Kingdoms of God.* Evanston: Northwestern UP, 1964.

Fletcher, Harris F. *Contributions to a Milton Bibliography: 1800–1930.* 1931. New York: Russell, 1967.

———. *The Intellectual Development of John Milton.* 2 vols. Urbana: U of Illinois P, 1956, 1962.

———, ed. *John Milton's Complete Poetical Works, Reproduced in Photographic Facsimile.* 4 vols. Urbana: U of Illinois P, 1943–48.

———. *Milton's Rabbinical Reading.* Urbana: U of Illinois P, 1930.

Forde, William. *The True Spirit of Milton's Versification Developed in a New and Systematic Arrangement for the First Book of* Paradise Lost, *with an Introductory Essay on Blank Verse.* London, 1831.

Fowler, Alastair, ed. *Paradise Lost.* London: Longman, 1968.

French, J. Milton, ed. *The Life Records of John Milton.* 5 vols. 1949–58. New York: Gordian, 1966.

Frye, Northrop. *Anatomy of Criticism.* Princeton: Princeton UP, 1957.

———. *The Educated Imagination.* Indianapolis: Indiana UP, 1964.

———, ed. Paradise Lost *and Selected Poetry and Prose.* New York: Rinehart, 1951.

———. *The Return to Eden: Five Essays on Milton's Epics.* Toronto: U of Toronto P, 1965.

Frye, Roland Mushat. *Milton's Imagery and the Visual Arts: Iconographic Tradition in the Epic Poems.* Princeton: Princeton UP, 1978.

———. Review of *Milton and the Baroque,* by Murray Roston. *Modern Language Review* 77 (1982): 410–12.

Fulghum, W. B., Jr. *A Dictionary of Biblical Allusions in English Literature.* New York: Irvington, 1977.

Fussell, Paul. *Poetic Meter and Poetic Form.* New York: Random, 1965.

Gardner, Helen. "Milton's First Illustrator." *Essays and Studies* 9 (1956): 27–38. Rpt. as app. in H. Gardner, *A Reading*.

———. *A Reading of* Paradise Lost. Oxford: Oxford UP, 1965.

Gennette, Gérard. "Langage poétique, poétique du langage." *Figures II*. Paris: Seuil, 1969. 123–53.

A Gentleman of Oxford (George Smith Green). *A New Version of the* Paradise Lost. Oxford, 1756.

Giamatti, A. Bartlett. *The Earthly Paradise and the Renaissance Epic*. Princeton: Princeton UP, 1966.

Gilbert, Allan H. *A Geographical Dictionary of Milton*. New Haven: Yale UP, 1919.

———. "Milton and the Position of Women." *Modern Language Review* 15 (1920): 7–27, 240–64.

Gilman, Ernest B. *The Curious Perspective: Literary and Pictorial Wit in the Seventeenth Century*. New Haven: Yale UP, 1978.

Grabar, André. *Christian Iconography: A Study of Its Origins*. Princeton: Princeton UP, 1968.

Graves, Robert. *Wife to Mr. Milton*. 1943. Baltimore: Penguin, 1954.

[Green, George Smith]. *A New Version of the* Paradise Lost *in Which Milton's Measure and Versification Are Corrected and Harmonized by a Gentleman from Oxford*. London, 1755.

Greene, Thomas. *The Descent from Heaven: A Study of Epic Continuity*. New Haven: Yale UP, 1963.

Grierson, H. J. C. *Cross Currents in English Literature of the Seventeenth Century*. London: Chatto, 1929.

———. *Milton and Wordsworth: Poets and Prophets. A Study of Their Reactions to Political Events*. Cambridge: Cambridge UP, 1937.

Grose, Christopher. *Milton's Epic Process:* Paradise Lost *and Its Miltonic Background*. New Haven: Yale UP, 1973.

Grossman, Marshall. "Dramatic Structure and Emotive Pattern in the Fall." *Milton Studies* 13 (1979); 201–19.

Gunn, J. A. W. *Politics and the Public Interest in the Seventeenth Century*. London: Routledge, 1969.

Hadfield, Miles, and J. C. H. Hadfield. *Gardens of Delight*. London: Cassell, 1964.

Hagstrum, Jean H. *Sex and Sensibility: Ideal and Erotic Love from Milton to Mozart*. Chicago: U of Chicago P, 1980.

———. *The Sister Arts: The Tradition of Literary Pictorialism and English Poetry from Dryden to Gray*. Chicago: U of Chicago P, 1958.

Halkett, John. *Milton and the Idea of Matrimony: A Study of the Divorce Tracts and* Paradise Lost. New Haven: Yale UP, 1970.

Hall, James. *Dictionary of Subjects and Symbols in Art*. London: Murray, 1974.

Haller, William. *The Rise of Puritanism; or, The Way to the New Jerusalem as Set Forth in Pulpit and Press from Thomas Cartwright to John Wilburne and John Milton, 1570–1643*. New York: Columbia UP, 1938.

Hamilton, Michael, ed. *This Little Planet*. New York: Scribner's, 1970.

Hammond, N. G. L., and H. H. Scullard. *The Oxford Classical Dictionary*. Oxford: Clarendon, 1970.

Hanford, James Holly. *John Milton: Poet and Humanist*. Cleveland: Case Western Reserve UP, 1966.

———. *Milton*. Goldentree Bibliography. New York: Appleton, 1966.

Hanford, James Holly, and James G. Taaffe. *A Milton Handbook*. Rev. ed. New York: Appleton, 1970.

Harding, Davis P. *The Club of Hercules: Studies in the Classical Background of Paradise Lost*. Urbana: U of Illinois P, 1962.

Harris, Thomas A. *I'm OK—You're OK: A Practical Guide to Transactional Analysis*. New York: Harper, 1969.

Harris, Victor. *All Coherence Gone*. 1949. Chicago: U of Chicago P, 1966.

Havens, Raymond D. *The Influence of Milton on English Poetry*. 1922. New York: Russell, 1961.

Haydn, Hiram. *The Counter-Renaissance*. New York: Scribner's, 1950.

Heninger, S. K. *The Cosmological Glass: Renaissance Diagrams of the Universe*. San Marino: Huntington, 1977.

———. *Touches of Sweet Harmony: Pythagorean Cosmology and Renaissance Poetics*. San Marino: Huntington, 1974.

Hesiod. *Theogony*. Ed. M. L. West. Oxford: Clarendon, 1966.

———. *The Works and Days. Theogony. The Shield of Herakles*. Trans. Richmond A. Lattimore. Chicago: U of Chicago P, 1959.

Highet, Gilbert. *The Classical Tradition: Greek and Roman Influences on Western Literature*. New York: Oxford UP, 1949.

Hill, John E. Christopher. *Intellectual Origins of the English Revolution*. Oxford: Oxford UP, 1965.

———. *Milton and the English Revolution*. London: Faber, 1977.

———. *Puritanism and Revolution: Studies in Interpretation of the English Revolution in the Seventeenth Century*. London: Secker, 1958.

———. *Society and Puritanism in Pre-Revolutionary England*. London: Secker, 1964.

———. *The World Turned Upside Down: Radical Ideas during the English Revolution*. London: Temple Smith, 1972.

Hollander, John. *The Untuning of the Skies: Ideas of Music in English Poetry, 1500–1700*. Princeton: Princeton UP, 1961.

Homer. *The Iliad*. Trans. Richmond A. Lattimore. Chicago: U of Chicago P, 1962.

———. *The Iliad*. Trans. Robert Fitzgerald. New York: Anchor-Doubleday, 1974.

————. *The Odyssey.* Trans. Richmond A. Lattimore. New York: Harper, 1968.

————. *The Odyssey.* Trans. Robert Fitzgerald. New York: Anchor-Doubleday, 1961.

Hoopes, Robert. *Right Reason in the English Renaissance.* Cambridge: Harvard UP, 1962.

Huckabay, Calvin. *John Milton: An Annotated Bibliography, 1929–1968.* Rev. ed. Pittsburgh: Duquesne UP, 1970.

Hudson, Gladys W. Paradise Lost: *A Concordance.* Detroit: Gale, 1970.

Hughes, Merritt Y., ed. *John Milton: Complete Poems and Major Prose.* New York: Odyssey, 1957.

————, ed. *Paradise Lost.* New York: Odyssey, 1962.

————. *Ten Perspectives on Milton.* New Haven: Yale UP, 1965.

Hughes, Merritt Y., and John Steadman, eds. *A Variorum Commentary on the Poems of John Milton.* 4 vols. to date. New York: Columbia UP, 1972–.

Hughes, Robert. *Heaven and Hell in Western Art.* London: Weidenfield, 1968.

Hunter, G. K. *Paradise Lost.* Unwin Critical Library. London: Allen, 1980.

Hunter, William B., Jr. "The Sources of Milton's Prosody." *Philological Quarterly* 28 (1949): 125–44.

Hunter, William B., Jr., C. A. Patrides, and J. H. Adamson. *Bright Essence: Studies in Theology.* Salt Lake City: U of Utah P, 1971.

Hunter, William B., Jr., John T. Shawcross, and John M. Steadman, eds. *A Milton Encyclopedia.* 8 vols. Lewisburg: Bucknell UP, 1978–79.

Huntley, John. "Teaching Milton: Some Thoughts on Manipulation and Mapping." *Milton Quarterly* 12 (1978): 144–45.

Ingram, William, and Kathleen Swaim. *A Concordance to Milton's English Poetry.* London: Oxford UP, 1972.

Jacobus, Lee A. *Sudden Apprehension: Aspects of Knowledge in* Paradise Lost. The Hague: Mouton, 1976.

Jakobson, Roman. "The Metaphoric and Metonymic Poles." *Fundamentals of Language.* By R. Jakobson and Morris Halle. The Hague: Mouton, 1971. 90–96.

Jameson, Fredric. *The Political Unconscious.* Ithaca: Cornell UP, 1981.

Johnson, F. R. *Astronomical Thought in Renaissance England.* Baltimore: Johns Hopkins UP, 1937.

Johnson, Samuel. "Milton." *Lives of the English Poets.* Ed. George Birkbeck. Oxford: Clarendon, 1905. 1: 84–200.

————. *The Rambler.* Ed. W. J. Bate and Albrecht B. Strauss. Vols. 3–5 of the Yale Edition of the Works of Samuel Johnson. Gen. ed. John H. Middendorf. New Haven: Yale UP, 1969.

Jones, R. F. *Ancients and Moderns: A Study of the Rise of the Scientific*

Movement in Seventeenth-Century England. St. Louis: Washington UP, 1936.

Jung, Carl G. *Archetypes and the Collective Unconscious.* Vol. 9.1 of *Collected Works.* 2nd ed. 1969.

——. *Collected Works.* Ed. Gerhard Adler et al. Trans. R. F. Hull. 20 vols. Princeton: Princeton UP, 1954–79.

——. *Man and His Symbols.* 1964. New York: Dell, 1968.

——. "The Undiscovered Self." *Civilization in Transition.* Vol. 10 of *Collected Works.* 2nd ed. 1964. 245–306.

Kelley, Maurice. *This Great Argument: A Study of Milton's* De doctrina *as a Gloss on* Paradise Lost. Princeton: Princeton UP, 1941

Kermode, Frank, ed. *The Living Milton: Essays by Various Hands.* London: Routledge, 1960.

Kermode, Frank, and John Hollander, gen. eds. *The Oxford Anthology of English Literature.* 2 vols. New York: Oxford UP, 1973.

Kirkconnell, Watson, ed. *The Celestial Cycle: The Theme of* Paradise Lost *in World Literature, with Translations of the Major Analogues.* Toronto: U of Toronto P, 1952.

Kliger, Samuel. *The Goths in England: A Study in Seventeenth and Eighteenth Century Thought.* Cambridge: Harvard UP, 1952.

Knott, John R., Jr. *Milton's Pastoral Vision: An Approach to* Paradise Lost. Chicago: U of Chicago P, 1971.

Kranidas, Thomas. *The Fierce Equation: A Study of Milton's Decorum.* The Hague: Mouton, 1965.

——, ed. *New Essays on* Paradise Lost. Berkeley: U of California P, 1969.

Kuhn, T. S. *The Copernican Revolution: Planetary Astronomy in the Development of Western Thought.* New York: Random, 1957.

Kurth, Burton O. *Milton and Christian Heroism: Biblical Epic Themes and Forms in Seventeenth-Century England.* 1959. Hamden: Shoe String, 1966.

Lawry, Jon S. *The Shadow of Heaven: Matter and Stance in Milton's Poetry.* Ithaca: Cornell UP, 1968.

Le Comte, Edward S. *A Dictionary of Puns in Milton.* New York: Columbia UP, 1981.

——. *Milton and Sex.* New York: Columbia UP, 1978.

——. *A Milton Dictionary.* New York: Philosophical Library, 1961.

——. *Yet Once More: Verbal and Psychological Pattern in Milton.* New York: Liberal Arts, 1954.

Legarde, André, and Laurent Michard, eds. *Moyen Age.* Paris: Danel, 1962.

Levin, Harry. *The Myth of the Golden Age in the Renaissance.* Bloomington: U of Indiana P, 1969.

Lewalski, Barbara K. *Protestant Poetics and the Seventeenth-Century Religious Lyric.* Princeton: Princeton UP, 1979.

Lewis, C. S. *A Preface to* Paradise Lost. Rev. ed. Oxford: Oxford UP, 1960.

Lieb, Michael J. *The Dialectics of Creation: Patterns of Birth and Regeneration in* Paradise Lost. Amherst: U of Massachusetts P, 1970.

———. *Poetics of the Holy: A Reading of* Paradise Lost. Chapel Hill: U of North Carolina P, 1981.

Long, Charles H. *Alpha: The Myths of Creation.* New York: Braziller, 1963.

Lovejoy, A. O. *The Great Chain of Being: A Study of the History of an Idea.* Cambridge: Harvard UP, 1936.

———. "Milton and the Paradox of the Fortunate Fall." *Essays in the History of Ideas.* Baltimore: Johns Hopkins UP, 1948. 277–95.

———. "Milton's Dialogue on Astronomy." *Reason and the Imagination: Studies in the History of Ideas.* Ed. J. A. Mazzeo. New York: Columbia UP, 1962. 129–42.

Lukács, Georg. *Theory of the Novel.* Trans. Anna Bostock. Cambridge: MIT P, 1971.

MacCaffrey, Isabel G. Paradise Lost *as "Myth."* Cambridge: Harvard UP, 1959.

Mack, Maynard, ed. *Norton Anthology of World Masterpieces.* 4th ed. New York: Norton, 1979.

Madsen, William G. *From Shadowy Types to Truth: Studies in Milton's Symbolism.* New Haven: Yale UP, 1968.

———. "The Idea of Nature in Milton's Poetry." *Three Studies in the Renaissance.* New Haven: Yale UP, 1958. 181–283.

———, ed. *Paradise Lost.* New York: Modern Library, 1969.

Marilla, E. L. *Milton and Modern Man: Selected Essays.* University: U of Alabama P, 1968.

Martz, Louis L., ed. *Milton:* Paradise Lost: *A Collection of Critical Essays.* Englewood Cliffs: Prentice, 1966.

———. *The Paradise Within: Studies in Vaughan, Traherne, and Milton.* New Haven: Yale UP, 1964.

———. *Poet of Exile: A Study of Milton's Poetry.* New Haven: Yale UP, 1980.

———. *The Poetry of Meditation: A Study in English Religious Literature of the Seventeenth Century.* Rev. ed. New Haven: Yale UP, 1962.

Masson, David. *The Life of John Milton: Narrated in Connexion with the Political, Ecclesiastical, and Literary History of His Time.* 7 vols. 1881–94. New York: Smith, 1946.

McAdoo, H. R. *The Spirit of Anglicanism: A Survey of Anglican Theological Method in the Seventeenth Century.* London: Black, 1965.

McColley, Diane. *Milton's Eve.* Urbana: U of Illinois P, 1983.

McColley, Grant. Paradise Lost: *An Account of Its Growth and Major Origins, with a Discussion of Milton's Use of Sources and Literary Patterns.* 1940. New York: Russell, 1963.

McCutcheon, Elizabeth N. "Bacon and the Cherubim: An Iconographical Reading of the *New Atlantis.*" *English Literary Renaissance* 2 (1972): 334–55.

Michels, T. J., and Nolan C. Hatcher. "Sociodrama in the Classroom: A Different Approach to Learning." *Teaching Today.* Ed. J. Michael Palardy. New York: Macmillan, 1975. 230–34.

Miller, Leo. *Milton's Portraits.* Special issue of the *Milton Quarterly* (1976): 38 pp.

Miner, Earl. "Milton's Laws Divine and Human." *The Restoration Mode from Milton to Dryden.* Princeton: Princeton UP, 1974. 198–287.

———. *The Restoration Mode from Milton to Dryden.* Princeton: Princeton UP, 1974.

Montaigne. "Apology for Raymond Sebond." *The Complete Works of Montaigne.* Trans. Donald M. Frame. Stanford: Stanford UP, 1958. 318–457.

Morford, Mark P. O., and Robert Lenardon. *Classical Mythology.* London: Longman, 1971.

Morrill, J. S. *Seventeenth-Century Britain, 1603–1714.* Critical Bibliography in Modern History. Hamden: Archon, 1980.

Myers, R. M. *Handel, Dryden, and Milton: Being a Series of Observations on the Poems of Dryden and Milton, as Alter'd and Adapted by Various Hands, and Set to Music by Mr. Handel, to Which Are Added Authenick Texts of Several of Mr. Handel's Oratorios.* Cambridge: Bowes, 1956.

Nabokov, Vladimir. *Notes on Prosody.* Princeton: Princeton UP, 1964.

Newton, Thomas, ed. *Paradise Lost.* By John Milton. London, 1778.

Nicolson, Marjorie Hope. *The Breaking of the Circle: Studies in the Effect of the "New Science" upon Seventeenth-Century Poetry.* Rev. ed. New York: Columbia UP, 1960.

———. *John Milton: A Reader's Guide to His Poetry.* New York: Farrar, 1963.

———. *The Microscope and the English Imagination.* Smith College Studies in Modern Languages. Northampton: Smith College, 1935.

———. "Milton and the Telescope." *English Literary History* 2 (1935): 1–32.

———. *Mountain Gloom and Mountain Glory: The Development of the Aesthetics of the Infinite.* New York: Norton, 1959.

———. "The Telescope and Imagination." *Modern Philology* 32 (1935): 233–60.

Oras, Ants. *Milton's Editors and Commentators from Patrick Hume to Henry John Todd (1695–1801): A Study of Critical Views and Methods.* Oxford: Oxford UP, 1931.

Ovid. *Metamorphoses.* Trans. Mary Innes. London: Penguin, 1955.

———. *Metamorphoses.* Trans. Rolfe Humphries. Indianapolis: Indiana UP, 1955.

Paley, Morton D. *Energy and the Imagination: A Study of the Development of Blake's Thought.* Oxford: Clarendon, 1970.

Panofsky, Erwin. *Studies in Iconology: Humanistic Themes in the Art of the Renaissance.* 1939. New York: Harper, 1972.

Parker, William Riley. *Milton: A Biography.* 2 vols. Oxford: Clarendon, 1968.

———. *Milton's Contemporary Reputation.* Columbus: Ohio State UP, 1940.

Passmore, John. *Man's Responsibility for Nature.* London: Duckworth, 1974.

Patrides, C. A., ed. *Approaches to* Paradise Lost: *The York Tercentenary Lectures.* Toronto: U of Toronto P, 1968.

———. *The Grand Design of God: The Literary Form of the Christian View of History.* London: Routledge, 1972.

———. *Milton and the Christian Tradition.* Oxford: Clarendon, 1966.

———, ed. *Milton's Epic Poetry: Essays on* Paradise Lost *and* Paradise Regained. Harmondsworth: Penguin, 1967.

———. *The Phoenix and the Ladder: The Rise and Decline of the Christian View of History.* Berkeley: U of California P, 1964.

Patrides, C. A., and Raymond B. Waddington. *The Age of Milton: Backgrounds to Seventeenth-Century Literature.* Manchester: Manchester UP, 1980.

Patterson, Frank A., gen. ed. *The Works of John Milton.* 18 vols. New York: Columbia UP, 1931–38.

Patterson, Frank A., and French R. Fogel. *An Index to the Columbia Edition of the Works of John Milton.* 2 vols. New York: Columbia UP, 1960.

Peter, John. *A Critique of* Paradise Lost. New York: Columbia UP, 1960.

Phillips, Edward. *The Life of John Milton.* Rpt. in Darbishire, *Early Lives of Milton.*

Pointon, Marcia R. *Milton and English Art.* Toronto: U of Toronto P, 1970.

Porter, William Malin. "A View from 'th'Aonian Mount': Hesiod and Milton's Critique of the Classics." *Classical and Modern Literature* 3 (1982): 5–23.

Potter, Lois. *A Preface to Milton.* 1971. New York: Scribner's, 1972.

Praz, Mario. "Milton and Poussin." *Seventeenth-Century Studies Presented to Sir Herbert Grierson.* Oxford: Oxford UP, 1938. 192–210.

Prescott, Anne Lake. *French Poets and the English Renaissance: Studies in Fame and Transformation.* New Haven: Yale UP, 1978.

Prince, F. T. *The Italian Element in Milton's Verse.* 1954. Oxford: Clarendon, 1962.

———. Rev. of *John Milton: Complete Poems and Major Prose,* ed. Merritt Hughes. *Modern Language Review* 56 (1961): 299–300.

Rajan, Balachandra. *The Lofty Rhyme: A Study of Milton's Major Poetry.* Coral Gables: U of Miami P, 1970.

————. Paradise Lost *and the Seventeenth-Century Reader.* London: Chatto, 1947.

Rapaport, Herman. *Milton and the Postmodern.* Lincoln: U of Nebraska P, 1983.

Richmond, Hugh M. *The Christian Revolutionary: John Milton.* Berkeley: U of California P, 1974.

Ricks, Christopher, ed. *John Milton:* Paradise Lost *and* Paradise Regained. New York: NAL, 1968.

————. *Milton's Grand Style.* Oxford: Clarendon, 1963.

Riggs, William G. *The Christian Poet in* Paradise Lost. Berkeley: U of California P, 1972.

Roach, John. *A Bibliography of Modern History.* New Cambridge Modern History. Cambridge: Cambridge UP, 1968.

Rogers, Katherine M. *The Troublesome Helpmate: A History of Misogyny in Literature.* Seattle: U of Washington P, 1966.

Rose, Millicent. *Gustave Doré.* Paris: Pleiade, 1946.

Roston, Murray. *Milton and the Baroque.* Pittsburgh: U of Pittsburgh P, 1980.

Rudrum, Alan, ed. *Milton: Modern Judgements.* London: Macmillan, 1968.

Ryken, Leland. *The Apocalyptic Vision in* Paradise Lost. Ithaca: Cornell UP, 1970.

Samuel, Irene. *Dante and Milton: The* Commedia *and* Paradise Lost. Ithaca: Cornell UP, 1966.

————. *Plato and Milton.* 1947. Ithaca: Cornell UP, 1965.

Sasek, Lawrence A. *The Literary Temper of the English Puritans.* Baton Rouge: Louisiana State UP, 1961.

Saurat, Denis. *Milton: Man and Thinker.* Rev. ed. Hamden: Archon, 1964.

Schilling, Harold K. "The Whole Earth Is the Lord's: Toward a Holistic Ethic." In Barbour, *Earth* 100–22.

Schultz, Howard. *Milton and Forbidden Knowledge.* New York: MLA, 1955.

Scoby, Donald R., ed. *Environmental Ethics: Studies of Man's Self-Destruction.* Minneapolis: U of Minnesota P, 1971.

Seigel, P. N. "Milton and the Humanistic Attitude toward Women." *Journal of the History of Ideas* 11 (1950): 42–53.

Seznec, Jean. *The Survival of the Pagan Gods: The Mythological Tradition and Its Place in Renaissance Humanism and Art.* 1953. Princeton: Princeton UP, 1972.

Sharratt, Bernard. "The Appropriation of Milton." *Essays and Studies* 35 (1982): 30–44.

Shawcross, John T., ed. *The Complete Poetry of John Milton.* Rev. ed. Garden City: Anchor-Doubleday, 1971.

————. "The First Illustrations for *Paradise Lost.*" *Milton Quarterly* 9 (1975): 43–46.

——, ed. *Milton: The Critical Heritage.* New York: Barnes, 1970.

Shepherd, Robert A., Jr. *John Milton's* Paradise Lost: *A Prose Rendition.* Somers: Seabury, 1983.

Shumaker, Wayne. *Unpremeditated Verse: Feeling and Perception in* Paradise Lost. Princeton: Princeton UP, 1967.

Sims, James H. *The Bible in Milton's Epics.* Gainesville: U of Florida P, 1962.

Spaeth, Sigmund G. *Milton's Knowledge of Music: Its Sources and Its Significance in His Works.* 1913. Ann Arbor: U of Michigan P, 1963.

Spencer, Hazelton, Beverly J. Layman, and David Ferry, eds. *British Literature.* 2 vols. 3rd ed. Lexington: Heath, 1974.

Spitzer, Leo. *Classical and Christian Ideas of World Harmony.* Ed. A. G. Hatcher. Baltimore: Johns Hopkins UP, 1963.

Spring, David, and Eileen Spring, eds. *Ecology and Religion in History.* New York: Harper, 1974.

Sprott, S. Ernest. *Milton's Art of Prosody.* Oxford: Blackwell, 1953.

Stanford, Gene. "Why Role-Playing Fails." *English Journal* 63.9 (1974): 50–54.

Steadman, John M. *Epic and Tragic Structure in* Paradise Lost. Chicago: U of Chicago P, 1976.

——. *Milton and the Renaissance Hero.* Oxford: Clarendon, 1967.

——. *Milton's Epic Characters: Image and Idol.* Chapel Hill: U of North Carolina P, 1968.

Stein, Arnold. *Answerable Style: Essays on* Paradise Lost. 1953. Seattle: U of Washington P, 1967.

——. *The Art of Presence: The Poet and* Paradise Lost. Berkeley: U of California P, 1977.

Steiner, George. *After Babel: Aspects of Language and Translation.* New York: Oxford UP, 1975.

Stevens, David H. *Reference Guide to Milton from 1800 to the Present Day.* 1930. New York: Russell, 1967.

Stewart, Stanley. *The Enclosed Garden: The Tradition and the Image in Seventeenth-Century Poetry.* Madison: U of Wisconsin P, 1966.

Strong, Roy. *The Renaissance Garden in England.* London: Thames, 1979.

Summers, Joseph H. *The Muse's Method: An Introduction to* Paradise Lost. Cambridge: Harvard UP, 1962.

Svendsen, Kester. *Milton and Science.* 1956. Westport: Greenwood, 1969.

Tayler, Edward W. *Nature and Art in Renaissance Literature.* New York: Columbia UP, 1964.

"Tercentenary Milestones." *Times Literary Supplement* 17 Apr. 1969: 406.

Thomas, Keith. *Man and the Natural World: A History of the Modern Sensibility.* New York: Pantheon, 1983.

Thorndike, Lynn. *History of Magic and Experimental Science during the First Thirteen Centuries of Our Era.* 8 vols. New York: Macmillan, 1923–58.

Thorpe, James. *John Milton: The Inner Life.* San Marino: Huntington, 1983.

———, ed. *Milton Criticism: Selections from Four Centuries.* New York: Rinehart, 1950.

Tillyard, E. M. W. *The Elizabethan World Picture.* London: Chatto, 1943.

———. *Milton.* Rev. ed. London: Chatto, 1966.

———. *The Miltonic Setting: Past and Present.* Cambridge: Cambridge UP, 1938.

———. *Studies in Milton.* London: Chatto, 1951.

Topsell, Edward. *The History of Four-footed Beasts and Serpents and Insects.* 1658. New York: Da Capo, 1967.

Trevelyan, G. M. *England under the Stuarts.* 1904. 19th rev. ed. London: Methuen, 1947.

———. *Illustrated English Social History.* 4 vols. London: Longman, 1944.

Triep, Mindele. *Milton's Punctuation and Changing English Usage, 1582–1676.* London: Methuen, 1970.

Vergil. *AEneïs.* Trans. John Dryden. Bridgeport: Airmont, 1968.

———. *The Aeneid.* Trans. Robert Fitzgerald. New York: Doubleday, 1983.

———. *The Aeneid.* Trans. Allen Mandelbaum. Berkeley: U of California P, 1982.

Waldock, A. J. A. *Paradise Lost and Its Critics.* Cambridge: Cambridge UP, 1947.

Walker, D. P. *The Decline of Hell: Seventeenth-Century Discussions of Eternal Torment.* London: Routledge, 1964.

Watkins, Walter B. C. *An Anatomy of Milton's Verse.* 1955. Hamden: Shoe String, 1965.

Webber, Joan M. "Jumping the Gap: The Epic Poetry of Milton—and After." *Milton Quarterly* 13 (1979): 107–11.

———. *Milton and the Epic Tradition.* Seattle: U of Washington P, 1979.

———. "The Politics of Poetry: Feminism and *Paradise Lost.*" *Milton Studies* 14 (1980): 3–25.

Wedgwood, Cecily Veronica. *A Coffin for King Charles: The Trial and Execution of Charles I.* New York: Macmillan, 1964.

———. *The King's Peace: 1637–1641.* London: Collins, 1955.

———. *The King's War: 1641–1647.* London: Collins, 1959.

———. *Milton and His World.* London: Lutterworth, 1969.

———. *Poetry and Politics under the Stuarts.* Cambridge: Cambridge UP, 1960.

———. *Seventeenth-Century English Literature.* London: Oxford UP, 1956.

West, Robert H. *Milton and the Angels*. Athens: U of Georgia P, 1955.

White, Lynn. "The Historical Roots of Our Ecological Crisis." *Science* 155 (1967): 1203–07.

Whitehead, Alfred North. *The Aims of Education*. 1929. New York: Free, 1967.

Whiting, George. *Milton and This Pendant World*. 1958. New York: Octagon, 1967.

———. *Milton's Literary Milieu*. 1939. New York: Russell, 1964.

Wiley, Margaret L. *The Subtle Knot: Creative Skepticism in Seventeenth-Century England*. London: Allen, 1952.

Wilkes, George A. *The Thesis of* Paradise Lost. Melbourne: Melbourne UP, 1961.

Willey, Basil. *The Seventeenth Century Background: Studies in the Thought of the Age in Relation to Poetry and Religion*. 1934. New York: Columbia UP, 1952.

Williams, Arnold. *The Common Expositor: An Account of the Commentaries on Genesis: 1527–1633*. Chapel Hill: U of North Carolina P, 1948.

Wilson, A. N. *The Life of John Milton*. New York: Oxford UP, 1983.

Wittreich, Joseph A., Jr. *Angel of Apocalypse: Blake's Idea of Milton*. Madison: U of Wisconsin P, 1975.

———, ed. *Milton and the Line of Vision*. Madison: U of Wisconsin P, 1975.

———, ed. *The Romantics on Milton: Formal Essays and Critical Asides*. Cleveland: Case Western Reserve UP, 1970.

Wolfe, Don M., gen. ed. *Complete Prose Works of John Milton*. 8 vols. New Haven: Yale UP, 1953–82.

———. *Milton and His England*. Princeton: Princeton UP, 1971.

———. *Milton in the Puritan Revolution*. 1941. New York: Humanities, 1963.

Wright, B. A. *John Milton: Poems*. Everyman's Library. London: Dent; New York: Dutton, 1956.

———. *Milton's* Paradise Lost: *A Reassessment of the Poem*. 1962. London: University Paperbacks, 1968.

Films and Recordings

Bronowski, Jacob, writer and narr. *The Ascent of Man*. Prod. Richard Gilling. Series ed. Adrian Malone. 12 programs. BBC, 1973.

Clark, Kenneth, writer and narr. *Civilisation*. Dir. Michael Gill and Peter Montagnon. 12 programs. BBC, 1969.

Quayle, Anthony. *Paradise Lost*. Selections from books 1–4. 2 records. Caedmon, TC-2008, 1950.

Rylands, George, dir. *Paradise Lost*. Selections from books 1–7, 9, 10, and 12. Read by Tony Church, Michael Redgrave, Prunella Scales, and others. 6 records. Texts provided. Argo, 431–432, 463–464, 508–509, 1965–67.

Speaight, Robert, and Robert Eddison. *Treasury of John Milton*. Selections from all the major poems. Spoken Arts, 3552–3557.

Taylor, Don. *Paradise Restored*. 90-minute videotape in color. BBC Classic Theater Series produced for *Omnibus* in 1967. Available from Time-Life Multimedia.

INDEX